Freedom in Meditation

DR. PATRICIA CARRINGTON is a clinical psychologist and lecturer in the Department of Psychology of Princeton University. She has been involved with meditation both personally as a regular meditator and professionally, using meditation with her patients and conducting research in this area. Dr. Carrington has developed her own method of meditation, Clinically Standardized Meditation, which is being used successfully in a number of organizations and by individuals interested in learning a simple, Westernized technique.

Born into a family of writers—her mother was an author and her brother is a prominent screenwriter—she was viewed by her parents as a "professional writer" at an early age. She rebelled against this, however, and opted for a career in an altogether different field—as a psychotherapist specializing in problems of adolescence and family life.

Ironically, she has ended up doing a good deal of writing. As co-author with her psychiatrist husband, Dr. Harmon S. Ephron, she has published numerous scientific articles on the new experimental studies of sleep and dreaming, and her research on the use of meditation as an adjunct to psychotherapy is a landmark in this area.

Dr. Carrington is also Director of Child Therapy at the East Brunswick Guidance Clinic in New Jersey and is in private practice. She divides her professional time between her work with patients, teaching, research, and writing. At home, she and her husband find time to enjoy a quiet Japanese garden.

Freedom in Meditation

By PATRICIA CARRINGTON, Ph.D.

1977
Anchor Press/Doubleday
Garden City, New York

Permission to quote from the following sources is gratefully acknowledged:
From M. Csikszentmihalyi, *Beyond Boredom and Anxiety*, San Francisco: Jossey-Bass, Inc., 1975, copyright © by Jossey-Bass, Inc.
From "Meditation As an Adjunct to Psychotherapy" by Patricia Carrington, Ph.D., and Harmon S. Ephron, M.D., from S. Arieti and G. Chrzanowski, *New Dimensions in Psychiatry*, New York: John Wiley & Sons, 1975, copyright © by John Wiley & Sons, Inc.

ISBN 0-385-11392-7
Library of Congress Catalog Card Number 76–6240

To my husband, Harmon
my thanks
for his help, and patience, and love

AUTHOR'S NOTE:
Throughout this book, you will come across what will seem to you to be a rather inconsistent and improper use of the pronouns "they," "them," and "their." I use these pronouns not only to represent the individual plural but also the "indifferent" singular. This was done to avoid gendered pronouns.

Some Words of Thanks

A book dealing with a skill such as meditation grows through the mingling of many people's observations, thoughts, and even musings. It takes shape through their challenges and achieves final form through their criticism. These are the people who have most directly taken part in this book:

Foremost is my husband, Dr. Harmon S. Ephron. His clinical wisdom and sensitivity to human values, and his ready ability to get in touch with the "meditative mood," supplied many of the basic ideas I have written about. He has also untiringly read and reread the manuscript, keeping me constantly alert to the psychiatric challenges involved.

Other important contributors are my students at Princeton who have conducted research on meditation: Susan Shackman; Christopher Ross; Hilary Brown; Wendy Zevin; Melissa Hines; Andy Rimol; DiAnna Tolliver; Douglas Moltz; Jocelyn Spector; and David James. Their enthusiasm and determination to get at the "truth" about meditation were contagious, and many aspects of this book grew out of our joint struggling to understand the issues involved.

Then there are the specialized contributors:

My good friend and colleague Bradford Wilson, whose valuable observations on the effects of meditation on those of his patients who are regular meditators and on the many people to whom he has taught various forms of meditation over the years suggested some of the principles and practical strategies presented in this book.

Melissa Hines's excellent thesis on "Meditation and Creativity" forms the basis for the theoretical discussion of the creative process in the first half of Chapter 13.

The information on Indian traditional thought, particularly that on Yogic customs and the meaning of the mantra in Chapter 9 (much of it unavailable from any published source), was largely assembled from conferences with Shyam Bhatnagar, teacher and practitioner of Swar Yoga, whose deep knowledge of the spiritual life of India and broad experience in teaching meditation make him an expert in the effects of sound and its uses to alter consciousness. The manuscript for the mantra chapter was also critically read by Raja Mrigendra Singh, Adjunct Professor of Philosophy at the City College of New York, and Dr. Ishwar Harris, Professor of Oriental Religion at Rutgers University; their helpful comments are incorporated in the final version. Dr. Samuel D. Atkins, Professor of Classics at Princeton University kindly supplied the information about the Sanskrit forms of the word "mantra."

Then there are the excerpts from personal meditation journals which I cite in the book: the perceptive observations of my colleague George Edington, of my husband, of a number of meditating patients, and of those who participated in our research.

There was also essential evaluative assistance. The keen editorial eye of my brother Robert Carrington first identified a number of organizational problems and put me on the track of major structural revisions; and I worked with an unusually gifted editor, Angela Iadavaia-Cox, who must become a research scientist if she ever switches careers! She relentlessly demanded, and pointed the way toward, the "best" that the book, and I, could produce.

Finally, there was the ever present support from my secretary, Donna Hyland, whose calm stance under pressure and wizardry on the typewriter piloted the detailed production of the manuscript through troubled waters to its eventual completion.

Contents

Contents

II *Managing Meditation*

Contents

Contents

IV Explaining Meditation

V Conclusion

Introduction

For meditation it is best to sit cross-legged either in full or half lotus posture.[1]

You should sit upright when meditating, with your back against a straight-back chair.[2]

The easiest way to practice the meditative exercises is to relax on a couch or bed, lying on the back, legs slightly apart and relaxed.[3]

You should meditate morning and evening but never late at night, unless you are planning to stay up all night.[4]

You should meditate at the darkest hour of the night, midway between sunset and sunrise.[5]

Never attempt to meditate when you feel any fever or have a cold or pain. Let them pass before you start.[6]

If you are ill in bed you should meditate as much as is comfortable.[7]

A trained instructor should select a specific mantra according to an exact procedure.[8]

A mantra can just be any interesting, or not interesting, sound notation.[9]

Meditating together, everyone sharing a single group mantra, can become a very, very high vehicle for group consciousness modification.[10]

If you tell your own mantra to anyone else it won't achieve the desired results with them and it might have a deterrent effect on that person.[11]

What are these conflicting instructions? Who is right? Why?

These statements and others like them are made by teachers of meditation who sincerely believe they are giving correct advice. Most of their directions are based on traditional practices—often ancient in origin. While innovations in teaching are occasionally made by creative teachers, none of these are backed up by scientific evidence on which modifications work best or are suitable for particular types of people.

I know of no meditation instruction available today that gives the student reliably documented research on whether following one routine when practicing meditation is any better than following any other routine. Because of the care with which they have been developed, the traditional meditative practices supply valuable information to anyone who takes up the practice of meditation, even in one of its simplified Western forms. But which pieces of information are soundly based and which are simply followed because of custom or sometimes even because of superstition?

These are some of the questions that forced themselves upon me when I started to investigate the field of meditation five years ago. The questions were a starting point for an investigation that has led me, on the one hand, through the fascinating field of traditional Eastern meditation and, on the other hand, through the rich productions of the Western scientific establishment as it has increasingly turned its awesome analytic tools to an examination of meditation.

One of the purposes of this book is to separate the useful instructions from the useless ones, the methods of handling meditation that may prove appropriate for our modern world from those that are suitable only for very small numbers of people under very special conditions—or those which may not be useful at all. There is a large and ever growing body of research on meditation comprising literally hundreds of research studies. Virtually all of it is directed to discovering what the meditative state "is"—that is, what its special characteristics are—or to how meditation affects people. I will refer to a good deal of this research as I go along in this book, but it does not answer certain urgent practical questions. Such problems as how difficulties arising from the practice of any form of popular meditation can best be handled; how blocks to meditation can be overcome; whether certain forms of meditation suit certain types of people better than they do others—all these remain largely unexplored territory.

At this point, research conducted by myself and my husband, Dr. Harmon S. Ephron, and by some of our participating colleagues in the field of psychotherapy, represents virtually the only attempts to investigate these aspects of meditation in a systematic way. In discussing various ways of *managing* meditation, therefore, I will draw mainly on our work. We have collected data from many sources: more than 100 meditating patients whom we have treated in clinical practice; over 1,500 people to whom my associates and myself have taught a simple form of mantra meditation; research studies conducted by my students at Princeton University; surveys on meditation practices among campus meditators and trainees in the general community; and finally the compelling experience of having been, myself, a regular meditator for more than four years, an experience shared by my husband and several other psychotherapists with whom I have worked closely in a joint exploration of the potential uses of meditation in the field of mental health. Putting together this information, we have assembled a body of knowledge which we hope will make meditation more satisfying and helpful to people who have learned one of the popular techniques yet may be having difficulty with it, or who still have unanswered questions; or those considering learning meditation. In the course of the book I will present a number of the findings we have unearthed. Hopefully they may stimulate other researchers to investigate these questions.

The contradictory instructions on how to practice meditation which opened this discussion reflect a surprising lack of agreement among techniques. This is what confronts the average person who approaches the subject of meditation. In order to explain these conflicting directives it is important to make a distinction. Meditation is a conglomerate word. Under its umbrella it groups a number of *different* techniques and intents. It is therefore helpful in approaching the area to recognize two main trends within the overall term "meditation."

First, there are the historic, centuries-old religious traditions of meditation in which the object is to attain spiritual development, to change the entire life of a human being undergoing the experience, and to use it as a profound tool for deepening the range of the human spirit. I call these traditional approaches "spiritual meditation."

There is also an essentially different form of meditation available today—meditation as it is frequently practiced in the West. It has its roots in the great meditative traditions, but is used to achieve quite different and more limited goals. This second form does not necessarily aim at changing one's life-style, nor is it intended as a profound spiritual adventure. It may of course inadvertently lead to the latter, but its intent is to affect those who practice it in certain practical ways without actually changing their lives in an essential fashion. Its object is to enrich the experience of the average Westerner who continues to function within the confines of ordinary society as we know it. I call this second form of meditation "practical meditation."

It is this practical meditation to which the flood of meditation books now crowding our store counters are largely addressed and it is practical meditation which is the central subject of this book. These chapters are intended, among other things, as a guide through the maze of information which is rapidly piling up on this type of meditation.

Many questions are being raised—questions that will become more important in the next few years as research zeroes in on some of the essentials. Although books such as those concerned with Transcendental Meditation (TM) present some of the research, we need to go further than a survey from only one point of view. It may even be necessary to go beyond meditation itself to find answers for these questions. There are other fast-growing areas of science which hold important clues. Some of the new research on biological rhythms; the studies of sensory isolation; even such unusual fields as biometeorology—these and similar disciplines supply leads which need to be investigated. They will be considered in this book in order to widen our understanding of meditation.

In searching for answers to some of the more puzzling aspects of meditation, it is also helpful to view meditation in a different light in relation to psychotherapy—not as a replacement for much of it as some recent authors have suggested it should become—but as a promising partner. Since I have had an opportunity in the intimate therapist-patient relationship, to observe the effects of meditation on the deeper levels of human experience, I will, where applicable, present some of my psychological case material which illustrates the effects of meditation on the lives and emotions of average people.

It also seemed wise to teach some methods of meditation to readers interested in this subject, so I have included a section in this book doing that. It is to be considered as an introduction to meditation for those who have never meditated, and an invitation for those who are already meditating to experience other techniques than their own. With a first-hand knowledge of the approaches we will be talking about, the reader should be better able to follow the discussions. I have included *several* methods because my experience has led me to feel strongly that the technique of meditation should be carefully adjusted to the particular person. There is no one "right" method. There are just different methods. Each individual should find the technique that is congenial to his or her personality.

As our exploration of meditation and its effects unfolds, there will be need to exercise caution. Promoting meditation has become big business, and advertising and public relations outfits can use scientific facts in startling ways. They are understandably eager to publicize scientific research which lends itself to testimonials—"four out of five doctors recommend *our* brand" is a familiar statement—and to ignore research that does the opposite. "Scientific tests show that Brand X does the same thing as *our* brand and maybe does it better" is not a popular slogan. If a meditation organization has a vested interest in research in this field, how can we be sure the research they report is objective? Does pre-selection of the scientific studies to be cited to the public play a part in the glowing picture presented for certain meditation techniques? We will look at these questions.

A problem in evaluating the research findings arises from the fact that while certain groups openly advocate religious forms of meditation on the basis of a special guru or "great seer," others promote religious forms of meditation and at the same time *deny* their religious basis. Words like "enlightenment," which are not scientifically defined or well understood, are often carelessly used for promotion purposes, causing confusion in the minds of the public. This commercialization of what we might call "transpersonal" concepts, is particularly unfortunate because these areas are interesting to investigate in their own right. Some scientists are involved in working to see that they are studied in the proper manner.

Transpersonal psychology is still largely unresearched and therefore considered, in the main, to be "unscientific," but there are examples of serious work in the psychology of consciousness, in parapsychology and in related disciplines: careful experiments on ESP and dreams conducted by Doctors Montague Ullman and Stanley Krippner at the Dream Laboratory of Maimonides Medical Center[12]; pioneering work on aspects of psychic healing headed by Dr. Lawrence LeShan[13]; research on altered states of con-

Introduction

sciousness with cancer patients being conducted by Dr. Stanislav Grof at the Maryland Psychiatric Institute[14]; theoretical and experimental work on various states of consciousness painstakingly pursued by Dr. Charles Tart.[15] These and similar studies deal with areas of inquiry that are largely uncharted, but their researchers never demand of us that we rely on their word as the "truth." Instead, they patiently subject their hypotheses to validation in the laboratory or in the psychiatric clinic. If they find that their method does not work, then they change their approach and pursue the research further. They are entitled to credit, respect, and encouragement for this, but such respect is scarcely due those advocates of Eastern philosophies who, even though they may sincerely believe in their own practices, demand that we take them at their word and proclaim their way as the "only" one. This latter approach cannot be called scientific.

The term "scientific" refers to a series of procedures by which information is first gathered and then, on the basis of preliminary information, a number of informed guesses (hypotheses) are made. These in turn are tested through experiments to see whether they will hold up, and only those that do are retained. This method rests on an interesting attitude on the part of scientists—they set out to *disprove* their own hypotheses or hunches, putting their ideas to the test by creating the most ingenious experiments possible, designed to give their pet theories a hard time. Only if the theories still stand up under this rough treatment are the experimenters justified in saying they have scientific "support" for their position.

This approach has an important bearing on meditation research. It implies that anyone who thinks that the form of meditation that he or she has developed, practices, or even admires has superior advantages for certain types of personalities or for dealing with certain problems must first set out to find out if they are *wrong* in what they think. They must for example seek to discover whether other forms of meditation or relaxation may not actually accomplish the same thing as well, or better than, their own particular form. If any school of meditation refuses to allow its method to be experimentally compared with other methods (I will be discussing the manner in which at least one leading meditation system sets up this sort of policy), this is therefore an unscientific attitude.

It cannot be overemphasized that meditation, as a Western experience, has only recently come to the attention of serious researchers. The information available to us at this point is therefore but the opening of a door. What is going to happen in this field in the next few years is not known, but I would scarcely be surprised if ten years from now much of our present research in this area is considered mere "beginners' exercises."

Conceivably, we could be on the verge of a breakthrough which will reach even beyond the present claims of the meditation hucksters, one which will place meditation and perhaps some of its allied disciplines on solid scientific ground for the first time. While it is to the near-term possibilities that I will give most attention in these pages—the ones that offer immediate promise for those of us in a tension-filled world—the mood of the future will be obvious in all that we consider.

I

Science
Explores Meditation

The Ageless Practice

Meditation is one of the most ancient of human activities. Man is the animal that uses language, responds to beauty, laughs, sheds tears . . . and meditates. What is unique about the ritual of "meditation" is the prolongation of the event, and the capacity to induce it at will. The experience that underlies it, however—the "meditative mood"—is familiar to all of us:

A mother holding her infant close is united with the child in a gentle rhythm as she rocks and sings to it.

A traveler leaning against a tree listens to the sounds of the breeze rustling the treetops and barely senses his own breath; it is as though he had "become" the wind.

An elderly Jew, draped in his impressively trimmed prayer shawl and black cubes of leather (*tefillin*) sways back and forth in the dawn light, monotonously repeating a simple prayer which brings him exaltation.

A vacationer lies on the beach, giving herself over quietly to the sun and the air, engulfed by the lulling rhythms of the sea.

A man hears organ tones cascading through a cathedral; as they vibrate through him, he is carried into a reverie where memories and images of childhood flood him—he has become a child again.

A camper gazes into a lowering fire following the trail of the glowing ashes as they drift upward and fade into darkness; she feels as though she, too, were floating gently through space.

A rock climber on a mountaintop breathes-in the silence above the earth; he is shaken by its immensity and his mind becomes as still as the snows in the mountain passes.

Except perhaps for the old man at prayer, these people experience meditative moods which they have not purposely induced. Their moods are spontaneous. They are welcomed as moments of unusual aliveness and include some of the profound states which Abraham Maslow[1] has referred to as "peak experiences." Are they different from the moments of inner stillness *intentionally* evoked by the ritual of meditation? An excerpt from the meditation journal of a colleague talks about this:

> Tonight at 8:45 P.M. I sat on the porch and watched the last twilight darken into night. I think I've learned to cheat on the TM* prohibition against "extra sessions." I would let a thought come popping into my mind and then gently replace it with some element of sensory perception—the dark line of treetops against the sky, the rushing of the overfed brook hurtling to the sea, the air against my face, the feel of my body against the chair, the smell of woods and growing things. . . . It was very soothing and peaceful.[2]

The writer clearly sees his experience in TM and his experience with an informal "meditative mood" as being so alike that during the latter it seemed as though he were "cheating" on his formal meditations. Actually such moods are like true meditation in many ways and one could even argue that they are meditations. Perhaps meditation as a discipline is no more than this spontaneous process developed into a *formal* practice.

Despite the fact that it frequently occurs naturally, people throughout the ages have nevertheless developed hundreds of ingenious methods for intentionally evoking this mood, methods which have been carefully cultivated and handed down over the generations. Perhaps spontaneous meditative moods occur less often than is desirable. Perhaps they are less intense when they occur naturally than human beings want or need them to be. In

* TM is the abbreviation for Transcendental Meditation, a popular Westernized meditative technique.

4

modern industrial society, based on machinelike efficiency rather than on natural rhythms, meditative moods may so seldom occur spontaneously that structured, formal types of meditation are particularly necessary. What are some of these methods that man has worked out for evoking and holding onto this fragile mood?

The Techniques

There are literally hundreds of practices which can be listed under the heading of "meditation."[3] All of these have in common the ability to bring about a special kind of free-floating attention where rational thought is bypassed and words are of far less importance than in everyday life. It is characteristic of this state that when in it, the person is completely absorbed by his or her particular object of meditation. If something else comes to mind, it will usually drift in with a sort of vague, faraway quality, then drift out again.

The devices used to bring about this state are as diverse as gazing quietly at a candle flame; attending to the mental repetition of a sound (*mantra*); following one's own breathing; concentrating on the imagined sound of rainfall; chanting out loud a ritual word or phrase; attending to body sensations; concentrating on an unanswerable riddle (*koan*); passively witnessing the flow of thoughts through one's mind; or whirling in a stereotyped dance. Whatever, the aim is the same: to alter the way the meditator experiences his or her own existence.

All these techniques close out the distractions of the outer world in much the same way as an "isolation chamber." In a sensory deprivation experiment the subject is removed from incoming sense impressions by being placed in a soundproofed room, by wearing goggles to eliminate patterned vision, or by undergoing other sense-reducing manipulations. In meditation, the meditator removes their attention from distracting sense impressions and thoughts by creating an inner "isolation chamber" of their own

5

making. It is when the outer world is removed that meditation can take effect and the individual is said to become "centered."†

Despite the fact that attention is directed toward a meditational "object," however, each technique copes with a basic property of meditation which can best be described as a *counter*-tendency, a need to pull away from the object of focus. Even the calm and centered mind is not entirely still. Periodically it reaches for renewed contact with the environment, either through sense impressions or thoughts, and each meditational system has its own way of dealing with this "outward stroke" of meditation.

Some systems are not permissive, or are even coercive with respect to the handling of "distractions of the mind" during meditation. A *nonpermissive* form of meditation will demand strict concentration on the meditational object. The practitioner will be directed to pinpoint their attention, to banish intruding thoughts from their mind by an act of will, and to return immediately and forcefully to the object of focus whenever they find their attention has wandered. This approach is seen in extreme form in instructions given to a meditator in a fifth-century Buddhist treatise dealing with thoughts that may intrude into the meditation:

> . . . with teeth clenched and tongue pressed against the gums, he should by means of sheer mental effort hold back, crush and burn out the [offending] thought; in doing so, these evil and unwholesome ideas, bound up with greed, hate or delusion, will be forsaken, then thought will become inwardly calm, composed and concentrated.[4]

In contrast, many meditative systems use varying degrees of permissiveness toward intruding thoughts. In these more permissive techniques, the meditator is instructed to return gently and without effort to the object of focus.

Although there are no experimental findings dealing with the effects on the meditator of permissive versus nonpermissive forms

---

† The words "centered" and "centering," as used in the meditative traditions, refer to a process of *psychological centering*—the reinstatement of a sense of inner balance through the use of devices which serve to focus the person's attention on some single point. This process is seen as acting like a psychological gyroscope to stabilize the mind and body and neutralize pulls away from the "center" of the self.

of meditation, it may well make a difference whether the meditator practices one approach or the other. The effects may even be different if they mistakenly *interpret* their form of meditation as being nonpermissive when it is not. Most techniques for meditation require that the meditator make no conscious effort, but "let things happen" rather than *make* them happen. Often, however, the average person automatically injects coercion into a meditative practice unless carefully trained otherwise. The result is roughly the same as it would be if a stern teacher were standing close by and commanding one to "shape up" the whole time one meditates.

A nonpermissive approach to meditation (self-produced or produced by instructions from someone else) can increase guilt in the meditator as he or she begins to blame themselves for not meditating "correctly," or for the kinds of intruding thoughts they are having. A permissive approach, on the other hand, because it encourages an accepting attitude toward the thoughts or feelings which may inadvertently arise during meditation, may help the meditator to handle previously unacceptable feelings which they might have been hiding or "repressing." It may also help release emotional tensions, because these have an opportunity to play themselves out in fantasy in this more permissive state.

Right now, however, I can only speculate about the effects on the meditator of different kinds of meditation instruction. There is no experimental evidence to shed light on the subject. As the study of meditation proceeds, no doubt this will be looked into and a good deal more will be known.

Meditation vs. Centering

In the great meditative traditions of both East and West, meditation is looked upon as a spiritual exercise, a means for attaining a special kind of awareness thought to be the highest state of consciousness of which man is capable. This supposedly advanced level of consciousness can only be arrived at as part of a total way of life. An ascetic life, special physical exercises, diet, and social arrangements, together with long hours of meditation each day, are the typical procedures followed. Even then it may take a lifetime (some people believe it takes many lifetimes) to arrive at or even approximate this desired state.

The average Westerner, however, approaches meditation on a different level—a practical one. Ordinarily he or she does not consider it a *deep* spiritual commitment, if they think of it as being spiritual at all. Usually it is learned to make life easier and more pleasant.

At first glance these different uses of meditation may seem merely a matter of degree—the mystic might be thought to be more intensely involved with meditation and the average person less so. Actually there is a fundamental difference. The typical modern meditator, not being tied to any particular belief system, can be flexible in his or her approach to practical meditation and can experiment with it. Such a person is free to use it effectively outside of the context of the traditional systems, and can, if need be, combine it effectively with other methods of self-improvement or with medical or psychological treatments.

The person seeking spiritual growth, on the other hand, must embrace a strenuous discipline. He or she must learn the delicate nuances of the technique assigned by their instructor so as to be able to apply it accurately and exactly. For this a highly skilled teacher is needed to guide the aspirant along the path of inner development, a teacher who knows exactly how and when to alter the meditative technique in order to produce further spiritual growth in this pupil. "Warming up" exercises such as the silent repetition of a mantra or concentration on one's breathing (or many others which are available) may be prescribed for such a pupil, but these are not considered "meditations." They are *devices* used to center the individual in preparation for the deep state of communion or oneness which is "meditation." The Hindu spiritual leader Bhagwan Shree Rajneesh points out that:

> . . . meditation has two steps: first the active, which is not meditation at all; second, that which is really meditation [and] is completely non-active . . . just passive awareness . . .[5]

Because of a limitation in our vocabulary, the West refers to the simple psychological centering devices, the *preliminary* steps,

8

as "meditation." We therefore give the same name to the techniques used to produce meditation as we do to the end state itself. According to the great meditative traditions, however, the centering techniques are not *meditation*. They are simply means toward the *goal*—which is meditation. These techniques are therefore more or less interchangeable, and the advanced practitioner will eventually discard all of them when he can achieve meditation directly.

The vocabulary of a society obviously reflects its preoccupations. We devise numerous words for technological processes—these are exact and informative—but we have only one word for "mind." Other societies, such as that of India, have many different words for "mind" according to its many functions as conceived by their ancient beliefs. As Western scientists continue to investigate the various meditative states and the devices used to reach them, we will no doubt create words to distinguish these states from each other and to identify different classes of techniques, or "centering devices."

In writing this book, I did not want to coin a new word to refer to these centering devices, although it is these devices which I will mainly talk about. Since most people think of them as "meditation," that is the term I use. When I speak of meditation, therefore (unless I specify otherwise), I will be referring to the centering techniques that constitute what I call "practical meditation." What I say about their use may or may *not* apply, in a given instance, to the rigorous disciplined forms of meditation used as roads to spiritual growth.

Despite my attempt to be clear about this, it will be obvious to anyone who has ever meditated by whatever technique, that there is no hard and fast line between the simple centering exercises and the deep meditative states. One can commence by naïvely using the simplest of centering devices (for example, mentally repeating a mantra with eyes closed) and end up having a profound experience which changes one's entire perspective on life. Or one can set out diligently to achieve deep spiritual awareness through meditation and wind up with a pleasant, relaxing centering experience and nothing more.

9

The boundaries, in other words, are permeable. Inner experience extends where it will. It resists control and refuses to be confined to categories; we cannot legislate the inmost segment of our lives. In discussing people's centering we will therefore inevitably find ourselves touching on the deeper implications of meditation as well.

We cannot of course discuss all the types of practical meditation available in the West today—for new ones are literally cropping up overnight and many are as yet entirely untested. Some of these may even fade before they have ever been studied. What will be considered are the *standardized* forms, because they are the ones most apt to become part of the new scientific body of knowledge about meditation. I will start with the most widely studied of them all, Transcendental Meditation.

Transcendental Meditation (TM)

Transcendental Meditation is a standardized form of mantra meditation adapted for Western use from an ancient Indian technique.[6] When instructed in TM, the student is assigned a Sanskrit word (*mantra*) said to possess soothing properties, which he or she is asked to repeat silently to themselves for twenty minutes, sitting quietly in a chair with eyes closed. This is done twice daily. When the meditator finds that their attention has wandered, they are told to make no effort to return deliberately to the mantra, but to resume its repetition in a passive manner by "favoring" the mantra over other thoughts. The TM instructors give considerable reassurance to practitioners with regard to the nature of thoughts which arise during meditation and the meditator is taught to look upon the spontaneous emergence of thoughts, feelings, images, or bodily sensations during meditation as evidence of a process said to have therapeutic properties which is termed *normalizing*. By means of normalizing, residual tensions produced by previous traumatic or stressful events in a person's life are said to be released spontaneously.

TM is readily available in the Western world, being taught by an organization of instructors, the International Meditation Soci-

10

ety (IMS)‡ using a uniform method of instruction. There are TM centers in and around most of the major cities of the United States and Europe; and the technique itself is easy to learn, being mastered in four lessons taught over a period of four days. It does not require adoption of any particular life-style for ordinary meditators (although it may for TM teachers) nor does it use special postures or methods of breathing.

IMS also claims that those who learn TM do not have to accept any particular set of beliefs. In actual fact IMS offers the meditator a chance to learn about a set of beliefs based on Hindu metaphysical assumptions about the cosmos, which they term the "Science of Creative Intelligence" (SCI). Although the TM trainee is not required to study SCI, it is offered as an additional course of instruction. Regular TM training also includes exposure to certain Eastern beliefs, as illustrated by the following quote from an authorized TM publication:

> We notice that in all creation, from the growth of the plants to the movement of the planets, there is great order, or intelligence. Since thoughts also exist, they must be made of the most basic form of energy as well. And they have their source, or basis, in the same field of creative intelligence and energy that underlies all creation.[7]

Quotes such as the above express the Hindu concept of *prana* (universal energy) and of *Brahman* (the irreducible essence of all creation). The ideas described are inherently interesting, and perhaps may ultimately prove to reflect some truth, but to call them at this point "scientific" is to stretch the boundaries of Western science beyond any ordinarily agreed upon meaning of the term.

Certain people, however, respond to the esoteric trappings of TM more positively then they would to the teachings of another technique which might be more pragmatic but less colorful. There are many people for whom the poetic *puja* (Hindu devotional ceremony) by which the learner is initiated into TM, is appealing. For others, however, the puja may be annoying or even embarrass-

‡ IMS is the education service of the U. S. World Plan Organization, the parent body of the TM organization.

ing and undoubtedly some people refuse to learn TM because of the aura of mysticism which surrounds it.

Regardless of individual reactions, however, such aspects of the TM training present disadvantages for *research*. If, for example, a subject is responding well to TM, it is difficult to tell whether this is because the technique is effective in and of itself or whether it is because the person is receiving emotional support from participating in a quasi-religious organization. Or is it because they have had expectations raised to such a high pitch by the TM teacher's earnest belief that this technique is a panacea? Sometimes all of these factors may be operating.

There are other difficulties as well for the researcher who is examining TM. IMS steadfastly refuses to reveal the "secret" mantras which they assign to their trainees. This is a serious drawback because it prevents the investigator from knowing what he or she is actually dealing with. It is contrary to scientific procedure to withhold information which may have bearing on a problem under investigation. In this case it prevents the experimenter from comparing the effectiveness of one type of mantra with another, one method of assigning the mantra with another, or exploring other crucial questions concerned with the effects of different sounds upon personality.

In addition, IMS will not sanction research comparing TM with any other technique of meditation.* When I inquired about the reasons for this, the American headquarters of the World Plan Organization in Los Angeles informed me that this directive is based on their leader "Maharishi"[8] Mahesh Yogi's opinion that other forms of meditation, particularly Benson's method, are damaging to their practitioners. Since official regulations require that all local TM chapters obtain the permission of the World Plan Organization before co-operating with any research on TM—formal research proposals are submitted to their central research department for approval—this means that comparative studies, the

* A few studies comparing TM with some other meditative techniques have been done but were conducted without official permission and the organization in the past approved some studies comparing TM to some *relaxation* techniques.

lifeblood of scientific inquiry, cannot readily be carried out using TM.

It was such considerations as these which first led me to search for another form of standardized meditation which could be used for research and clinical purposes. It had become obvious to me that not only was TM often unsatisfactory for use in research but also that a form of meditation which psychotherapists could teach to patients was essential when using meditation as an adjunct to psychotherapy. As we will see when we come to consider the use of meditation in psychotherapy, TM is not flexible enough to be suitable for all clinical purposes. It is also out of the reach of many patients and treatment institutions because of the cost of instruction.†

Clinically Standardized Meditation (CSM)

The form of meditation I decided upon as an alternative was developed by selecting a classical Indian form of mantra meditation, modifying it so that it became a relaxation technique suitable for Western use, and developing a standardized set of instructions. This is, I imagine, similar to the steps which the developers of TM followed when refining their technique. There is actually nothing new about any of the meditation techniques in current use; they are all well-known systems that have passed the test of time.

The first group of people to use the form of meditation that I had put together from these traditional sources were Princeton students who were attending a meditation seminar. The students were enthusiastic about the technique, and on a series of personality tests administered before learning this type of meditation, and again after they had practiced it for ten weeks, they showed changes similar to subjects who had been practicing TM in a comparable study being conducted on the campus. Both groups showed clear-cut evidence of anxiety reduction over a ten-week period.

The basic technique was then revised, elaborated, and given the name Clinically Standardized Meditation (CSM) to indicate its

† At this writing, $125 for an adult.

research and clinical nature. A teaching manual was prepared, and since then the technique has been taught to a number of other psychotherapists for their use with patients.[9]

CSM is closer to TM than to the other currently used forms of meditation but differs from it in some important respects. Our trainees select their own mantra from a list of sixteen Sanskrit mantras presented to them,‡ or if they wish to make up their own, they do this instead by following some simple rules. Regulations of length of meditation sessions to suit individual requirements is a key aspect of the teaching, and we do not explain the effects of meditation in terms of any belief system, or use esoteric terms such as "transcending," "cosmic consciousness," or the like. Where explanations are needed, we refer to whatever scientific evidence is presently available. Our course of instruction is shorter than that of TM because we dispense with the process of building up expectations through preparatory or follow-up lectures; CSM is taught in two lessons.

CSM's ritual for imparting the mantra does not involve chanting or any special ceremony; merely the use of a quiet room, some plants pleasantly arranged, and (if the person wishes it) some incense and a candle on a small table. We then use a short, standardized, soothing means of transferring the mantra (which he or she has personally selected) to the trainee. We devised this ritual because we found that the dignity and emphasis lent to the occasion by a ceremony, however rudimentary, is an important part of the learning process. Meditation is, in a sense, a rebirth. It is a new beginning, a significant commitment to one's own growth.

Since our instructions emphasize the effortlessness of the meditation technique and its permissive nature, CSM lies, with TM, at the permissive end of the scale relative to other meditation techniques which require at least some degree of discipline and concentration.

‡ Because the impact of specific sounds on human beings is as yet an unresearched area, and because the meditative traditions often claim that certain word-sounds may be harmful, we asked three experts on the Yoga tradition of mantra meditation to check the mantras on our list. They assured us that the specific sounds we had chosen could be safely used for practical meditation.

To date we have used CSM successfully with a sizable number of patients in clinics, hospital settings, and private practice. The main advantages of this form are its standardization, its flexibility, and its sensitivity to the special needs of the various people who learn it. As research develops in this area, however, we will in all likelihood discover that no *single* meditative technique is appropriate for all people or all occasions. A number of different standardized forms will probably need to be developed. Teachers of the classical forms of meditation have in fact followed such a principle of diversification for thousands of years.

Like all other meditative methods, CSM has its drawbacks. It is time-consuming, requiring a private lesson of one hour for each person being trained, although the following day's group meeting gathers together all current trainees. In an attempt to correct this, we have developed a type of self-regulated meditation similar to CSM which can be taught by tape-recorded instructions. Preliminary tests with this new form are encouraging, and further research is planned.

Benson's Method

Boston cardiologist Dr. Herbert Benson's TM studies (carried out in collaboration with Dr. R. Keith Wallace) are landmarks in the area of meditation research—the first laboratory proof that a form of practical meditation can lower metabolism in a profound manner.[10] Although his original investigations were based solely on TM, Benson later developed his own form of meditation, an unnamed method generally known as "Benson's technique," which he devised in order to check on whether other meditative techniques besides TM could evoke the same generalized state of relaxation, a condition Benson refers to as the Relaxation Response.

He discovered that they could. His technique, a simple form of breathing meditation where a person thinks the word "one" (or any other sound they choose) to themselves on every out-breath, brought about exactly the same physiologic changes in laboratory studies which had been noted during TM: decreased oxygen consumption; decreased carbon dioxide elimination; and decreased rate of breathing.[11] As a result, Benson concluded that "any one of the age-old or newly derived techniques [for meditation] produces the same physiologic results regardless of the mental device used."[12]

Benson describes his method as a "noncultic" meditative technique. It requires some initial relaxation of the body muscles from toes to head, a quiet environment, a mental device (attending to one's breathing) and a "let it happen" or "passive" attitude. It is a scientific form of meditation which can be studied openly in the laboratory without strings attached and used at a clinician's discretion in any manner he or she feels is appropriate in the consulting room. Because of this Benson's method can be taught without cost, as can CSM.

Is Benson's technique interchangeable with TM, however? Are the two techniques merely different versions of one basic mental procedure capable of eliciting the Relaxation Response? Benson seems to believe that the specific mental device used is of little importance, a mere matter of personal choice. I agree that the type of meditation used should be based on personal preference, but I feel we do not have enough experimental evidence as yet to conclude that all the practical meditative devices are interchangeable.

Benson's technique, for example, differs from both TM and CSM in that it requires a greater degree of *concentration*. Benson gives his trainees the following instructions: "When distracting thoughts occur, try to ignore them by not dwelling upon them and return to repeating 'ONE'—the word is to coordinate with the out-breath." He does not require his practitioners to *force* these thoughts out of their mind (as some nonpermissive forms of meditation do), but simply calls for them to "ignore" them, and return their attention to their breathing and their mantra. This is different, however, from the even *more* permissive directions of CSM, which do not suggest that meditators ignore their thoughts at all but rather that they flow with them, at least up to a point, simply keeping in mind the possibility of returning to the mantra periodically to touch home base. Clearly this is a different mental attitude.

Both TM and CSM also teach a somewhat more easygoing way of handling the mantra. In these techniques the meditator is instructed to allow the mantra to proceed at its own pace, to get faster or slower, louder or softer, or even to disappear if "it wants to." This is different from trying to link the mantra with one's breathing, as in Benson's method. When we link the two in this fashion, the breathing *controls* the mantra. Benson's technique therefore operates within much tighter limits than TM or CSM— it is less of a free-floating self-determined experience.

This is not to say that Benson's technique cannot be useful, but simply that it is different and the difference may be of importance. Some people may prefer Benson's method to TM or CSM because it is more structured and follows set rules. These may be people who prefer to have things "spelled out" for them, who feel comfortable with clear-cut regulations. On the other hand, a more poetic, artistic, or sentimental person might find such rules stifling and prefer a freer, more open-ended form of meditation. By the same token, a more religious or a more dramatically inclined person might prefer the Sanskrit ceremony of initiation offered by TM to the strictly secular ceremony of CSM or to the somewhat impersonal instructions of Benson's method.

It may be that the personality of the meditator is the most important factor of all when judging the "merits" of any of these techniques. On the other hand, certain "easier" techniques may have more popular appeal. This possibility has recently been investigated at Princeton University.[13] As part of an experiment, researcher DiAnna Tolliver set out to discover which of two meditation techniques (TM or Benson's) twenty-six subjects would rate as preferable after they had practiced both techniques for a period of two weeks each. She first gave the subjects a test to determine their basic personality characteristics,* and then taught them the meditation techniques, in random order. Later these subjects evaluated their reactions to the two forms of meditation by filling out detailed questionnaires.

As often happens with experiments, this one had to be altered because of an unexpected occurrence. It turned out that Tolliver

---

* Cattell's *16 Personality Factor Inventory.*

could not compare the personalities of those who preferred Benson's technique to those who preferred TM because every one of the twenty-six subjects reported that they liked TM better! Whether they had scored on the personality test as High-Anxious or Low-Anxious, as Extroverted or Introverted, Dependent or Independent—this seemed to make no difference—they all preferred TM, saying it was "simpler to do." Most of the subjects found Benson's method pleasant, but none elected to continue with it. Three months after the commencement of the study, over 80 per cent of the subjects were still practicing TM.

Such a reaction is difficult to evaluate. TM obviously carries with it a considerable build-up of expectations. Was this the reason for the subjects' greater enthusiasm for this technique? While this is possible, it is doubtful if it was the sole reason because the usual TM presentation was intentionally omitted in this study. In order to insure that the experimenter did not bias the subjects in any way, preliminary group discussions for *both* TM and Benson's technique were conducted in a joint meeting lasting for an hour. The lecturer described each method of meditation as being short, simple, and easy to learn, and explained that on the basis of the work of Drs. Keith Wallace and Herbert Benson, it had been shown that both techniques yielded exactly the same results. She did not use testimonials, graphs, or charts as part of her presentation.† Although we cannot be certain that the subjects remained uninfluenced by publicity on TM to which they may have inadvertently been exposed through the mass media, 81 per cent of them later reported on a questionnaire that they had not had greater expectations for this technique than for Benson's—in fact, had not expected too much from either. A comparison of CSM (as yet unknown to most students) with Benson's method, should help to clarify this point and is planned for the future.

The present experiment suggests that many people find TM a less demanding task than Benson's method, scarcely surprising in that it is a more permissive technique. This finding may explain

† These innovations were possible because although this comparative study was carried out by a qualified TM teacher, it was done without the sanction of the World Plan Organization.

the impression that several of my colleagues who have taught Benson's method, have conveyed to me—namely that it seems harder for a number of people to "stick to" Benson's method than to TM. Naturally, reports of this sort are not scientific evidence, but they do point the way for some careful studies on the long-term effects of these different methods in terms of their holding power. Can it be that Benson's method, because it demands more concentration than, say, TM or CSM, will prove to be less well adhered to *over time* than certain other techniques? Only careful experimentation can answer this.

Other Methods

TM, CSM, and Benson's method are the main types of meditation we will be talking about because they are standardized and form part of a growing body of scientific evidence. There are other promising techniques on the horizon however.

Psychologist Dr. Lester Fehmi has developed a standardized form of meditation called Open Focus,[14] which simulates a Zen experience of oneness with one's surroundings. While most forms of meditation are studied in the laboratory long after they are created, Dr. Fehmi went about developing his technique the other way around. He tried out a number of different sets of directions for meditation on subjects hooked up to an electroencephalograph (EEG) machine and observed the effect of each set of directions on their "alpha" and "theta" brain waves. In this way, he discovered that certain directions having to do with imagining "objectless space" had the most dramatic effect on the brain. These directions were then elaborated into Open Focus, a guided-imagery meditation which is proving highly effective.

Also through trying out a number of types of meditation on his subjects in preliminary tests, psychologist Robert Woolfolk[15] developed a form of breathing meditation which is quite similar to Benson's method in some respects, but different from it in that he asks his subjects to pay attention to both the in *and* out breath, something which seems to be easier for certain people to do than noticing the out-breath only.

A number of Westernized zazen techniques have also been used in various experiments. These are usually forms of breathing meditation, but without the strict seating requirements and other rigorous demands of true Zazen. Most of them have not been too carefully standardized but are nevertheless useful. They do require some considerable concentration to master, however, which may prove a drawback for many people.

Where do we stand with respect to the similarities and differences, the ease and difficulty of the various forms of practical meditation? The answer seems to be that at this point, since our experimental evidence is scarce, each person will still have to judge individually how he or she responds to any particular technique. I teach a type of mantra meditation which has much in common with CSM and TM, and Woolfolk's breathing meditation, which is much like Benson's method, in Chapter 6. This way, if you like, you will be able to experience both mantra and breathing meditations, and see how each *feels*. Your opinion, based on first-hand experience, can then become a piece of scientific data which you can use while reading this book. You will, in effect, be conducting your own experiment on meditation.

2

Is Meditation Unique?

People often ask whether meditation is merely "another relaxation technique" or simply a form of prayer, a type of self-hypnosis, or so similar to some other method of self-development as to be indistinguishable from it. While some teachers of meditation dismiss these questions lightly, this is not very helpful. Meditation, particularly in its practical forms, does have a number of points in common with some of the other methods used to promote personal growth and the line is not always easy to draw between them. We will look at a few of the related techniques to see what the similarities and differences between them and meditation may be.

Religious Meditation and Prayer

The formal discipline of meditation originated in religious practice and the use of meditation as a spiritual exercise still outstrips by far its use as a practical technique in most parts of the world. The Hindu and Buddhist religions and that of the Sufi sect among the Moslems have developed meditation into a fine art, but other religious traditions through the ages have also developed their own highly effective meditative practices.

Some form of Christian meditation, particularly those practiced in monasteries, are true "meditation" in the sense in which we are using that word in this book. Other Christian practices loosely termed "meditation" are, however, actually "contemplations." Rather than evoking the meditative mood, they create an atmosphere where thought is directed in a disciplined manner to a specific theological problem or religious event. This process often ends with an effort to apply the religious idea contemplated to one's own life.

Much more commonly used by the religious lay person than meditation (at least in the West) is simple prayer, and the relationship of prayer to meditation is an elusive one. While profound prayer probably cannot take place without entering what we have called the meditative mood, mechanical repetition of standard prayers in order to fulfill religious obligations does not require this special mood at all.

Prayer is nevertheless closely related to meditation in many ways. It is usually an inward, contemplative state, undertaken in quiet, often in solitude. As in meditation, so in prayer, outward stimuli are reduced and a special kind of soothing, monotonous environment is created. The echoing intonation of ritual words and phrases chanted over and over again; reverberating music; candlelight; votive offerings; incense; the sound of bells; awe-inspiring architecture with symbolic decorations; a special posture held for a period of time; the closing or partial closing of the eyes —these are all traditional accompaniments of prayer intended to evoke a sense of reverence and union with the deity. Through them the meditative mood is evoked in a highly effective manner.

Although prayer relies upon the meditative mood, it is nonetheless a *goal-directed* activity. In prayer, a person calls upon a deity in some manner. They give praise or offer thanks; seek forgiveness, consolation, or assistance, or enter into some other relationship with the deity. This goal-directed form of praying, by far the most common type, is quite different from the nonstriving, relatively *goal-less* absorption of meditation.

As we turn to other forms of prayer, however, the distinction between them and meditation is not so clear. Prayer *can* be used as a genuine form of meditation in the sense in which we have been using this term. Maupin has described silent, contemplative prayer as having been for a long time the West's only widely used,

22

socially approved "form of meditation."[1] He suggests that with the lessening of prayer in the West in recent years, we have lost important benefits of this form of "meditation" that have little to do with religious belief—psychological quiet and contact with inner experience and our deeper resources.

In some instances prayer is intentionally structured in a form belonging strictly to the realm of meditation. In Western monasteries, the repetition of words in praise of God has been widely used to evoke a special state in which the outer world is shut out and the person is transported into an exalted sense of closeness with God. The "Prayer of the Heart" used by Russian monks and devout lay people in prerevolutionary Russia is an example of this. This prayer was used to "purify the intellect" by means of a passive attitude and the repetition, on each successive out-breath, of the phrase "Lord Jesus Christ, have mercy on me." By this means the mind was thought to become emptied of all thoughts, images and passions. In this instance, a Christian religious phrase was being used in the same manner as mantras are used in India. Sanskrit mantras are either the names of deities or religious phrases.

Used as a form of silent inner communion, or coupled with a mantra-like repetition of religious words, prayer can be seen to blend imperceptibly into meditation. Although we cannot equate prayer and meditation, we cannot fully separate them either. The two states are closely related, not only historically, but often in their spirit or purpose, and both practices are in some sense related to another familiar method which evokes the meditative mood—that of self-hypnosis.

Self-Hypnosis

It is often asked whether meditation and hypnosis are not the "same thing" because they both involve entering a "trance state." The word "trance" often brings a negative image to mind. According to Webster's Dictionary, it implies an inability to function or being in a state of daze or stupor. It is also frequently thought of in the sense of the trances of deep hypnosis, where a person has only limited contact with her or his surroundings and may be quite unable, afterward, to recall what went on during the trance.

These are certain kinds of trance, to be sure, but in actual fact they are neither the only ones nor the most prevalent. *Light* trance states, which are familiar to everyone, do not ordinarily possess these alarming qualities. Dr. Ronald Shor has pointed out that these light trances are actually daily, commonplace occurrences for all of us.[2] They involve sharp narrowing of our attention, which becomes focused on one or on a few objects or events or thoughts. Because of this narrowing of attention, our generalized-reality-orientation—that is, our awareness of our surroundings and of our usual ways of thinking and perceiving—begins to fade, creating a "trance" effect. Shor describes his own experience with such a spontaneous trance:

> I was reading a rather difficult scientific book which required complete absorption of thought to follow the argument. I had lost myself in it and was unaware of the passage of time or my surroundings. Then without warning, something was intruding upon me; a vague, nebulous feeling of change. It all took place in a split-second and when it was over I discovered that my wife had entered the room and had addressed a remark to me. I was then able to call forth the remark itself which had somehow etched itself into my memory even though at the time it was spoken I was not aware of it.[3]

Obviously many other everyday occurrences involve entering a state of light trance, although we may not label the state we experience by that name. We all know, for example, how artists may be intensely absorbed in their work during its inspirational phase and become practically oblivious to their surroundings. The same absorption can occur when one is deeply involved in some majestic scene or in an engrossing game, or in viewing a work of art, listening to music, making love . . . or meditating. Does this mean that we should think of all these activities as being forms of self-hypnosis?

Although both involve some degree of trance, there are also some important differences between meditation and self-hypnosis. One of the identifying characteristics of self-hypnosis is the increased receptiveness of subjects to self-administered suggestions about mental or physical behavior which they want to bring about. The hypnotized person acts (or thinks) in the way he or she believes *themselves*, or the hypnotist is directing them. Self-hypnosis is therefore *goal-directed* and psychologist Robert White, discussing the theory of hypnotism, has suggested that goal-directed striving is one of the primary characteristics of *all* hypnotic states.[4]

This description of hypnosis is very different from most descriptions of meditation. In the great traditions, meditation is looked upon as a goalless, nonstriving state. Though in actual practice the meditator may make some effort during meditation (perhaps in an attempt to reach some spiritual goal), this is usually only a minor aspect of the experience and often discouraged by meditation teachers. Self-suggestions such as telling oneself to relax during meditation, or the implied "suggestion" involved in repeating a mantra which has become a signal to oneself to enter a state of deep relaxation, do of course play some role in the meditative experience, and certain forms of Yoga require the meditator to employ some suggestions to help him or her reach Brahman, the highest state of consciousness—but these minor uses of suggestion can scarcely be compared to the central position given to suggestion in self-hypnosis. With respect to *active striving towards a goal*, these two states seem very different.

Meditation and self-hypnosis do not necessarily show the same kind of physiological changes either. As we shall see in the next chapter, meditation typically brings about a lowering of metabolism, a deep quieting of mind and body. By contrast some hypnotic states *raise* metabolism, as when an athlete uses self-hypnosis before a game to "psych" himself up. Other hypnotic states bring about no physiological changes at all, including no changes in brain waves,[5] and a number of researchers have shown that hypnotized subjects usually have an activated brain wave pattern which is no different from ordinary wakefulness.[6] The only time hypnotized persons show wave patterns similar to those seen during meditation is when they are given specific suggestions to enter a meditation-like state. If they are *directed* to become deeply relaxed, they will usually obligingly do so, just as they will do many other things, including going to sleep, under hypnosis.*

The relationship between meditation and hypnosis is not entirely solved, however. It is possible that in the *broadest* sense of the term, meditation *is* a form of "hypnosis," although it is certainly not the kind of hypnosis we know in the West. Western hypnosis is a highly motivated state where the subject plays a "role," acting out certain prescribed actions or thoughts. Abraham Maslow,[8] who has called this Western form "striving-hypnosis," points out that a much less familiar type, "*being*-hypnosis," allows the subject to move away from role playing and enter an intense absorption similar to that of "peak experiences" or mystic states of contemplation. This being-hypnosis is used almost exclusively for certain spiritual disciplines such as Yoga or Zen. It is possible that it *is* a form of meditation, or vice versa.

Because striving-hypnosis and meditation, while not the same thing, do have some points in common, however, it is perhaps not surprising that one of the most prominent of all the modern relaxation techniques, autogenic training, had its origin in the study of hypnosis as practiced in the West.

Autogenic Training

J. H. Schultz, a Berlin psychiatrist, published the first accounts of a new form of deep relaxation in 1926. It combined Western methods of self-suggestion with some ancient Yoga techniques and he referred to it as "autogenic," meaning, in essence, "self-generated." It was to become the world's most widely used and extensively researched method of relaxation training, with almost 3,000 research studies presently in print dealing with innumerable medical uses of autogenic training, as this technique came to be called.[9]

Schultz's method arose out of research on sleep and hypnosis. In Berlin around the turn of the century, the renowned brain

* It is interesting to note that Zen monks are taught to suppress the hypnotic trance. The name they give to it is *sanran* (meaning "confusion"), because they feel that it interferes with their practice of meditation.[7]

physiologist Dr. Oskar Vogt had observed that a number of patients who had undergone a series of hypnotic sessions under his guidance began, quite on their own, to put themselves into a state very similar to hypnosis during the day when they were alone, and that these self-hypnotic exercises seemed to be having a remarkable recuperative effect upon them. Patients who had practiced the exercises several times a day were reporting marked improvement in their ability to manage stress, they were also experiencing less fatigue and tension, a clearing up of numerous physical symptoms, and gains in overall efficiency.

Dr. Schultz became intrigued by Vogt's findings. Exploring this technique of self-hypnosis with his own patients, he soon discovered that when they practiced it regularly they almost invariably reported two things: a feeling of *heaviness* in their limbs and sometimes in the whole body, and agreeable feelings of *warmth*. Because of this Schultz reasoned that people might be able to induce effects like that of self-hypnosis merely by thinking of "heaviness" and "warmth," without any formal hypnotic induction at all.

He discovered that they could. By simply concentrating on verbal phrases suggesting heaviness or warmth, his subjects were able to bring about a state which seemed to have remarkable healing properties. This discovery launched the large body of work on autogenic training which is still accumulating. Schultz was soon joined by another physician, psychophysiologist Dr. Wolfgang Luthe, and together these men brought autogenic training to hospitals and health clinics throughout Europe, many parts of Asia, Australia, and Canada. Only the United States remained conservatively unreceptive to this technique, so widely acclaimed elsewhere. In recent years, however, autogenic training has begun to attract the interest of Americans as well, particularly since it has been combined with biofeedback training, apparently an effective combination.

Autogenic training typically uses a series of graded exercises involving successive concentration on various bodily states. Such phrases as "my right arm is heavy" (used for right-handed people) are first repeated for very short periods of time, then as the trainee becomes accomplished, more advanced phrases are added, dealing with warmth in the arms, legs, and body, or cooling of the forehead, and so on. Certain trainees, who have been undergoing autogenic training for a year or more, are taught to concentrate on producing certain mental as well as physical states. These mental exercises are called autogenic "meditations," but are far more controlled than the usual forms of meditation. They involve exact instructions such as asking the trainee to visualize certain colors in a particular sequence, and are probably better described as a form of Guided Imagery, rather than meditation.

Regular autogenic training (comprising the basic relaxation exercises) does have much in common with the meditative states, however. The exercises must take place in a quiet room with reduced lighting, clothes loose, the body relaxed, and the eyes closed. The trainee either lies down on their back, leans back in a chair, or sits on a stool in a "rag doll" posture.

The entire process is "meditative" in the sense we have been using that term because to perform the exercises the subject must enter an almost dreamlike state known as "passive concentration," where they do not force any effects but simply "let them happen." If the trainee does not use "passive concentration," their autogenic exercises will not be effective. Because of this, many of the observations made by the autogenic training people are directly applicable to the study of meditation. As we shall see later, this is an advantage for meditation research because tens of thousands of autogenic training records, giving step-by-step accounts of persons practicing this relaxation technique, have been collected over the past half century. This forms a staggering body of information telling us what happens when people place themselves in a state of deep relaxation. We shall take a look at some of this carefully recorded evidence when we come to consider tension-release during meditation.

Free Association

Psychiatrists often compare another technique to meditation—the method of "free association" which is regularly used with patients in psychoanalysis. Like autogenic training, this technique also originated in the study of hypnosis.

In their joint work on the treatment of hysteria, published in 1895,[10] Drs. Sigmund Freud and Josef Breuer reported what was to turn out to be the first step in a major breakthrough in the treatment of psychiatric disturbances. They had discovered that when certain types of patients were able to discharge repressed emotions under light hypnosis, their hysterical symptoms frequently disappeared quite suddenly. When working further with this technique, however, Freud soon found that it had certain drawbacks. Many patients were unreceptive to hypnosis and he began to feel that a method where the doctor had such overriding control of the patient was undesirable.

Perhaps these same results could be brought about by simply having the patient consciously recall and express his or her thoughts and emotions without being put into a hypnotic trance. Trying out this alternate plan, Freud soon discovered that it worked and the method of "free association" was born.[11] In this procedure the patient was directed to relax on a couch and verbalize any thoughts which crossed their mind, no matter how trivial or embarrassing. Using this technique Freud was able to obtain the same kinds of cures for hysterical neuroses that had been possible under hypnosis, and the new technique could be expanded for use with other types of patients as well. Later it was to become a cornerstone of the psychoanalytic method.

The atmosphere necessary for the free associative state is similar in many ways to that needed for meditation. In order to bring about either of these states, stimulation must first be reduced. The free associating patient is placed in a quiet room (the analyst's office) with few distractions. She or he does not look directly at the analyst but allows their mind to wander freely while lying on a couch. Neither the free associating patient nor the meditator is to judge the nature of the thoughts which occur during the session but to accept whatever enters their minds.† In this way, in both situations, emotionally "charged" material not ordinarily available to consciousness is encouraged to rise to the surface.

† This nonjudgmental attitude toward "distractions" or thoughts during meditation is particularly characteristic of the permissive forms of meditation.

There are some important differences between the two techniques, however. During free association the patient is required to *verbalize* all of their thoughts—putting them immediately into words. While this is useful for therapy, doing so automatically excludes all those aspects of experience which cannot be converted rapidly enough (if at all) into word-symbols. There are thus a host of images, sensations, and feelings available to the meditator which free associating patients must ignore because they are continually translating their experience into language *while the experience is still going on.*

Another difference between the two techniques is that free association is used for pinpointing special trouble areas, while meditation seems to handle more general areas of tension. For this reason many nonverbal reactions—feelings which may have developed in early childhood before we had the use of words—seem to be handled by the meditative state, which may escape the patient in psychotherapy.

There is another difference. The psychoanalytic patient free associates with a clear *purpose* in mind—he or she is trying to reveal to the analyst certain concerns. The situation of the meditator is entirely different. During meditation they have no immediate goal in mind, the thoughts which drift through their heads need serve no purpose, and there is no attempt to contemplate their meaning. In this sense, free association might be compared to a type of "work" and meditation (at least "practical" meditation) to a type of "play."

The final distinction between meditation and free association is that free associating requires a relationship between two people, while meditation involves a lessening of all outward ties. The patient in therapy is never totally free from his or her need to please or defy the therapist—they are always in some manner concerned with what the therapist thinks. The meditator, however, is beholden to no one while on their "inward journey."

Despite these important differences between the two techniques, there are moments during free association when the meditative mood must be evoked. This mood may be disrupted by the patient's effort to put their thinking into words, but it is still a necessary component in the psychoanalytic process. If the patient can slip into this meditative mood easily, progress in psychoanalysis will presumably be better. Freud observed that people differ sharply in their ability to free themselves from what he called "intentional" (directed) thinking and learn to free associate. Their capacity to do this may be a function of the degree to which they feel comfortable entering the meditative mood, a reason why patients undergoing psychoanalysis may benefit from practicing meditation. We will discuss this possibility when, later on, we take up the question of using meditation as an adjunct to psychotherapy.

Progressive Relaxation

In the mid-1930s psychophysiologist Dr. Edmund Jacobson developed a method for combating tension and anxiety which involved an interesting notion. He reasoned that since anxiety (as he had demonstrated in his laboratory) involves muscular tension, then turning the situation around and eliminating tension in the muscles should remove anxiety.[12]

To reduce muscular tension turned out not to be so easy, however. People who are chronically tense often have no awareness of the fact that they are tensing their muscles or in which part of the body they are doing so. Perhaps if they were to be made aware of the process of tensing various muscle groups then they would gain control over the tensing-relaxing process. What Jacobson had hit upon was a rudimentary form of "biofeedback," the process of becoming aware of bodily processes and bodily controls.

On the basis of his theory, Jacobson commenced to teach patients to "feel the tension" in various muscle groups, one at a time. They were asked to tighten their muscles intentionally in each area of the body and then were directed to let the muscles relax suddenly and pay close attention to how this felt. Through this method his patients were eventually able to eliminate almost all muscle contractions and experience a feeling of deep relaxation.

Jacobson's training, which he named "progressive relaxation," was long and arduous. It required a total of fifty-six one-hour training sessions to learn his basic technique, and further sessions were often desirable. This made his method too cumbersome for most research purposes, although it was undeniably effective, as Jacobson himself was able to prove over a long series of careful laboratory studies.[13]

In order to overcome this time drawback, behavioral psychologist Dr. Joseph Wolpe later modified Jacobson's technique. In the new version, tensing and relaxing of the muscles was done much more rapidly and the training course was reduced to a total of six twenty-minute sessions.[14] Like many other quick methods, this shortened version lost some of the spirit of the original. Jacobson cautions against having the trainee tense and relax his muscles more than two or three times each hour, because this can result in too much effort being expended and might counteract relaxation. Wolpe and his followers ask their subjects to tense and relax their muscles repeatedly during each twenty-minute period. This is important to realize, because Wolpe's modification of Jacobson's technique is the one widely used today. When we speak about a high dropout rate from progressive relaxation, it will be well to remember that the Wolpe modification calls for real effort. Not everyone may be up to expending that kind of effort for fifteen minutes twice a day.

Are there similarities between progressive relaxation and meditation? Aside from the fact that they both bring about relaxation, progressive relaxation also calls for the atmosphere which is by now familiar to us in all the relaxation techniques—the quiet room, dim lighting, a comfortable position, and an easy, receptive attitude. But despite these points in common, there are important differences between this form of relaxation and meditation.

Wolpe's therapists often use goal-directed suggestion and even hypnotic procedures to bring about awareness of bodily sensations when teaching progressive relaxation. Directions such as the following are typical:

> . . . Completely and totally relax. . . . Just let your muscles go. . . . Enjoy the feeling of deep relaxation. . . . Relax more and more. . . . Focus your attention on how it feels to have your muscles completely and totally relaxed. . . .[15]

Such phrases, repeated over and over again to the trainee in a soothing voice, are often mentally rehearsed by the trainee when they practice this technique at home. Subjects also typically repeat muscle-tensing and relaxing commands to themselves when practicing progressive relaxation. This makes this technique a much more active one than meditation, with the exception of certain inevitable moments (longer or shorter according to the specific directions) when the practitioner remains entirely still.

In a study at Princeton University we compared progressive relaxers with TM meditators and found out something interesting about these "silent" periods which the progressive relaxers experienced. During the ten minutes that our subjects spent lying still and relaxed after completing their muscle tensing, about 65 per cent of them reported that during at least a portion of this time, they usually experienced states of mind which were unfocused, floating, passive, and filled with shifting imagery. It seems as though they may have been entering a meditative mood during these still moments, a point to remember when we look upon the two techniques as distinct and then wonder why sometimes they have quite similar effects.‡

Biofeedback

The most recent of the relaxation techniques does not rely on a mental device for obtaining its effects but on a mechanical one. Biofeedback can be applied to brain waves as well as to other physiological systems to produce a relaxed state. A subject who is hooked up to an EEG machine need only attend to a signal which goes on when their brain is producing a strong burst of the desired type of brain wave and with this information can usually learn to produce the desired brain wave pattern on command, often within fifteen sessions or less.

This kind of biofeedback has important implications for the study of states of consciousness. Brain rhythms are characterized by their frequency—so many cycles or peaks per second. The alpha rhythm, measured from the back of the head, is between eight and twelve cycles per second. The theta rhythm is slower—

‡ Another technique used in behavior modification, the "calm scene," where the trainee vividly imagines details of a pleasant, relaxing scene, may bring out the meditative mood even more strongly.

between five and seven cycles per second. These two kinds of brain waves are of particular interest to scientists because they seem to reflect specific mental states.

Alpha waves typically accompany drowsy relaxed states where the mind is drifting in a somewhat unfocused manner. Subjects in the laboratory variously describe the alpha state as "relaxing," "passive," "anxious," "letting go," "submissive," "high," "pleasant," or by other adjectives. Although it is not, then, experienced in the same way by everyone, it is often present in abundance in the brain wave tracings of experienced meditators during their meditation, and sometimes outside of it as well.[16]

Theta is the state people reach just before sleep and some research even suggests that it may be the time when creative people receive some of their important inspirations.[17] Like alpha, theta also appears in the brain wave tracings of meditating persons, but usually only in very experienced meditators and following a previous period of alpha.[18]

What are the implications of these findings? Do they mean that a person can bypass meditation and achieve what has been jokingly referred to as "Instant *Satori*" (enlightenment) simply by bringing about certain changes in their brain waves? At first this seemed as though it might be the case and the public was eager to purchase the portable alpha biofeedback machines which began to come on the market. It was soon discovered, however, that alpha does not do all of the things that had been promised. While meditation may produce alpha, going into alpha does not necessarily produce meditation. Apparently a meditative state is more than the mere sum of its accompanying brain waves.

According to Dr. Gary Schwartz of the Department of Human Relations at Harvard,[19] one of the most important things to realize when trying to influence various bodily systems is that they typically operate in patterns, something which in the first flush of enthusiasm about biofeedback may not have been properly appreciated. To take a single aspect of the body's operation, such as heart rate or blood pressure or a particular brain wave pattern, *out of context* and train it by itself to respond to a signal (as has usually been done in biofeedback) may be a "second-rate" imitation of nature.

Schwartz found, for instance, that he could train a subject in his lab to reduce his blood pressure a few points in response to a signal sent to him whenever his blood pressure lowered itself even slightly, but if the subject was taught this and *nothing else*, his blood pressure would go down while his heart rate remained the same. Under natural conditions, however, we see lowered blood pressure *accompanied* by a slowed heart rate more than half the time.

Do these systems (heart rate and blood pressure) naturally link up because in a sense they "prefer" to move together rather than singly? To find out, the Harvard researchers then rigged the biofeedback signal so that it sounded only when both blood pressure and heart rate were being lowered at the *same time*. When this was tried the results were clear. Blood pressure fell more sharply when the subjects were responding to a blood pressure-plus-heart rate signal than when they were responding to a blood pressure-alone signal. The subjects were also able to learn more rapidly when their task was to move *both* blood pressure and heart rate in the same direction (whether this direction was up or down).

This and other research suggests that body systems operate more efficiently when acting in unison with one another than when acting alone. Since these systems are interrelated, a training procedure which gets to all of them at once and tries to move them as a whole, the way a chord is transposed in music to another octave, may be the most effective. Schwartz has gone so far as to suggest that perhaps the main importance of biofeedback will be its potential as a research tool rather than the use of it as a form of therapy. Biofeedback training can give us extremely important information about physiology which previously we have not been able to identify. When a change in the functioning of body systems is desired for health reasons, however, it may be easier to bring it about by methods which automatically stimulate a *cluster* of physiologic systems—the same systems that tend, in nature, to vary in a co-ordinated fashion. This is what seems to happen with methods such as meditation which automatically bring about full relaxation in many systems at the same time. It may be the harmony between a number of different bodily processes that is responsible for a state of maximum calm.

In light of this reasoning, it might be a wise strategy in the long run to find ways of understanding, using, and encouraging the relaxation response of the human body *as it occurs in nature*, rather than imitating it by machines, and this can probably be done best by using the various mental techniques for relaxation. Among these techniques, meditation ranks high as an effective tool. For certain purposes, in fact, it may well be the most useful tool of all.

Looking back at the various techniques for personal growth reviewed here, we can see that virtually all of them require special conditions such as lowering of external stimulation or the presence of monotonous stimulation. In addition, every one of them sometimes evokes a meditative mood—with the possible exception of self-hypnosis, which only does this if the specific directions which the person gives her or himself are to "relax."

Despite the fact that they often involve a meditative mood, however, none of the techniques seem to be the *same* as meditation. They do not set out purposely to create the nonstriving, goalless experience of meditation, and none seem to achieve it in quite the same manner. We might view meditation therefore as a method which is related to, but also different from, the other techniques for relaxation or personality growth.

Knowing what meditation is *not*, the door has now been opened to proceed to the next puzzling question. Why has *science* become so interested in this state?

3

The Scientist Takes Note

Seated in a chair in the Biomedical Electronics Laboratory of the famed Menninger Foundation in Topeka, Kansas, a forty-five-year-old Indian yogi, Swami Rama, intentionally "puts himself into" various states of consciousness, seemingly able to alter his brain waves at will. As he does this, an electroencephalograph (EEG) machine receives minute electrical messages from electrodes attached to various cites on his head and conveys them to recording equipment in an adjacent room. A research team, headed by psychophysiologist Dr. Elmer Green, there collects the mass of data which will later be analyzed. The team is making a careful record of some of the unusual abilities which the swami has learned during his long years of practicing meditation. This information is to be used to refine methods for teaching Westerners to alter their own states of consciousness at will, to achieve a sense of inner peace and tranquillity, perhaps even to tap the source of their creativity.[1]

The Swami's behavior is striking, but this project is all the more impressive if we realize that not too many years ago an investigation of this sort would never have taken place. Until recently meditation was considered a subject unsuitable for serious scientific research. It was classified among the so-called "occult" disciplines and looked upon, at best, as an appropriate subject for students of anthropology or religion, but certainly not of interest to experimental scientists. In the past few years the picture has changed. The interest of the scientific community has been awakened and research in meditation has become respectable. What happened?

The first crack in the barrier which prevented the meditative disciplines from being considered as bona fide ways of altering mental states was the "psychedelic revolution" of the 1960s. This era of experimentation with mind-altering drugs resulted in radical changes in the way altered states of consciousness were looked at in the West. These states of consciousness had held the attention of people in Eastern countries for thousands of years but ironically, as "rational" Westerners, we seemed to require the specific introduction of drugs to blast through our defenses and make us notice these different ways of experiencing. Once aware, research could no longer ignore them.

As time went on, an increasingly significant number of people, including scientists, began to experiment with altered states of consciousness in themselves and for a short while there were laboratory experiments on the effects of the mind-altering drugs. Researchers set out to discover whether the major psychedelics such as LSD, psilocybin, or mescaline could be used in the treatment of chronic alcoholics, criminal offenders, or others who were difficult to treat by the usual therapeutic methods. Marijuana was also studied in the laboratory, since scientists wanted to know what its effects on health and personality were. Then, in 1966, almost as abruptly as it had begun, such experimentation came virtually to a halt as a result of new and stringent regulations by the United States Government. Since then only a handful of researchers in special hospital settings have been permitted to conduct a small number of experiments in this area.[2]

After the government regulations took effect, some of the scientists who had been interested in exploring consciousness in the laboratory now turned their attention to finding drugless means for inducing these unusual states of consciousness. Foremost among these other methods were the various forms of meditation. A new group of researchers also joined in this research when meditation became the subject of study and when a more practical reason became evident—the general public was taking meditation up at an unprecedented rate.

As the 1970s were ushered in, a growing number of people in the Western world had by now reported that the elusive, ill-defined process known as meditation seemed to "work" for them. They said they felt more inwardly peaceful since they had been meditating and claimed to have less anxiety and to have developed fewer tension-related diseases. In a society known for its driving pace, where illnesses which are related to stress are rapidly increasing, this is not an insignificant achievement.

Other things were also happening to make meditation an acceptable subject for scientific investigation. We in the West had long held the belief that involuntary processes such as heart rate, blood pressure, body temperature, brain waves, and others, could not be altered by an act of will; they were said to be "autonomic," outside of conscious control. In the mid 1960s and early 1970s however, this entire view of mind-body relationships was upset. Psychophysiologists began to show through ingenious experiments that humans and animals alike *can* learn to control their autonomic functions, and that they will do so in an extremely accurate manner, provided they are given adequate feedback information about how well (or how poorly) they are doing at the time they are learning.[3]

The result has been a host of scientific studies on biofeedback. People have been taught to alter their brain waves "at will" with the aid of an electroencephalograph machine hooked to an electrical device which sounds a beep when they are producing the correct waves. Others have learned to control their finger temperature, lower or raise their blood pressure, slow down or speed up their hearts, or perform a number of other feats, simply by being informed on how they are doing *while* they are doing it.

It is interesting that before the discovery of biofeedback, for nearly two hundred years, physicians serving with the British Army or Civil Service in India had been sending back reports on a few people whom they had studied there who seemed to be able to regulate their "involuntary" body processes, such as heart rate, body temperature, or pain. The doctors claimed that these unusual individuals, called yogis, were able to do so because of their long practice in special Indian mental and physical techniques, yet we in the West did not pay much attention to these scattered reports. It seems that we first needed to develop the technology to measure this capacity. When we could deal with it through a machine, it became "real."

The new interest in biofeedback undoubtedly contributes to the rising interest in meditation. Biofeedback and meditative techniques have much in common: both are based on a *delicately attuned awareness of inner states*. In each of these techniques one deals with experiences occurring within the self which are sensed, but cannot be defined. With the advent of machines which can measure changes in subjective states, "inner space" has become respectable scientific territory.

Another trend lending unexpected support to the study of meditation is a form of behavior therapy known as "systematic desensitization," which relies on the production of a deep state of relaxation for its effects. During this relaxed state, various stimuli which ordinarily produce anxiety for the patient are presented to them in small measured amounts. If the technique works properly, the relaxation "takes the charge off" the patient's fears.

Systematic desensitization is an increasingly popular form of treatment and because it makes use of a relaxation technique, the concept of *relaxation* is suddenly of interest to a great many psychologists. In systematic desensitization several standard methods for achieving relaxation have been used, but the search is on for other, even more efficient means of bringing about this quiet state. Since meditation is one of the most effective known methods for bringing about relaxation, the scientific study of meditation is not only becoming acceptable in psychological circles, it is even in style.

Studying the Masters

Scientific investigation of meditation commenced appropriately enough with the study of traditional meditative techniques in natural settings. Since the original studies were done in the late

1950s and early 1960s, a little before the era when meditation began to be widely used in the West, the obvious sources of meditators at that time were trained yogis or Zen monks. A person who has devoted many years or a lifetime to mastering a technique can be expected to demonstrate it better than anyone else. By studying these people the researchers hoped to learn about "pure" zazen or "pure" Yogic meditation.

These investigations were not easy to conduct. It is difficult to locate a sufficient number of adequately trained and dedicated monks who are willing to be hooked up to machines and it is awkward to transport complex recording instruments. In India, neurophysiologists Drs. Bagchi and Wenger carted a portable electroencephalograph machine 4,000 miles across the country and were only able to locate thirteen subjects.[4] Surprisingly such obstacles were eventually overcome, and the result was several interesting studies.

Because of the inherent difficulties in such research, some investigators used very small numbers of subjects. Drs. Anand, Chhina, and Singh, a team of Indian physiologists, for example, studied only a single meditator sealed in an airtight box in their laboratory.[5] The subject, an experienced yogi, remained meditating inside this contained space for ten hours while the researchers periodically sampled the air in the box for its oxygen content. They were startled to find that over a ten-hour period this yogi practitioner consumed oxygen at a rate 30 per cent *below* the amount considered necessary to sustain life, and that during one period (halfway through the experiment) he was consuming oxygen at a rate as low as 50 per cent below the presumed minimum. However, he emerged from the experiment healthy. Obviously he had been in an unusual state.

In another study, by Indian neurophysiologists Drs. Bagchi and Wenger,[6] various physiological practices were monitored in forty-five subjects who assumed Yogic postures accompanied by meditation. The researchers found that these subjects' heart rates slowed down by 6 to 9 per cent (although they never went below sixty-two beats per minute) during meditation and their respiration rates decreased by an average of 23 per cent. In some instances,

41

respiration dropped by 50 to 60 per cent and occasionally became so shallow that it was unmeasurable. Other studies have shown yogis easily able to maintain themselves during meditation by breathing only once or twice a minute. At the same time, Bagchi and Wenger's subjects showed an increase in the electrical resistance of the skin, a measure generally considered an indication of lessening stress. Their brain waves also showed some unusual patterns which we will discuss later.

At around the same time that the research groups in India were conducting their field studies, a team of Japanese neurophysiologists were studying the brain waves of meditating Zen monks in a Zen monastery. They gathered material which later was to be used for the first experimental comparisons between two traditional schools of meditation—Zen and Yoga.

Both research teams were interested in the same thing: the response of trained meditators to distractions that might be expected to disturb a person in a normal state. We all experience immense amounts of stimulation all the time; if we were conscious of all of it we would never be able to focus our attention on any one thing. Fortunately we automatically "tune out" sensations once we are fairly sure they do not require action. We are not ordinarily aware of a clock ticking unless it is particularly loud and therefore threatening to our peace of mind. If we should become curious about whether the clock is still running, then the ticks are "tuned in" and we hear them clearly. This entirely automatic process which insures that familiar things will eventually not be responded to, is called "habituation." The investigators wanted to find out whether their meditating subjects would habituate to distractions presented to them *while they were in meditation.*

By recording the brain waves of four yogis, Anand, Chhina, and Singh studied their alpha rhythm during a normal resting state and found it to be unusually high.[7] They also studied two of the yogis to see how their alpha pattern behaved when certain sounds and sense impressions were introduced during a stage of meditation called *samadhi.* This is a deep state of meditation specific to Yogic tradition: Yogis claim that during it they are oblivious to both external and internal stimuli and that their higher nervous system is in a state of ecstasy, or "bliss." Accordingly the researchers chose to introduce strong stimuli at regular intervals while the yogis were in samadhi—bright lights, loud banging noises, touching the subjects with a hot glass tube, and ringing a tuning fork close to their ear. Two yogis even requested that their hands be immersed in icy water just above freezing point. They claimed that when in samadhi they were oblivious to this ordinarily painful procedure.

When distracting stimuli are introduced during the alpha state, the alpha rhythm normally "blocks" (temporarily disappears) and a more alert pattern takes its place. This is what happened with the yogis, but with an important difference—when the same stimulus was presented to them *repeatedly* they did *not* habituate to it. No matter how many times a distracting sound or other sense impression was introduced, *each time* the yogi would react by total alpha blocking as though it were the first time he had heard it.

During samadhi, however, there was a dramatic change in their reaction pattern. When they entered this profound state of meditation, the EEG machine showed persistent alpha waves with well-marked increases in amplitude. As the waves became deeper and more rhythmic the experimenters introduced the various distractions one by one and kept repeating them, but none of these intense stimuli presented to these subjects at this time produced any blockage of the alpha rhythm whatsoever. It was as though the subjects were oblivious to sense impressions. Lights, sounds, burning rods, freezing temperatures—they simply did not respond. The two yogis that had asked that their hands be immersed in icy water showed no response to the presumed painful effects of the cold. Yet none of these subjects showed any evidence of sleep patterns during samadhi and were obviously alert.

When two Japanese neuropsychiatrists, Drs. Kasamatsu and Hirai, studied meditating Zen monks, they asked essentially the same questions in their experiment.[8] Using a click as a distraction, they had their subjects meditate in a soundproof room while listening to a click repeated every fifteen seconds.

A group of average Japanese subjects (who were not Zen monks) were first introduced to the experiment. As might be expected, these people showed the usual reaction to clicks. After the third or fourth click, the brain's response to the sounds became less intense until finally it had habituated completely. Now each time the click occurred, the brain gave no evidence of responding, the sound had been tuned out.

When meditating Zen monks were exposed to these same repetitive clicks they reacted differently. The Zen monks showed no habituation to the clicks *during their entire meditation.* They responded to the last click in the series just as strongly as if it had been the first click they had ever heard! While the yogis in samadhi seemed oblivious to any stimulation, the meditating monks seemed open to *all* sense impressions at this time. This same openness to stimulation continued when the Zen monks were not meditating. They responded to all sense impressions without habituation.

The comments by the monks on their subjective experiences when hearing the clicks were interesting. They reported that they had perceived each sound more clearly than they would have in their ordinary waking state but that even though it was remarkably clear they were never disturbed or involved with it in any way. One monk described his state of mind as being similar to noticing every person one sees on the street, but not looking back with emotional curiosity at any of them.

While in these studies samadhi and the zazen state seemed to have the opposite effects *during* meditation, the *after* effects of both forms of meditation were similar. When not meditating, both yogis and Zen monks seemed unusually open to stimuli. Is this perhaps the physiological parallel of "expanded awareness?"

Kasamatsu and Hirai had also asked Zen masters to evaluate the degree of proficiency of each one of the meditating Zen monks by indicating whether they considered them "advanced" in their training or not. Without knowing how the masters had rated these subjects, the researchers then independently classified the monks according to how pronounced the brain wave changes had been. They found a surprising correspondence between the two groups of ratings. The more years the monk had spent in Zen training, the more striking were his brain wave changes during meditation and the more "proficient" that monk had been judged to be by his Zen master. In this study, machine and master-teacher were in agreement.

While these first studies of Zen monks and yogis proved extremely interesting, they soon arrived at somewhat of a dead end. Investigators could not rely for subjects on a few practitioners scattered around the world, some of whom might take twenty years or more to master the art of meditation. A simple Westernized form of meditation was necessary before wide-scale studies could be undertaken.

That form was found in TM. While, as we have seen, TM is not ideal for research purposes, it lent itself more easily to wide-scale systematic study than any previous form of meditation and made possible the launching of a new era of investigation which gathered momentum in the late 1960s. For the first time, meditation came to the laboratory, instead of the laboratory having to travel to it.

TM was useful because it was taught in a *standardized* manner —this insured that wherever it was taught and whoever the particular teacher might be, the *method* was exactly the same and groups of subjects could accurately be compared with one another. People practicing TM were also widely available. As a result of these advantages, experimental studies of TM have so far led the field by a wide margin and are still proliferating, thanks both to the zeal of IMS and to the current interest of the scientific community in the study of relaxation techniques. Information on these TM studies is widely available[9] and so we will review them only briefly here.

The Physiology of Meditation

Some current researchers consider meditation a unique physiological state, different from both sleep and ordinary wakefulness, although sharing some attributes of each.[10] Their studies suggest that during meditation the body enters a profound state of relaxation which resembles in certain respects the deepest stages of sleep, while the mind remains alert and wakeful. More recent research, however suggests that meditation may actually be an artificially prolonged *pre*sleep (hypnagogic) state[11] If so, this is different from the presleep states that we ordinarily experience and may offer unique advantages in terms of re-energizing the organism.

The first studies on the physiology of meditation showed that the heart rate tended to slow down slightly during meditation, just as it does during the quiet phases of sleep, but that this physiological quieting down was achieved much more *rapidly* in meditation. Oxygen consumption (the amount of oxygen the body uses regardless of speed of breathing) was also sharply lowered during meditation.[12] Oxygen consumption is at its highest during intense physical effort such as running or jumping and at its lowest during sleep, when activity is at an absolute minimum. For the sleeping person, however, it takes a number of hours before oxygen consumption settles down to its lowest level. After four or five hours it is about 10 to 20 per cent lower than during wakefulness. In meditation, a similar reduction in oxygen consumption can occur within a matter of minutes after the subject enters meditation, and this drop usually lasts for the duration of the meditation session.

In addition to consuming less oxygen in a natural manner, subjects also tended to breathe more slowly when meditating.[13] On occasion a TM meditator has been reported to breathe at about half the rate they show when simply resting with eyes closed, and one researcher has reported that a single meditating subject's breathing slowed down so much that only about four breaths per minute were recorded (a rate comparable to that observed in certain meditating yogis and Zen monks).[14]

Brain Waves During Meditation

The findings from different laboratories seem to agree that when meditating, subjects tend to show a predominance of alpha waves.[15] These waves are particularly prominent during meditation in the frontal and central regions of the brain. It is as though the motor were idling as the brain drifts along in a peaceful, rhythmic fashion. These trains of alpha waves are sometimes followed by bursts of theta waves.[16] The Zen monks mentioned before showed an ability to remain for extended periods of time in "theta" without going to sleep at all—somewhat of a feat—and TM meditators also occasionally show theta waves without any deterioration into a sleeping pattern.

Increasingly, however, we are getting reports that the brain waves during meditation are remarkably similar to those in states of drowsiness. The mind seems to hover between sleep and wakefulness during meditation and it is not even unusual for actual sleep to occur at this time.[17] A group of TM teachers studied at the Stanford Research Institute, for example, showed definite sleep patterns during TM, although these apparent "catnaps" did not result in full descent into "deep" sleep.[18] While subjects in other studies occasionally have entered *deep* sleep during meditation, we most frequently see brief periods of light sleep alternating with a drowsy but awake state.

In observing meditators, I have noticed that these brief naps that may occur during meditation seem to have a special subjective quality. People often report them as not feeling like sleep. They seem to have a more beneficial and alerting effect than a regular nap. Meditation has certain special properties which set it apart from ordinary drowsiness. We do not ordinarily sustain a delicate balance between sleeping and waking for long periods of time, but tend either to wake up fully or fall asleep. Yet a capacity for hovering between these two states of consciousness for an indefinite period seems to be a distinguishing characteristic of meditation. Perhaps it is the source of much of its value for human beings. We will consider this possibility when we look at the ways in which meditation acts to restore a natural balance.

The most interesting aspect of the meditator's brain activity, however, may not be one specific brain wave or pattern of waves which is identified with meditation, but the unusual evenness and rhythmicity of *whichever* wave form is occurring—the tendency for all areas of the brain to harmonize and pulsate together. Neurologist J. P. Banquet investigated this possibility in a novel fashion. He studied TM meditators who had buttons near their fingertips which they could push to record different "stages" of meditation.[19] A different push-button signal was designated for each of five types of meditative experience. These were body sensations; involuntary movements; visual imagery; "deep meditation"; and an objectless mental state which TM teachers refer to as "pure awareness." During the course of the study, four advanced meditators pushed the button to show that they were either in "deep meditation" or "pure awareness." Looking over their EEG records later, Banquet found that at the exact moments they had sent these signals, an unusual pattern was occurring in their brain wave tracing. The alpha wave patterns shifted at these moments to fast beta waves (a wave form typical of active, awake states), but the beta that these subjects showed was different from the usual waking type—it was entirely "in phase" in each lead of the scalp. That is, the recordings from a number of different areas of the brain were *synchronized*. Ordinarily beta waves are of random length, uneven, and unpredictable.

Banquet called this occurrence *hypersynchrony* and concluded that it is *the* outstanding EEG characteristic of meditation. Not only did alpha waves tend to spread synchronously from the back to the front of the brain during meditation, but after the subject had been in meditation for a few minutes, the separate hemispheres of their brain also tended to come "into phase" with one another. The random and chaotic brain waves of ordinary waking consciousness seemed to be replaced by co-ordinated rhythmic patterns.

At the Hartford Institute of Living, a team of researchers has found essentially the same thing in their EEG studies of TM meditators,[20] and neurophysiologist Dr. Leonide Goldstein of the New Jersey College of Medicine and Dentistry reports having observed synchronous beta wave activity lasting for eighty seconds, occurring in one subject immediately following the ending of a Yoga chant intended to induce deep meditation.[21]

GSR During Meditation

The galvanic skin response (abbreviated GSR) is generally considered a measure of stress. It is recorded by placing electrodes on the skin surface and then attempting to conduct a mild electric current across the skin. If the person is in a calm state, the skin tends to resist electric current. In the presence of anxiety or stress, this "skin resistance" takes a precipitous drop and an electric current flows easily. This is the measurement used in the well-known "lie detector" test, supposedly to indicate if a particular question has made a person feel anxious.

In quiet states such as sleep, skin resistance typically rises. Not surprisingly, therefore, it sometimes rises during meditation. When it does, the rise is much faster than in sleep. One researcher, Dr. R. Keith Wallace, reported that within minutes after starting meditation, his subjects' skin resistance increased on the average by 160 per cent.[22] Recent studies[23] have failed to attain any such dramatic rise in skin resistance during meditation, but all have reported a rise of at least 30 to 40 per cent.

Does regular meditation change the way a person *handles* stress? Psychologist David Orme-Johnson, then at the University of Texas in El Paso, reasoned that meditators should in general be calmer than nonmeditators and therefore able to recover more quickly from disturbances. To test this possibility, he assembled a group of experienced meditators and a group of nonmeditators. He then presented each group with intermittent noise which was about as loud as a pneumatic hammer drilling pavement.[24]

As he presented each new burst of noise, he tested the subjects' skin resistance to find out how long it would take them to habituate to the sound so that they would no longer react with a startled drop in GSR (a stress response). His results showed that the meditators stopped reacting to the loud sound after about eleven repetitions of it and the nonmeditators kept right on reacting the same way for thirty or forty repetitions.

In another study the same research team investigated "spontaneous GSRs" in meditators and nonmeditators.[25] These are fluctuations in skin resistance which occur without any apparent reason. The average person seems to fire little "alarm signals" (GSRs) at intervals, as though they were alerting themself to possible danger even when there is none. In general, the more anxious people are, the more of these subliminal "alerting" GSRs they produce. Again meditators seemed less anxious than non-meditators. The *non*meditators produced about three times as many of these spontaneous GSRs when simply sitting resting as did their seemingly calmer meditating friends.

The next step was to allow the nonmeditators (the ones who had shown three times as many GSRs as the meditators) to be instructed in TM. Within two weeks after learning meditation, this group's spontaneous GSRs were then looked at again. This time they had less than half as many spontaneous GSRs as they had before, their scores were in fact almost as low as those of long-term meditators, an example of the surprising rapidity with which meditation can affect the central nervous system.

In a more recent study, psychologists Daniel Goleman and Gary Schwartz studied the ability of subjects who were given a chance to meditate beforehand to cope with a stress-producing film and compared their reactions to the film with those of subjects who simply relaxed for twenty minutes beforehand. The experimenters found that the subjects who meditated just before seeing the film showed a greater alerting response to the announcement that the film was going to be shown. Their hearts beat faster, their GSRs showed a more exaggerated alarm response, and yet these same subjects also recovered much more rapidly from the stress during the showing of the film and after than did those who did not meditate beforehand. This suggested to the experimenters that meditation may bring about greater alertness to possible danger (on the whole, a desirable characteristic) while at the same time the person who has meditated recently is more able to calm down rapidly once they perceive that the danger does not apply to themselves. This research is in agreement with Orme-Johnson's findings on the greater "recoverability" of meditators under stress conditions.[26]

Other changes occur during meditation too. Blood lactate levels may drop sharply at this time[27] and according to certain research studies (although not to others) this may indicate a reduction in anxiety.[28] Blood flow also tends to increase in forearms and forehead as meditation proceeds, allowing blood vessels to dilate and circulation to operate more easily.[29] While no consistent changes in blood pressure have been identified *during* meditation, long-term studies have shown that some hypertensive patients have been able to reduce their blood pressures significantly over *time* after commencing meditation.[30]

To sum up the physiological research on meditation, a great many different studies suggest that meditation is a low-stress state. Obviously, not all meditators find meditation restful on all occasions, but the averages are impressive, and the beneficial effects are apparently not confined to any one form of meditation. Dr. Herbert Benson, for example, was able to repeat his original TM physiological studies using his own method of meditation and obtained equally impressive drops in body metabolism. As a result, he concluded that he was measuring a fundamental response which was not exclusive to any particular meditation technique.[31]

Psychological Effects

It is usually easier to measure physiological changes than to study psychological ones. Psychological tests are often not as exact as physiological measurements and are not as well accepted as evidence of genuine change. In addition, many psychological tests fail to measure the changes which may be most important when studying meditation, such as the subjective feelings of well-being. Despite this, some tests are simple enough to use right on the spot and investigators have in this way been able to measure some psychological changes which occur right after meditation.

After lounging or taking a brief nap we are not usually at our best on tasks which require speed or concentration. After *meditating*, however, subjects in some experiments have done better on tests requiring manual skill and the ability to observe accurately than they did after a period of simple rest.[32] They could move faster and more nimbly and their scores were significantly higher than they had been before meditating.

TM meditators have also been studied to find out how well they could identify subtle differences in the length of tones sounded just after they had finished relaxing with eyes closed and again just after they had meditated. One group of subjects showed

a keener ability to discriminate pitch and loudness of tone following a twenty-minute session of meditating than after twenty minutes of resting.[33]

In another interesting study, meditators were monitored physiologically to find out if they were really in a state of deep relaxation
during their meditation.[34] It turned out that some were and some
were not. It was those meditators who had been more deeply
relaxed who could afterward discriminate more accurately between different degrees of visual brightness and who had
significantly faster reaction times. The meditators who did not
fully relax did not do so well. It seems then that the degree of
relaxation one reaches during a particular meditation session may
have an effect on the immediate benefits that come after the meditation.

Some long-term psychological changes may also take place with
meditation. The most commonly seen one is a reduction in anxiety. There is virtual agreement among researchers that by whatever test used, meditation reduces anxiety in many who practice
it.[35] What has *not* been proven is that meditation has a clear
advantage over other relaxation techniques in doing this. When
groups practicing other techniques such as progressive relaxation
or alpha biofeedback have been studied, reduction in anxiety has
also been found. It seems that if deep relaxation can be achieved,
by whatever means, anxiety is likely to be reduced.

There is one important practical difference between meditation
and those other techniques, however. Only relatively few of the
meditators in the experimental studies just described (about 20 to
30 per cent on the average) quit before these studies were over,
while the percentage of people who stopped using the other techniques was so great that it often brought the research to a halt.
Several investigators[36] have reported that anywhere from 70 to
100 per cent of the persons practicing either progressive relaxation
or alpha biofeedback stopped these practices before the research
studies were completed, complaining that their techniques were
"tiresome" or "boring." The response to meditation was usually
quite different. In general, subjects tended to look forward to
meditation as a positive part of their day. It was, in effect, its own

reward. This is an important difference. If people do not enjoy performing a certain technique, they will not continue with it long enough to get lasting benefits from it. Many people do enjoy meditating. This seems to give it a clear lead, for practical purposes, over many other relaxation methods.

As for the effects of meditation on habitual behavior, a number of questionnaire surveys have suggested that the regular practice of meditation has what might be called an "anti-addictive" effect. Possibly it reduces the abuse of drugs such as marijuana, LSD, barbiturates, amphetamines, alcohol, and cigarettes. We will consider some of the studies that suggest this later on.

A host of other TM-based psychological studies also indicate that such diverse activities as memorizing lists,[37] solving arithmetic problems,[38] and thinking creatively[39] may improve with meditation. In addition, practicing meditation is reported to have improved academic performance in college students,[40] increased job performance and job satisfaction among workers over an eleven-month period,[41] and increased the sense of having control over one's own life.[42]

These are only some of the research reports which are being used to support claims of meditation's benefits. The list also encompasses more lofty aspects of personality such as self-regard, spontaneity, capacity for intimate contact, and self-actualization.[43] It includes studies on the effects of meditation in prisons[44] and in drug rehabilitation programs[45]; the use of meditation for diseases such as bronchial asthma,[46] hypertension,[47] aphasia (loss of capacity for speech),[48] cancer,[49] and certain speech disorders[50]; and the possibility of using meditation with psychiatric patients in hospitals or in the community.[51]

Meditation looks impressive indeed if we take all these reports at face value, yet even a casual observer may feel somewhat uneasy with the fact that all this research seems so positive. Where are the adverse reports? What about those failures to "replicate" (repeat) these studies in other laboratories? What do nonmeditating scientists think about the meditation research? Negative findings, contradictions, unresolved questions—these are the everyday fare of experienced investigators in other fields and the feedback on which scientific discovery thrives. Why is it we do not hear more about them in the field of meditation?

The fact is that healthy "contradictory" evidence has only recently begun to be published in this field and as far as the general public is concerned, it is still eclipsed by the original TM studies, which have received more extensive publicity. In the long run, however, this newer research will probably be more important than the former studies because it is more constructively *critical*. We will now look at this controversial side of meditation research.

4

The Other Side of Research

When a new area in science begins to be studied intensively enough to disprove some of its original findings, this is a signal that it is being taken seriously by experimenters. Contradictions in the research pave the way for a deeper understanding of the processes being looked at. This appears to be happening with meditation with some exciting results.

Wallace's Work Seen Differently

In the course of their research at the Department of Anaesthesiology of the Royal College of Surgeons in London, Drs. John Bushman and Peter Fenwick[1] have explored the dramatic drops in oxygen consumption and carbon dioxide output during meditation originally reported by Wallace and Benson. Wallace, for example, found a drop in oxygen consumption during meditation of between 16 and 18 per cent when meditation was compared to the resting states which came before and after it.[2] A contrast is, however, always relative—the results found depend on what is being contrasted. If, for instance, we were to compare the level of oxygen consumption of a woman running with her level while sitting in a chair engaging only in occasional minor movements, we would find that her oxygen consumption had dropped. The statement "sitting in a chair lowers oxygen consumption" could then be made, but only relative to *these particular conditions*. If we were to measure her level of oxygen consumption when lying down quietly, we would find an even greater reduction in oxygen consumption, and if she were to sit up again and begin once more to move occasionally, then "sitting in a chair" could *now* be said to have *raised* her oxygen consumption.

The British research team was concerned with this problem. Could some of the dramatic physiological changes that Wallace and Benson had noticed in meditating persons have been due to a failure to take this contrast factor into account? To find out, these investigators carefully recorded all effortful behavior, as well as all changes in oxygen consumption and carbon dioxide output, made by a group of TM meditators during their period of premeditation resting in the laboratory, and then during and after their sessions of meditating.

What they discovered was that any movement made by the subjects during their premeditation resting period raised oxygen consumption. If the subjects merely lifted a leg, for example, their oxygen consumption might be raised by as much as 50 per cent, and even minor things such as being spoken to or closing their eyes caused a rise in the premeditation figures. When they measured the degree of tension or relaxation in their subjects during the premeditation period, they also found out something else. Those subjects who were tense before meditation showed large drops in oxygen consumption during their subsequent meditation sessions, while those who were relaxed beforehand showed only small drops.

The polygraph records of those people who were relaxed beforehand were revealing. Even before meditation started, their carbon dioxide output would begin to drop steadily. During meditation the drop simply continued, and after meditation it went up again because of body movement. This suggested to the experimenters that if they could find a group of meditators who were relaxed *enough* before meditation, these people might not show any drops at all in metabolic rate while meditating.

Such a group was found. It consisted of experienced TM meditators who came to the laboratory just after rising in the morning, and before having eaten. When they were studied, it turned out that these people were already so relaxed that they could not produce any further metabolic changes at all, even during meditation. This strengthened Bushman and Fenwick's opinion that many of the reported drops in metabolism during meditation in the past may have been due to a contrast effect.

By the time their experiment ended, the research team reported having found an overall drop in oxygen consumption during meditation in their regular subjects of about 7 per cent, less than half the size of the drop reported by Wallace. They attributed this difference in their findings to the fact that they had taken particular care not to disturb their subjects before and after meditation, making sure that they remained completely still during *all three* experimental conditions.

It is important to understand the implications of such a "failure to replicate." This new research does not mean that meditation is not deeply relaxing—the subjects *were* extremely relaxed during their meditation. It also does not mean that the earlier studies were not well conducted. Failures to replicate are a universal occurrence in research and are welcomed as an opportunity to learn more about the subject being studied. In this case, the British experiment means that future experimenters investigating changes in metabolism during meditation will now need to prove that the effects they obtain are not simply the result of muscle movement preceding meditation vs. muscle stillness during it, but due to some unique quality of the meditative state *itself*. Approaching the task from this standpoint should produce more precise information about meditation.

There is the possibility that formal meditation is only one of a larger group of physiological and mental states, all of which share at times what I have called the meditative mood. Perhaps whenever this meditative mood is present, even if the state in progress is not termed "meditation," the physiology may be affected in a manner that causes a lowering of metabolism. Some further evidence from the Royal College of Surgeons suggests this possibility.

When Drs. Bushman and Fenwick piped soothing music to their subjects over earphones, the drop in oxygen consumption while listening to the music was found to be as great as it had been during meditation. Music of course can induce the dreamy reverie state which I have classified as a meditative mood. Could this be the reason the drop in oxygen consumption with music was equal to that during formal meditation? It may be that the meditative mood runs like a connecting thread through all the relaxation techniques, a potential which all of them can offer. If the mood is evoked by the technique, then metabolic changes may follow; if it is not, they may not occur. It is possible that future researchers may find it is more important to study the meditative mood than the specific technique for achieving meditation or relaxation.

The Experimenter Effect

Another area challenged by some of the newer research is that which concerns the experimenter's effect on his or her own research. A strong interest on the part of experimenters in their subject of research can be a mixed blessing. Such interest can make for hard work, dedication, and inspiration on the part of an experimenter, but occasionally it can be a drawback to well-balanced research. Not that these investigators will be less honest or conscientious when conducting their experiments, but simply that they must beware of a well-known stumbling block in science called the "experimenter effect."

Every piece of scientific research is affected in some way by human limitations and by the expectations of the experimenter and this distorting influence can never be totally eliminated. Up until now, however, a number of the meditation experiments, particularly those done on TM, have not taken sufficient trouble to *reduce* this effect to a point where it is reasonably certain that it is not affecting the results.

When Michael West of the University of Wales Institute of Science and Technology studied the effects of TM on memory tasks administered directly after meditating, he was particularly aware of the fact that his own expectations and hopes might inadvertently creep in and influence his results.[3] His solution to this was to keep his experiment almost entirely automated. Even the numbers which the subjects were to repeat in the memory tasks were tape-recorded rather than given in the experimenter's own voice. At the end of the experiment, West found that his subjects had done no better on these tasks after meditation than they had prior to meditation. This contradicts the results reported by graduate student Allan Abrams on improved memory following TM.[4] Were West's results due to his care in removing the experimenter effect?

A recent study at Princeton University was also so tightly designed that the hopes of the chief investigator, Mark Shook, who is an enthusiastic TM meditator, were not borne out by the results, possibly a credit to the care with which he conducted the study. TM literature features a study on reaction time where researchers Shaw and Kolb studied eighteen subjects (nine meditators and nine nonmeditators) to find out how rapidly they could respond to a flash of light.[5] They discovered that the meditators had reaction times which were 30 per cent faster than those of the nonmeditators. After the meditators had meditated for fifteen minutes and the nonmeditators had rested for that amount of time, all subjects were then retested. All had better scores after the recess, but the meditators had improved slightly more (their reaction time went up another 15 per cent) while the nonmeditators had improved by only about 10 per cent. It looked as though meditators in general may be faster "reactors" than nonmeditators.

When researcher Mark Shook conducted his experiment on reaction time, he planned it differently.[6] Instead of nonmeditators, he studied a group of people who had just recently signed up to learn meditation but had not yet started, another group who had been practicing meditation for one to three months, and still another group who had been practicing it for six months or more: a total of forty-two subjects. He then measured *two* types of reaction time—"simple" reaction time, which is a response to a single flash of light (the same measure Shaw and Kolb had used), and "complex" reaction time, which requires a quick decision between *two* lights. When the results were tabulated, those subjects who had been practicing meditation did no better on either of these reaction time tasks than the people who were waiting to learn the technique, nor did the more experienced meditators do better than the less experienced ones.

Shook next looked at the reaction times of all eighty-five subjects just *before* they meditated (or in the case of people about to learn meditation, before they rested) and then measured them once again after they had meditated or rested for twenty minutes. Once more there was no change in any of the scores. Neither simple nor complex reaction time improved with either meditation or rest. What are we to conclude from this?

Since this was a more extensive experiment using a much larger number of subjects and a more cautious approach, its results seriously challenge the Shaw and Kolb findings. At this point, the effects of meditation on reaction time must be considered unproven—a typical example of the reversals that we so often see in scientific work. At the same time, however, we must not lose sight of the fact that capacities such as visual-motor co-ordination, an important ingredient in athletic and other types of performance, *have* been shown to improve after meditation and that such results have been replicated in several laboratories. In other words, the result of the widening scope of meditation research is that some of the original findings have become more firmly established, while others are being disproved.

A Comparison

A number of the findings from the newer studies do not directly contradict earlier results, but suggest that the effects seen apply to a *range* of meditative and relaxation techniques, rather than any single technique.

At the University of Exeter in England, Dr. Denver Daniels compared TM meditators with long-term practitioners of Hatha Yoga, subjects practicing progressive relaxation, and nonmeditators.[7] He set out to discover whether these various groups would respond differently to a stressful stimulus. For his stress stimulus Daniels chose a sharp grating noise, the kind that "sets your teeth on edge." Such sounds usually change the electrical resistance of the skin, bringing about a drop in skin resistance. When he played these shrill scraping noises to his subjects over a loudspeaker, those practicing progressive relaxation reacted with a sharp drop in skin resistance. The same was true of the ordinary nonmeditators; they too were unable to resist reacting automatically whenever they heard the scraping. The group of TM meditators responded differently, however. They seemed able to tolerate the noise easily; the poloygraph needle recording their skin resistance hardly moved at all, showing only a minimal reaction to the sound. The only subjects who were as relaxed as the meditators when presented with the sound were the long-term practitioners of Yoga. These people, who had been practicing Yoga for nine years or more, also barely reacted and a few of them even seemed totally unresponsive to the sounds.

Daniels feels that his results are due to "greater relaxation" produced by both TM and Hatha Yoga. This is a plausible explanation, but is it possible that the presence or absence of something else helped determine whether any particular subject could withstand the noise without distress?

We can imagine that during the experiment, the progressive relaxers, who were occupied with tensing and relaxing their muscles periodically, probably had little or no opportunity to drift into a full meditative mood. The nonmeditators, on the other hand, with nothing to occupy their minds except their discomfort, may well have spent *their* time listening for the next painful sound and perhaps hoping the experiment would soon be over. Probably the only people who were able to establish a full meditative mood were the meditators and the experienced practitioners of Yoga. There is, therefore, a possibility that the meditative mood played an important role in insulating these subjects from the painful stimulus, serving in a sense as a mental "cushion" to protect them from it.*

Basic Designs

We might look at the meditation research that has been done thus far from the standpoint of how well it has been designed. A

---

* This could be checked out in the future by researchers asking subjects how they felt, and what type of thoughts were going through their minds, during the experiment.

poorly designed study is like a house constructed from inadequate blueprints. No matter how much care goes into the actual construction of such a house, or how fine the materials used, it may collapse. Those readers who are curious about the attractive charts of the TM findings publicized by the World Plan Organization, may want to read the following account in order to obtain a perspective from which to judge these reports. Those who do not care about the pros and cons of experimental design or the problems involved in meditation research, can simply skip to the next chapter. Doing so will not interrupt the continuity of this book.

What are the basic designs used in meditation research? How adequate are they? I will commence by considering the easiest study to conduct in this area—a comparison between meditators and nonmeditators. *The TM Book*, a paperback put out under the auspices of the World Plan Organization,[8] is a good measure of the kind of information the general public is getting about meditation. Thumbing through its pages, I counted fifteen charts describing studies based on this type of comparison, a greater number than that for any other approach.

This method is a straightforward one. When meditators are compared with nonmeditators, if the meditators do better on certain tasks, it is assumed that this is because they meditate regularly while the other people do not, and the results are then reported as showing the benefits of meditation.

In science, however, we have to beware of hidden factors. There is a problem with these meditators vs. nonmeditators comparisons; namely, that people who undertake to learn meditation may have *always* been different from those who do not undertake to learn it.

Unfortunately, no research has been done to find out the special characteristics of people who decide to learn meditation vs. those who do not, but we do have some indirect evidence. In a large-scale study on the effects of TM on the use of nonprescription drugs, Dr. Mohammad Shafii of the University of Louisville School of Medicine asked meditators and nonmeditators to indicate on an anonymous questionnaire how often they had used marijuana during a period of time *before* the meditating group had learned TM.[9] The reports of the meditators showed that they had been regularly using *twice* as much marijuana as the non-meditators before they started TM. Was this because the people who were later to become meditators were a less conventional group, more willing to experiment with drugs? Or was it because they were a more anxious group who had a greater need for marijuana or other outside aids to relax them? While we do not know the answers to these questions, what we can learn from this experiment is that these two groups—the meditators and the non-meditators—must have been composed of somewhat different kinds of people to begin with.

A study conducted at Princeton University also sheds some light on this question. Researcher Susan Shackman compared college students who had chosen to learn TM right away with another group who said they were willing to postpone learning it and agreed to study a simple relaxation technique in the meantime.[10] On personality tests administered to these subjects before they learned their respective techniques, Shackman found that both groups scored about the same with respect to the amount of anxiety they showed. On a test for self-image, however, the subjects who had chosen to learn TM without delay had significantly higher "disparity" scores—that is, there was a greater contradiction between the way they presently saw themselves and the way they would, ideally, have liked to be. Discrepancy of this sort often means discontentment with the way one is.

The about-to-learn-meditation group also differed from the non-meditators in one other respect. On the California Personality Inventory (a well-known test of personality) the prospective meditators scored significantly *lower* on Dominance, Capacity for Status, Sociability, Self-Acceptance, and Sense of Well-Being. This suggests they may have been more insecure people than those who were willing to postpone learning meditation. If they were, perhaps some of the glowing reports we hear from meditators arise from the fact that in general they tend to be more troubled than those who do not learn meditation, and therefore have more room for improvement in their emotional state. More stable people might not show as much improvement with meditation and perhaps are less likely to learn it in the first place. We might have arrived at this same conclusion through a common observation—people usually do not go out of their way to learn something for which they do not feel a particular need.

If meditators and nonmeditators are basically different kinds of people, then how do we know whether any differences reported between these two groups in those studies which simply compare meditators with nonmeditators, are the results of *meditation?* The answer is we do not know. We very well may be comparing fundamentally different personalities. Nevertheless, *some* of the differences found may be genuinely due to meditation and nothing else. The trouble with the research that relies on the meditator vs. nonmeditator comparison is that it does not give us any way of telling which findings are true results of meditation and which are not.

A second type of research compares regular meditators with people about to learn meditation ("beginning meditators"). Here both groups have signed up to learn meditation, the only difference between them being that subjects in one group have been randomly assigned to a meditation group and are practicing their technique, while the other group has been randomly assigned to a waiting list and will learn meditation sometime in the *future.*† For this reason we can be certain that in these studies we are dealing with people who are more or less the same in one important respect—they are equally attracted to learning meditation.‡ This makes this type of design preferable to the meditators vs. nonmeditators one. In looking over the TM research charts, all other things being equal, this latter type of study can be taken more seriously.

Whenever two separate human beings are compared with each other, however, it is somewhat like comparing an apple with an

---

† In Shackman's Princeton study her subjects were not randomly assigned to the meditation or relaxation groups—for practical reasons they had to be allowed to choose their group. This represents an unavoidable weakness in the study, but was the source of interesting information about the differences between subjects who chose meditation immediately and those who could wait.

‡ The same advantage is seen in those studies that compare regular meditators with *irregular* meditators. Here both groups are already meditating, making a comparison between them well matched.

orange. People differ from each other in many ways and we can never be certain just what all these ways are in any particular instance. A method which compares two groups of subjects can therefore never be as exact as one which compares each subject with his or his *own self* under varying conditions.

An increasingly popular research approach compares regular meditators with *themselves*—before learning to meditate and again after some time has lapsed, making this a "before and after" or "longitudinal" design. This is in many ways an ideal method for studying meditation. For practical reasons, however, it is often not possible. It takes a great deal of time, effort, and money to follow subjects over a period of months, and even more if the study extends for years, and it is discouraging to have subjects drop out of such an experiment in ever increasing numbers, so that the study may yield only meager data in the end. Despite these difficulties, however, an encouraging number of studies are now being reported which use this longitudinal design.

Still another way of comparing subjects to their own selves is a "before and after" study which is completed in a *single* experimental session. This is easier and obviously less expensive than the longitudinal approach. By this method, a subject is tested before she or he meditates, again right after the session, and perhaps during the session as well. When it is appropriate to the particular problem being studied, this is a highly desirable way of going about research. Everything takes place in the laboratory and is under the experimenter's control. It is the design used for most of the physiological studies and for the psychological ones which deal with performance on simple tasks such as visual or auditory discrimination, reaction time, memory, and the like.

In many studies also, measurements taken before and after meditating are compared with measurements taken before and after the same subject rests quietly with eyes closed. This is done to check on whether or not any changes which may have occurred after meditation are really due to the meditation itself, rather than being simply a result of the subject having taken it easy for a few minutes. Like so many other strategies, however, this one has a subtle "catch" to it.

Meditators usually consider meditation to be particularly beneficial and are much less likely to think of a simple rest period as being able to do them much good. Because of this difference in attitude toward the two states, an "expectancy effect" may be created. If the subjects are TM meditators, this effect can be especially strong because they have been taught to view meditation as possessing benefits no other state can possibly offer.

Expectations are potent forces. If we expect that a particular doctor will be able to cure us of an ailment while another will be unable to, we are more likely to recover quickly under the first doctor's care. If we believe that medicine X is a wonder drug and that medicine Y is a sugar pill (placebo), then medicine X may cure us of our ailment (*even* if it is really only a sugar pill) while medicine Y may have little effect on us.

If subjects consider a period of meditation more beneficial than a period of rest, how can we be sure that the different effects we see when we compare these two conditions may not merely be due to the convictions the meditating subjects had that one condition would be better for them than the other? In scientific language, how can we be sure this is not a placebo effect?

We cannot, and for this reason we need to recognize that expectation effects may be present. If we cannot eliminate them (we never can completely) then they must be taken into account. Are there some other expectations that affect the results of meditation research?

Tracking Down the "Placebo"

In a typical TM training course, new meditators receive two introductory and three teaching lectures during which a vast array of exciting promises and scientific facts "proving" the beneficial effect of meditation are paraded before them. By the time the meditators are left on their own, they are now deeply embedded in a belief system about the benefits TM brings. Of course, other forms of meditation have their indoctrinations too. The power of religious or quasi-religious ceremonies, incense, and the like is considerable. Any trained meditator is therefore expecting certain results and perhaps because of this he or she is more likely to find them.

There is no easy answer to this problem of the placebo effect in research, but an interesting effort to grapple with it has recently been made by psychologist Jonathan Smith.[11] Dr. Smith devised a fictional self-improvement technique which consisted of nothing more than sitting quietly with eyes closed twice a day for fifteen to twenty minutes, but which had an elaborate psychophysiological rationale for its supposed effectiveness, following closely the reasoning given for TM's effects. Similarly, as we have seen, in her study comparing TM with Benson's method, researcher DiAnna Tolliver, who is herself a trained TM teacher, took responsibility for modifying the presentation of the TM teachings so that expectations for the two methods were equalized. Still another way of coping with this problem is to compare relatively unknown forms of meditation with each other, types for which expectations are assumed to be equal.

The placebo effect is, however, an elusive quarry. Often the more we pursue it, the more it seems to evade us. In trying to reduce the expectation factor in our experiments we run the risk of creating some new problems for ourselves. This is because the *state* of meditation and the techniques or exercises used to bring this state about are quite separate things. A person can do any meditation exercise according to instructions, but if the fragile meditative mood is not evoked by the exercise, then they will not have been meditating. In order to reduce the influence of expectations, experimenters could strip the teaching of meditation down to its "bare bones" and use nothing more than a curt set of directions such as "Just shut your eyes and think the following word silently to yourself for twenty minutes." What then would the subject be doing when thinking this word?

The person would certainly be performing a mental exercise, but this could not be said to be genuine "meditation" unless he or she brought to the experience some *emotional* component of central importance. If the experience did not take on a special meaning for this new meditator, if it did not become part of an almost nostalgic closeness with their own self and feelings, it probably would not evoke the meditative mood. Perhaps the expectations and colorful "buildups" surrounding the learning of meditation are essential in establishing this singular mood. If so, then they may be a very real and central part of the experience, something we should leave intact when teaching meditation. If we eliminate suggestions which are conveyed through a simple ritual or an encouragingly respectful attitude toward the technique on the part of the teacher, we may congratulate ourselves on being "scientific" and "objective," but in the process we may have eliminated the process of meditation.

Meditation research seems then to tread a very fine line. We need to find a way of reducing all *unnecessary* expectations without going so far as to eliminate the touch of magic and dream, the hopeful mood, the sense of warm contact with the teacher that makes meditation what it is—something apparently quite different from mere physical relaxation.

The Search for the Opposite

Smith's experimentation brings up another question that troubles researchers in this field—what state is enough *like* meditation so that it can be reasonably contrasted with it while at the same time it is enough *unlike* it so that we can be sure this "control" condition is not really just another kind of meditation?

At one stage of his study, Smith compared a form of mantra meditation similar to TM to a condition which he termed "anti-meditation," a technique which was designed to be the "near antithesis of meditation." Anti-meditation involved sitting with eyes closed and actively generating as many *positive* thoughts as possible. If the subject felt that he or she was lapsing into a "lazy trance state or daze" at any point, he was to snap himself out of it by blinking his eyes. Thinking was to be *deliberate* and to consist of a fantasy-daydream, telling oneself a story, or "listing" positive qualities of something.

This ingenious effort to find an adequate "control" for meditation nevertheless created certain difficulties. While the anti-meditation technique which Smith devised may be the opposite of some forms of mantra meditation, it seems closely to resemble certain forms of *concentrative* meditation; as, for example, keeping the mind purposely occupied with positive thoughts, often of a religious nature, such as "God is good, God is kind, God loves me" repeated over and over again. A peculiar fact about meditative techniques is that two different methods, seemingly opposite on the surface, can often bring about identical results. The ceaselessly whirling dervish and the motionless yogi in samadhi both arrive at a state of objectless absorption. Perhaps Smith assigned not a meditation antithesis, but simply a different type of meditation to his control subjects.

The condition most commonly compared with meditation is obtained by asking control subjects simply to rest with eyes closed on the assumption that they are doing something quite different from meditating by following these directions. That seems reasonable, but it is nevertheless merely an assumption. Different people with eyes closed may be in many different places mentally. Some may be occupying their minds figuring out the dinner menu or planning how they will ask their boss for a raise. Others may hover on the edge of sleep. Still others may enter a meditative mood which is virtually indistinguishable from the state of mind of the meditator, even though they are not repeating a mantra or performing any other centering exercise and have never learned meditation. What the examiner *thinks* is a single condition—resting with eyes closed—may then be any one of a number of different conditions.

There is a way to deal with this problem: ask the subject what was going on in his or her mind. In a long-term experiment, this means having the subject fill out a daily checklist after each meditation session which is designed to find out if they were in fact in a meditative mood. If they are the kind of person who often slips into a meditative mood when shutting their eyes, we might expect that several months of sitting twice daily with eyes shut would affect them much the same way as meditation does a meditator. On the other hand, if closing the eyes does not tend to evoke a meditative mood in a person we might expect them not to change in the same way a regular meditator would over a corresponding period of time. The presence or absence of the meditative mood may be one explanation for what often seems to experimenters to be puzzling and even contradictory findings.

This problem might be summed up by recognizing that there are several assumptions underlying much of our present research on meditation. We tend to assume (1) that because a meditator is sitting and repeating a mantra or using some other meditational device, he is necessarily "meditating"; (2) that because a subject is sitting for twenty minutes with eyes closed, he is necessarily *not* meditating; and (3) that people who have never been *taught* to meditate ("nonmeditators") do not meditate.

All three assumptions can be challenged. To test them it is necessary to record the experiences of the participants along with measurements of their psychological change or performance. The measurement of both the experiential and the objective components of the meditation experience is crucial in clarifying the real meaning of meditation and the only way to avoid being trapped by the labels we have attached to various states of consciousness.

How Dropouts Affect Meditation Research

Whenever an activity is undertaken by a large number of people on a regular basis, no matter how beneficial they find it to be, a sizable number sooner or later abandon the practice. This is the case with regimens of daily exercise, dieting, mental practices for self-improvement, and even the taking of necessary medicines. People terminate self-administered programs for a number of different reasons, but the dropout rate is always a factor to contend with in any program which leaves people on their own to accomplish their own goals. Meditation is no exception. While IMS claims to have no official figures on the dropout rate for TM, several independent studies have been done to determine this and they show that from 30 to 50 per cent of adults sooner or later stop practicing this technique, and that up to 70 per cent of high school students may quit the practice.[12] The majority of these studies cite a dropout rate which hovers around the 50 per cent mark.*

* For more detailed information on the TM dropout rate, see Appendix.

This is not surprising, nor does it reflect on the intrinsic value of TM. It is simply another factor to keep in mind when considering the validity of meditation research. If a long-term study is being conducted and a group of meditators have dropped out along the way, then the final testing procedures will obviously include only those subjects who had the stamina, determination, motivation, or whatever else was necessary, to keep them meditating—while those who may not have had these qualities were automatically excluded from the final results. Under such conditions we have no way of knowing how much the "quitters" might have improved if they had continued to practice meditation for the same period of time as the "persisters." Perhaps the quitters dropped out precisely because they were *not* improving and so were discouraged. If so, leaving them out of the final results will make the research on the effects of meditation look more positive than it should. All we can legitimately conclude from such studies is that *among those who stayed with meditation,* a certain improvement has occurred. This is an acceptable enough statement from a scientific point of view—the only trouble is, it is seldom made. The reader looking over meditation research almost always has to supply such qualifications for him or herself. They should therefore be aware of this pitfall, keep an eye on the dropout rate in any particular experiment, and notice whether the researcher has taken this factor into account when interpreting the results.

Where We Stand

Meditation research, particularly that dealing with TM, is being presented to the general public in books and pamphlets which display experimental findings in attractive charts. These charts report bona fide scientific research, but as we have seen, not all the studies they depict are equally reliable. I have described some ways that someone reading about the research in the field can judge for him or herself how likely it is that any particular study will stand up under challenge; that is, how well designed it is. But are such considerations useful in terms of the *practical* value which meditation has for the meditator?

Actually, they may not be. The newer, more challenging research has not reversed the basic finding that meditation relaxes people, reduces tension, and may bring about a number of side benefits. Because of this, the *reasons* why it is restful, or the knowledge that other states may also be relaxing or beneficial, may be beside the point for the person who finds meditation to be a particularly compatible and effective means for inducing tranquillity in him or herself. With this perspective in mind, we will now turn to the experience of meditation itself.

II

Managing Meditation

5

Learning How to Meditate

Because we will be discussing several different types of practical meditation in this book, it might be interesting at this point for you to learn a representative technique from each. This way you will have a better basis for judging the discussions that follow. If you are already a meditator you may want to skip over the technique which most resembles your own and try the others to broaden your acquaintance with the field.

Although meditation instructions in this chapter are intended as an introduction to some of the basic techniques, you may decide to build one of them into a regular practice. This can easily be done and directions for doing so are given, but before learning meditation with the intention of adopting it as a regular practice, you should be aware that a *few* individuals practicing well-known forms of meditation have had sufficiently unsatisfactory experiences with meditation so that their own "psychic wisdom" has prompted them to abandon it. In the absence of a personal meditation teacher, my recommendation is that if for any reason you find one of the techniques of meditation described here in any way unpleasant, you should quietly give yourself permission to set it aside. Perhaps at some future time you may feel it is desirable to give it another try, perhaps not. The wisdom of your inner self on these matters is remarkable and each person should respect his or her own deepest intuition as to whether this practice is suitable for them.

If you decide you want to sample some forms of meditation now, a useful method might be to learn one of the techniques presented here on each of four consecutive days. You can look upon this either as being an interesting experiment, or as a means of learning meditation for your permanent use. If you plan to meditate regularly with one of these techniques, be sure to read the comments later on in this chapter.

Preparation

For all four meditative techniques taught here, the same preparations apply:

1. Plan your meditation sessions so you will not be meditating within an hour's time after having eaten a meal, and avoid stimulants such as coffee, tea, or Coca-Cola for two hours beforehand. A small glass of orange juice, milk, or decaffeinated coffee can be taken before meditating. . . . The meditative traditions insist that meditation is relatively ineffective (if not actually harmful) on a full stomach and the reasons for not taking a stimulant are obvious—meditation is for calming down.

2. Choose a relatively quiet room to meditate in where you can be alone, and silence the telephone. Meditation should be undertaken in a serious manner with few distractions. Explain to others that you are not to be interrupted. The only reason for interruption should be an urgent situation which demands your attention—even children, who can usually understand what "napping" means, can soon learn not to interfere with your meditation.

3. Meditate seated before a green plant, flowers, or some other natural object where it is pleasant to rest your eyes. If you enjoy the smell of incense, lighting it can add to the meditative experience, but it is not necessary. If you do use it, avoid overly sweet or artificial scents; ideally it should be a natural, unobtrusive scent which gives you a sense of being close to nature.

4. Face away from any direct source of light. The room need not be dark, but it's pleasanter if the lighting is subdued.

5. Sit on a chair or on the floor, whichever you prefer, in an easy,

comfortable position. If you are experienced in using the lotus position, that's fine, but it is not necessary for our purposes—a straight-back chair will do just as well. It will help you to relax if you remove your shoes and loosen all tight clothing before commencing to meditate.

6. If during meditation you find yourself uncomfortable at any point you can always change your position slightly, stretch or yawn, or scratch an itch. The point in this type of meditation is to be comfortable. You are not learning the more rigorous forms of meditation such as a Zen monk or a yogi might practice, so you do not have to be concerned with learning to *master* distractions as they do. This is to be an easy, quiet time with yourself—that is all.

7. Follow the instructions given for the specific type of meditation you are using. If, despite all precautions, you are interrupted during the meditation, remember one thing: *to play for time*. Try not to jump up out of meditation suddenly any more than you would jump up from a deep sleep if you could avoid it, your body is likely to be as relaxed during meditation as during the deepest stages of sleep. If someone is knocking on the door or calling to you, answer only after a pause (if possible) and say you will be there in a minute or so. Move slowly, yawn, stretch—and *then* get up. If feasible, return to your meditation after the interruption to finish off the remainder of your meditation time.

8. The best way to time your meditation is by occasionally looking at your clock or watch through half-closed eyes, squinting so as not to alert yourself. While you may, if you wish, use a timer placed beneath a pillow to muffle its sound, many people find that it is too startling and peremptory. Sometimes you may need to take a minute or two longer for a particular meditation. The timer will not "know" this, but you will.

9. After finishing meditation, remain seated for a minute or two with your eyes closed. During this time allow your mind to return to everyday thoughts. After a couple of minutes of just sitting, open your eyes *very* slowly. You may want to rub your

hands together gently and run them lightly over your cheeks as though in a face-washing motion, or to stretch. Then rise in a leisurely manner.

Attitude

The techniques described here are easy forms of meditation and you should not have difficulty with them, even if you are quite unfamiliar with meditation. Some of these techniques are relatively more concentrative than others, although for all of them you will adopt a gentle nonforcing attitude. The main thing to remember is not to try to do any of these meditation exercises "correctly," but to let each meditation "do" itself. Whether it turns out "good" or "bad": this is not your concern. Just go along with the meditation, drift with it, and find out what happens.

In these forms of meditation you will not be *focusing* your mind or forcing it to "stick to the point." Whenever thoughts enter your mind (and they will often do so because that too is part of the meditative process) simply treat these thoughts as you might clouds drifting across the sky on a summer's day. You don't try to push the clouds away. You don't hold onto them. You simply watch them come and go. When you realize that your mind is drifting far away and is caught up in thoughts, gently come back to your object of focus. No forcing—you do this pleasantly, the way you would come home again to greet a good friend. The extraneous thoughts which you had are a natural and useful part of the meditative process.*

Keep in mind that you are not to try to make anything "happen" during meditation. Trust the meditation to "know" best. Some people have compared these forms of meditation to the experience of being in a rowboat without oars, gently drifting on a quiet stream. Let the stream take you where it will.

Now let's turn to the first form of meditation you will learn. We have already spoken about the use of the *mantra* as a focusing device in TM and CSM. While some forms of mantra meditation call for *concentration*, neither TM nor CSM requires this

---

* Why this may be so will be discussed in Part V of this book, when we consider theories of meditation.

and neither does the meditative method taught here. Having tried it, you will understand more about the permissive forms of mantra meditation.

Mantra Meditation

Directions: Select one of the three mantras suggested in the list below, or, if you wish, substitute a word of your own choosing which has a pleasant ringing sound. If you decide to create your own mantra, be sure to avoid using any word which is emotionally "loaded." No names of people, no words that bring too intense or exciting an image. The word should ring through your mind and give you a feeling of serenity. If it has a touch of unfamiliarity or mystery to it, this can help remove you from everyday thoughts and concerns.

If you decide to tell someone close to you the mantra you have chosen, be sure this person understands that regardless of his or her personal reactions to it, your mantra should be respected. Your mantra will come to have a special meaning for you and will soon be a signal to turn inward toward a peaceful state if you do not lessen these effects by using it lightly or casually.

When choosing your mantra, first repeat each of the suggested mantras to yourself (either mentally or out loud in a soft voice) and then select the one that sounds the most pleasant and soothing, or make up one of your own. In these mantras, the letter *a* is usually pronounced "ah," but do whatever pleases you.

MANTRAS†
Ah-nam
Shi-rim
Ra-mah

Having selected your mantra, sit down comfortably. With eyes open and resting upon some pleasant object such as a plant, say

† *Ahnam* means "nameless" (literally "without name") in Sanskrit. *Ramah,* referring to the Hindu deity "Rama," is a highly esteemed Sanskrit mantra. *Shirim* (Hebrew for "songs") was chosen as a CSM mantra because of its euphonious quality and the fact that many people found it unusually soothing. Since we have been using it, several TM meditators have informed me that a Sanskrit mantra that sounds quite similar to it is also used in TM.

the mantra out loud to yourself, repeating it slowly and rhythmically. Enjoy saying your mantra. Experiment with the sound. Play with it. Let it rock you gently with its rhythm. As you repeat it, say it *softer* and *softer*, until finally you let it become almost a whisper.

Now stop saying the mantra out loud, close your eyes, and simply listen to the mantra in your mind. *Think* it, but do not say it. Let your facial muscles relax, do not pronounce the word, just quietly "hear" the mantra, as, for example "Ah-nam" . . . "Ah-nam" . . . "Ah-nam" . . . That is all there is to meditating—just sitting peacefully, hearing the mantra in your mind, allowing it to change any way it wants—to get louder or softer—to disappear or return—to stretch out or speed up. . . . Meditation is like drifting on a stream in a boat without oars—because you need no oars —you are not going anywhere.

Continue meditating for twenty minutes. When the time is up sit quietly *without* meditating for at least two or three minutes more (or longer if you wish) then follow the instructions in Point 9 for coming out of meditation.

Meditation on Breathing

There are a number of forms of meditation on breathing, all of which are variations of ancient techniques. Some of these methods make more demands on the meditator than others. The instructions given here are a modification of those developed by psychologist Dr. Robert Woolfolk and his associates for a study of insomnia to be described later. These researchers found this kind of meditation to be effective in reducing the amount of time it took insomniacs to fall asleep. As described here, it can be considered a permissive meditation technique.

Directions: Sit in a comfortable position and take a single slow deep breath, thinking to yourself the word "in" as you breathe in, and the word "out" as you breathe out. After taking this first deep breath, do not intentionally influence your breathing. Let your breathing go its own way, fast or slow, shallow or deep, whatever way it wishes. As it does so you will think to yourself "in" on every in-breath and "out" on every out-breath.

While doing this breathing meditation, you can try to extend the sound in your mind so that at all points during the meditation you are either thinking "in . . . n . . . n . . . n . . ." or "ouuuuuuuut . . . t . . . t" in long, easy sounds. If the word "out" feels too abrupt because it ends in *t* and this is distracting (as it is for some people), substitute the syllable "ah" for the word "out"—saying "in" as you breathe *in*, and "ah" as you breathe *out*.

Do this meditation naturally, with no concern about its correctness. If you skip an "in" or "out" because your mind has wandered (as it will), you can always pick up the words on the next breath whenever you are ready. If the words fade away and you are just sensing the breathing alone, that is fine. It simply means you are becoming quieted down. The words are really only there to help you focus your attention on your breath; often during the quieter phases of meditation they fade out if they are not needed. But don't *expect* them to disappear—simply *let* them go if they want to. When twenty minutes are up, come out of the meditation gradually according to the instructions in Point 9.

Moving Meditation

Two types of moving meditation are described here. You can select the one you prefer after trying both, or you may want to make up one of your own according to the instructions given.

Method 1: Sit with a pillow on your lap so that your hands are resting comfortably on the pillow and cup your hands together in a "prayerlike" position with fingers lightly touching (Figure 1). Then gently open your palms

while still keeping their lower edges resting against the pillow and in contact (Figure 2). Now once

again bring your palms together so that all fingers touch lightly, returning to the position shown in Figure 1. This meditation consists of opening and closing your palms over and over again, gently and easily. As you do this you can be looking at your hands or resting your eyes on some pleasant object in the vicinity, or you can close your eyes. Use as little energy as possible for this exercise and let your motions be easy and rhythmic.

Method 2: Sit comfortably with your eyes open or closed. Slowly and gently begin to bob your head very slightly. At the same time tap one foot lightly in time with the movement of your head. Keep all motions small, easy, and comfortable. If you tire moving one foot, shift to the other, or allow your feet to remain still. Use little energy, let yourself flow with your own natural rhythms.

Do not be discouraged by the fact that at first a moving meditation may seem clumsy, awkward, or even "silly." If you keep doing it, you will find that at some point your body "gets into" the rhythm. At that point you will feel "pulled together" and your gestures will be easy and comfortable.

Allow the moving meditation to proceed as it will. Your motions may change in rhythm, intensity, or duration, or in the amount of muscular energy you use. If you are very relaxed, your motions may become almost imperceptible. Let them change any way they want to. Your body is telling you what it needs; respect it.

Instead of the types of moving meditation described here, you may prefer to invent a method of your own. That is fine. Just remember to keep your repetitive movement—whether of hands, feet, or head—easy. It must be a movement which calls for a low expenditure of energy.

Continue meditating for twenty minutes. At the end of this time allow your body movements to taper off, becoming gradually less forceful and less definite until the muscle movements finally disappear entirely. After all motion has ceased, remain sitting absolutely still for a minute or so to allow the effects of the meditation to permeate, then finish as instructed in Point 9.

Visual Meditation

Directions: Select a pleasant natural object such as a plant, flower, piece of fruit, bit of driftwood, or some simple vase. Although a candle flame is sometimes used for visual meditation, it is not suggested here because its glare may cause eye strain if not properly used.

Place your chosen object on a table at or near eye level and at a distance of two to four feet from you. Adjust this distance according to the most comfortable focus for your own eyes and eliminate distracting objects in the immediate background.

Sit comfortably and allow your eyes to come to rest on the object, but do not *try* to see it. Make no effort to focus. Instead, *allow* the object to come into your vision, *let* it enter your awareness. Do not make any conscious attempt to think about it in any way—what it is, what it means, its name, the class of objects it belongs to—although if such thoughts come to your mind *spontaneously*, that is fine. Just look at your object innocently as a child might.

Avoid staring at any time, for this can cause eye strain. During this meditation your eyes will spontaneously want to move about, travel over the object. Allow them to do this. Do *not* stop your eye movements—this is part of "seeing."

Because most of us can only look at things with "the eye of the beginner" for a few seconds at a time (unless highly trained) this meditation consists of a series of new beginnings. After allowing the object to remain in your field of vision for about seven to ten seconds (this interval may be longer or shorter according to your own inclinations), purposely shift your eyes to a more distant place in the room. At this time you can remove your mental attention from the object as well, and let it wander where it will.

Continue repeating this process—gazing away from the object for a few seconds (you will "feel" the right length for this time interval) and then, when you are ready, bringing your eyes and your attention back to it easily. Each time simply allow yourself to become absorbed in the object once more (again for about seven to ten seconds) and then systematically remove your gaze once again. Continue in this way—looking at the object, looking away from it, and then returning to it refreshed—for five minutes (this is a shorter meditation than the other forms). At the end of five minutes close your eyes for a minute or so and sit quietly, then finish off as described in Point 9.

Comments

While the instructions given here for these forms of meditation call for a permissive, nonforcing attitude, any of these same methods can be conducted in a more concentrated, disciplined manner and frequently are taught that way. For purposes of relaxation, however, I find the permissive approach to be more easily learned, more effective, and more apt to be faithfully practiced by the average Westerner. This does *not* mean that the more rigorous concentrative approaches are either wrong or harmful—merely that they are different. Usually these more difficult approaches are for advanced students who have acquired a considerable degree of self-discipline and who are working with a teacher to achieve goals somewhat different from those we are seeking here.

The mantra meditation given here is the most permissive of the four techniques since it requires an absolute minimum of effort on the part of the meditator. It follows almost exactly the instructions we use in teaching CSM, with the difference that the teaching of CSM is taught in person and followed up by group and individual consultations.

The meditation on breathing is similar to the zazen techniques which are mentioned in this book in that it is *derived* from them, but it differs in its degree of rigor. In classical zazen meditation, meditators must sit in the lotus or half-lotus position in a carefully prescribed manner. They cannot move during the sitting, even if a fly should crawl over them, their legs become numb, or if they have a burning itch—and they must keep their eyes open throughout, resting on a spot about two to four feet in front of them. In some forms of zazen, meditators follow their breathing by counting each out-breath from one to ten, at which point they commence over again with "one," "two," etc.

The moving meditation, suggested by a classicial Indian form of meditation known as *mudra*, is a far less exacting technique than the stylized Indian one. Mudra meditation makes use of ritualized gestures which are structured in a certain way in order, it is said, to trap "vital energies." The repetitive movements I have described are not based on traditional Indian mudras, but are designed for the Westerner. With thousands of gurus training disciples in various forms of meditation, however, it is impossible to know whether any particular gesture has or has not been used for purposes of centering during spiritual training. Perhaps the moving meditations presented here have at times been used that way. They also seem to resemble some forms of prayer.

The visual meditation described here differs from *tratak* (Hindu meditation upon light), in one form of which the meditator is required to stare unblinkingly at a small flame until the eyes tear. Allowing the sight to come *to you* (rather than actively seeking to "see") is a familiar part of many exercises designed to relax the eyes. The process of looking away from and then back at the object is a device created here to bring about a perpetual sense of "freshness" of vision. I consider this "returning" process to be basic to this particular form of meditation.

Meditating as a Regular Practice

If you want to continue using any of these four techniques as a regular form of meditation, this can be done effectively if the following points are kept in mind:

1. It is important to schedule your meditation sessions into your life so as to make them a regular daily routine—occasional use of the technique, while pleasant, will not bring about any lasting benefits. It is best to meditate twice daily, but if this is difficult, you should try to do so at least once daily.

2. Your meditation should always be done in a reasonably quiet place without distractions. If someone else is present, he or she should be meditating. Nonmeditating adults, children, or animals should not be in the room. A "signal" that meditation is in session is a good idea: it can be put on the outside of your door to let family, friends, or roommates know that you are in a meditation session—other people often do not realize this.

3. Morning and late afternoon are very good times for meditating, but there are many other satisfactory times as well.‡

4. Always come out of meditation slowly, taking a full minute or more to surface gradually—this helps carry over the tranquillity of meditation into your daily life.

5. If you plan to begin regular meditation with one of these techniques, it is wise to finish reading Part II of this book, "Managing Meditation." before commencing. In this way you can become familiar with some of the difficulties that you may encounter and some possible solutions.

6. If after commencing meditation, you experience any discomforts during or following meditation that do not seem merely

‡ For a discussion of meditation and time of day, see Chapter 9.

temporary (see Chapter 6), immediately cut your meditation time to only ten, or even five minutes per session and continue on that level (visual meditation should be cut to one or two minutes). Usually the problem clears up with this reduction in time. If meditation continues to present difficulty, give yourself permission to stop the practice of meditation, without feeling either distressed or guilty; or you may want at this point to seek instruction from an experienced meditation teacher.

7. If you are undertaking meditation in the hope of alleviating a physical condition which may be related to stress or tension, you should do this with the knowledge of your physician and remain under his or her careful supervision. Do *not* neglect going for regular medical checkups just because meditation may seem to be making you "feel better"—this can be both misleading and dangerous.

8. If you are presently undergoing any form of psychotherapy, you should first discuss plans to start meditation with your therapist and decide in consultation with him or her whether it seems wise for you to practice meditation on a regular basis at this time. Part III of this book, which deals with the use of meditation as as adjunct to psychotherapy, may be of use to you in making this decision.

9. If you elect to practice visual meditation on a regular basis, it should feel relaxing to your eyes afterward. If it does not, or if you feel any eye strain, cut the meditation time in half. If the eye strain persists, stop doing this form of meditation. On the other hand, if you find that your eyes feel relaxed and rested after five minutes of visual meditation, then you can proceed cautiously to build up your visual meditation time by adding two minutes per day to the original five minutes, and observing the effect on your eyes. If this form of meditation continues to be relaxing to your eyes, you may gradually increase the amount of time spent meditating with it until you are doing a full twenty minutes of visual meditation.

10. If you have not found any of the four forms of meditation described here to be effective or to your liking, but still feel you want to obtain the benefits of meditation, *do not be discouraged.* There are other fine forms of meditation, one of which might be right for you. It may also be that you are one of those people who respond excellently to a teacher but cannot learn a nonverbal technique from a book. *Some* people can learn beginning piano from a book alone and do very well with it; others need to work with a teacher. If you are the type of person who finds it hard to learn from written instructions, I would urge you first to seek out reliable personal instruction in meditation before assuming that the practice is not for you.

Others' Experiences

Ever since we commenced meditating, my husband and I and a number of our colleagues and friends have intermittently kept regular meditation journals. The participants in my meditation seminars at Princeton have also documented their meditation in the same way. These journals show that each meditation session tends to be a new and different experience, just as each dream is unique. Each meditator also appears to have his or her own characteristic style of meditating. This style may change and develop over time, as the following entries in my own meditation journal indicate:

> When I first learned meditation, I would hear in my mind the two-syllable Sanskrit mantra as a distinct word, usually personified. At first it seemed to come from a graceful feminine presence, a mermaid who swam before me during my meditation, calling to me in some strange yet intensely meaningful language —the language was the sound of my mantra. Sometimes the image was a bird soaring in the sky, leading me forward with its beautiful cry.

After several weeks of meditating, I no longer saw these "guiding images" except when under particular stress, and the mantra became more indistinct, less wordlike. After nine months of meditation I wrote:

> Often my mantra is now present during a large portion of my meditative session as a faint but steady background beat continuing beneath my foreground thoughts and preoccupations. It goes its own way yet it harmonizes like the contrapuntal rhythms in Bach's music. When it finally "takes over" at some point during the meditation, the mantra becomes no longer a word but now just a pulsating rhythm, like slow rolling waves on the shore. The first syllable is the receding of the water, the second syllable is the long roll of the sea washing over the beach.

In the various forms of mantra meditation, the mantra itself may be experienced with seemingly infinite variety. At different times it may be loud, soft, fast, slow, melodic, harsh, resonant, muffled, clear, barely discernible, or be experienced in some other fashion. One meditator described a form of thought during meditation which he said was deeply absorbing—during it the mantra was absent for long periods of time. When he found himself engaging actively with such thought, however, rather than flowing with it, the mantra reappeared spontaneously and continued along with his thinking, seeming to lead him back into his quiet state.

At certain times, meditators may experience a string of memories drifting through their minds during meditation. Sometimes these are scenes of tranquil, nostalgic places from childhood, carrying with them a strong sense of pleasure. At other times disturbing images may arise. These usually tend to lose their painfulness as the meditation continues, changing under the soothing rhythm of the mantra or the peacefulness of one's own breath quietly attended to, or just dissolving in the stillness.

Memories that emerge during meditation are often sensed as unusually vivid; it may seem to the meditator as though he or she is *reliving* the experience rather than remembering it. Meditators can almost smell the scents, taste the food, feel the touch on their skin, see the remote details of the scene involved—details they may not have previously recalled since the original event. These kinds of relivings do not seem to be stories with plots and do not have the structure of dreams. They are vivid *impressions*.

Aside from the imagery which may occur during meditation, the entire meditative session may be experienced in a manner which can best be described by comparing it with familiar images. My husband has variously referred to his more positive meditative states as being like sitting high up on a mountainside listening to the wind; being by a fireside sipping fragrant tea; or watching a baby nursing peacefully. Others report that meditation has evoked in them a feeling of pleasant days in a quiet meadow, a boat rocking lazily at anchor, or a shower of cherry blossoms drifting toward the earth. The similes are endless and highly individual, but they also have certain things in common. Most of them depict tranquil moods and often water, mist, and rhythmic motions feature prominently in them.

The mantra, or any other object of focus used for meditation, may play a significant orienting and synthesizing function during meditation. As one meditator put it:

> . . . I searched for the mantra, and having found it, felt "pulled together" (as being oriented by the North Star). I was coalesced.

The experience of yielding to internal rhythms, of not "trying" is also commonly reported:

> . . . I am in a state of alertness, yet without grasping or making any effort to cope. I do not try to succeed nor can I fail. Distant feelings, images, uninvitedly float into my ken, but there is no effort to define what I hear, see, sense . . .

Occasionally during meditation, a meditator will have a spontaneous insight which may bring about a change in their life. I find these insights to be essentially similar to the deeper insights which may occur during psychotherapy, but with one difference—the preliminary conscious "work" leading up to the therapeutic insight is not present during meditation. The meditative process can even foster insights in people who have no previous experience in searching for meanings or causes for things that happen in their lives.

One other aspect of the meditative experience should be mentioned here. A meditation session will often follow a certain progression. Starting with an active type of thought, it may move toward more quiet types of thinking, and sometimes this process leads to a state where no thinking seems to occur at all. In mantra meditation, the mantra may become increasingly soft and indistinct as the meditation session continues, until, no longer needed, it gives way to profound quiet. In breathing meditation, awareness of the breath may recede until it becomes almost imperceptible and silence is the all-encompassing experience.

According to meditative tradition, at this point the mind is not focused on either thought or image, but is fully aware, conscious. The mind is said to be alert without having any *object* of alertness. This experience of utterly still awareness is one of the goals of the more advanced spiritual disciplines, although it is not necessarily a goal of the practical forms of meditation. "Transcending," as TM teachers call this state, is not by any means experienced by all meditators who practice the simple centering techniques, perhaps not by the majority of them. Many people, if they have experienced it at all, have not identified it as being any special state of consciousness.

While attaining such an "objectless" state is not necessary in order for personality change to take place, for those who do experience it, it seems to be deeply meaningful. One investigator has described this fleeting state, possibly the ultimate goal of meditation, as follows:

> When, in full wakefulness, all inner activity comes to a stop, all thinking, all fantasy, all feeling, all images—everything—even the urge to think or to feel or to act; when all of this stops, stops on its own, without suppression or repression, one thing remains: a vast, inner stillness—a clear peace, and the firm realization that this, at the very least, is how it feels to be, simply, alive.[1]

Aware of what meditation as *experience* can be, we will now turn to the question of its management in everyday life. Understanding certain practical aspects of meditation can make the difference between a successful practice of this technique and a frustrating one. The next chapters in this section will look at ways of handling meditation.

6

The Challenge of Tension-Release

One of the striking features of the meditative state is its tendency to go its own way—sometimes not at all in the direction the meditator consciously intends. A person may learn all the correct procedures, obey all the rules of a particular form of meditation, and still be unable either to "produce" an altered state of consciousness at will or legislate its contents. The meditative mood *may* emerge—or other things may happen.

These other things—the surprising alternatives to the expected peaceful state—are probably the most frequent source of discouragement for new meditators. Temporary side effects or discomforting sensations are a common result of deep relaxation. Usually disappearing spontaneously, often within a matter of minutes, these side effects occasionally require alterations in the meditation routine before they disappear, and teachers of all the various relaxation techniques have had to find ways to help their students cope with them.

The relaxation process (particularly if a formerly tense person is the one who is relaxing) is not always an even or smooth one. What occurs is somewhat analogous to what happens if we release a tightly wound metal spring abruptly. There may be sudden jumps, jolts, or tremors as the spring uncoils, adjusting itself by stages to each new reduced state of tension. Our mind and body behave much like the tightly wound steel spring. The unwinding process is often awkward and uneven. Most of us remember a time when we went to bed after a tension-filled day. As we began to relax in the presleep state, we experienced a sudden involuntary jerk that awakened us fully again. In the deep relaxation techniques, similar temporary startles or other forms of discomfort may appear. Often these are so mild that we hardly notice them and they usually require no special attention. Occasionally they are prominent enough to attract our interest.

This unwinding phenomenon has been given various names. IMS calls it "normalizing."* The teachers of autogenic training refer to the side effects as "autogenic discharges." Other relaxation techniques such as progressive relaxation or alpha biofeedback, while describing such effects in their training manuals, do not give the process a specific name. I prefer to use the term "tension-release" as it is simple and descriptive of what actually happens.

Side effects from tension-release are more apt to be noticed in the first ten minutes of any meditation session and after that to disappear gradually. It usually takes this much time for the body and mind to become thoroughly quieted down. An initial period of throwing off tension should be viewed as both natural and useful, *not* as a signal to reduce meditation time. Only if side effects persist throughout the whole session and are distinctly *uncomfortable* to the meditator, should the suggested reductions in meditation time be made. By being persistent and simply returning to the object of focus, any period of brief discomfort can almost always be weathered pleasantly, tension dispersed, and deep relaxation obtained.

It is useful to know about the forms these side effects can take, however. The single largest body of evidence dealing with them has been compiled by the autogenic training researchers. As indicated before, teachers of autogenic training have collected vast numbers of carefully recorded training accounts of people practicing their relaxation technique. These are of particular interest because this method also evokes the meditative mood. Since autogenic trainees are usually required to report each sensation that arises during their relaxation session to their trainer, when present,

* Originally they referred to it as "unstressing," but later abandoned that term.

or to write them down immediately after their home practice, the reports contain information on many different types of reactions experienced during these training sessions. The mass of information which has been collected is invaluable in exploring the side effects of relaxation.

Tension-Release Effects

The list of tension-release side effects compiled by the teachers of autogenic training coincides remarkably with those we see in meditators.[1] Though they are entirely normal occurrences, the person who experiences these effects can sometimes be upset by them if not warned ahead of time and may need advice on how to handle them.

The relaxing person, may, for instance, feel unaccountably heavy in the relaxed state, as though "sinking down through the floor," or may feel quite the opposite—weightless, as if "floating away." Such sensations may affect the whole body, or only one specific part, such as arms, legs, or head. After the relaxation session is over, there is usually no carry-over of these effects into daily life.

During deep relaxation, sensations of intense heat, icy cold, or a burning feeling sometimes occur. The deeply relaxing person may have a sudden itch that comes and goes. They may experience feelings of tingling or even a temporary numbness in some part of the body, or may feel pulsations coursing through the body or over the top of the head. Often these sensations are pleasant. Occasionally they are disturbing, as if an "electric current" was running through the body or as if there were "a steel band around the head" or a sudden tightness in certain parts of the body. Relaxers sometimes even perspire profusely, shiver, or find themselves trembling, or if tension-release is particularly intense, their hearts may pound or they may breathe rapidly. These reactions seem ultimately to be useful in "unwinding," because the result of such a seemingly difficult session is often deep relaxation afterward.

A person in a state of deep relaxation sometimes has other experiences as well. They may have the impression that they can almost "smell" certain scents, as though they were "in a barn and there is hay which smells good," or "on a beach feeling the wind and breathing in the strong salty smell of the sea," or "in grandmother's kitchen breathing the scent of freshly baked bread." Smells—pleasant, unpleasant, or neutral—can seem startlingly real at this time. In the same way, the relaxer may experience vivid sensations of taste, such as that of freshly ground pepper on the tongue, or of milk, or honey, or mustard, and the like.

The person's concept of their own body may also change during deep relaxation: their hands may feel as though they were "as large as the room" or their head "like a blown-up balloon." They may even feel as though their legs, arms, or head were separated from their body or that they had no body; or they may experience themselves as incredibly "tiny." Such sensations are often a kind of pleasant "trip." On the other hand, the relaxer sometimes has momentary discomforts such as pains that come and go, a headache, a stinging sensation in a toe or finger or elsewhere. Their throat may suddenly feel sore and then clear up again within a matter of minutes. Saliva may pour so that they must continually swallow, their mouth may dry up, their nose run, or they may sneeze or cough. Some may sigh involuntarily or yawn repeatedly or make automatic sucking movements with their lips, or their stomach may growl unmercifully. In rare cases of extreme tension-release, individuals sometimes experience some nausea or have a strong urge to urinate.

The relaxing person may also notice small muscle twitches or jerks or involuntary movements, or "see" all kinds of fascinating images—showers of sparks, spirals, whirls, geometric forms, textilelike patterns, vivid colors, bright lights.

She or he may also "hear" inner "sounds" such as a humming in their head or a rushing, whirring, or ringing. Often these sounds are experienced as rare and beautiful, as "a thousand crickets chirping" or "a tinkling chorus of tiny bells." At other times it seems as though the body were tilted over at an extreme angle, falling over, or upside down. Again these experiences may be either pleasant or unpleasant according to whether or not the person is threatened by their unusual quality.

It is not exceptional for someone in deep relaxation to experience intermittent waves of intense restlessness where they feel they "simply can't stand it another second without getting up," or they may have strong emotional reactions or burst into laughter or tears. They may also feel intense rage or have pleasurable sexual sensations or even experience orgasm.

These are but some of the forms that tension-release during deep relaxation can take. Very few of these side effects are experienced by any one person, however, and they are usually most noticeable for about two weeks after commencing meditation, after which they fade rapidly. Some people, in fact, experience such mild forms of tension-release, even at first, that they never notice this process. Each person's particular *pattern* of stress-release also varies. Some may experience certain specific side effects over and over again in a number of meditations until these are eventually replaced by other characteristic effects (or none).

It should be emphasized that side effects need not be present for a person to benefit from meditation, although they can be beneficial when they occur. A meditator should neither expect them nor be surprised if they do not appear. Usually they will take care of themselves. If not, then there are several effective ways to handle them which we will discuss later.

Relation of Tension-Release to Life History

Not only does every meditator have a characteristic pattern of tension-release, but the particular pattern they experience may be meaningful in terms of the person's unique life history. The autogenic training specialists have reported some striking parallels between patients' past experiences and the tension-release patterns they characteristically report.

They found that particularly intense side effects were most apt to occur in very anxious people who had at one time or another in their lives experienced severe accidents. Their pattern of tension-release was related to the site of the injury and often involved the sensations that were originally associated with the accident.

A young man of twenty-four who had come for autogenic treatment because of anxiety reactions and some troubling depression is reported to have suddenly burst out laughing during his relaxation session. Later he told his therapist that he had been experiencing a feeling as though a stick were being pushed into his left upper abdomen just below the ribs and that his eyelids had been very tense, as though held together. At the same time he had had a feeling as though his heart were beating more strongly. Interestingly enough, this young man felt quite comfortable after the relaxation session was over, a response which is not unusual following intense tension-release. When he discussed these side effects with his therapist, he then recalled three minor hockey accidents which had occurred to him between the ages of thirteen and eighteen. During one collision a hockey stick had been pushed into his upper abdomen and he had lost his breath and almost fainted.

This patient's tension-release paralleled the feelings and experiences he had during his accidents. Not only did he repeatedly feel the stick pushed into his abdomen below his ribs during relaxation, but his eyelids had also been pressed together, possibly in response to the shock of the accident which was being "re-run" during the relaxation session. This particular side effect is reported to have recurred a number of times during this patient's autogenic training sessions, as though a trauma had to work off its effect by being repeated.[2]

Other traumatic situations as well may be reflected in specific tension-release patterns. Women with a history of an abortion carried out under particularly unfavorable circumstances, or who had had a traumatic delivery, showed disagreeable kinds of stress-release involving their abdominal region and their lower back when they relaxed in autogenic training.[3] These side effects diminished and often ceased later on, again as though the physical

97

traumas had been "worked out" of their systems in the deep relaxation of the autogenic state.†

Another group who showed tension-release patterns related to previous trauma were schizophrenic patients who had received long series of electroshock treatments. These patients reported many more side effects which involved a *loss of balance* (floating, sinking, etc.) when in autogenic relaxation than did schizophrenic patients who had *never* had shock treatments.[4]

Another area of trouble which may reflect itself in specific side effects is sexual deprivation. In a study conducted by autogenic training researchers, sexually deprived people were compared with people who had fairly normal sex lives and "satisfying affectionate relationships with persons of the opposite sex."[5] The sexually deprived people showed a great many more side effects of *all* kinds than did the nondeprived people.‡ They also had more sexually oriented visual experiences and thoughts. The sensations and movements during relaxation which happened to involve thighs, lower abdomen, and genitals were almost six times as frequent in this deprivation group as in people who were not sexually deprived.

What was striking about these studies was the way in which the stress-release process seemed to "select" patterns of expression which related directly to deep conflicts and unconscious concerns in these persons. This sort of occurrence is not confined to autogenic training. It can happen during meditation in the same way although such dramatic types of tension-release are usually seen in persons with either traumatic backgrounds or with long-standing emotional problems.*

† No comparable studies of tension-release patterns during the various forms of practical meditation have as yet been done, so it is uncertain whether such specific reactions as these would be seen during meditation. A colleague of mine reports that a patient of his who at age twelve had been confined to bed for a year as a result of severe skull injury, experienced *no* unpleasant side effects during TM. Further research in this field is needed.

‡ This is not always the case with meditators. A colleague reports that a patient of his, virtually celibate during all of his adult life due to severe anxiety about any sexual contacts, has shown *no* unpleasant side effects from CSM.

* For accounts of two psychotherapeutic cases where specific tension-release patterns occurred during meditation, see Appendix.

The Management of Tension-Release

Fortunately, enough is now known from our practical work with meditation so that we can begin to offer considerable guidance to meditators who are experiencing temporary discomforts. The first step in the management of tension-release is to become aware of the "initial adjustment period," an interim period which lasts for roughly the first two to three weeks after beginning meditation. Its exact duration depends on the personality of the meditator and the life-pressure he or she has recently had to face.

Too rapid "unwinding" can take place in certain people when they first learn to meditate because the changeover from a consistently tense state to a relaxed state is too sudden to be assimilated. The switch to a more peaceful state can be a mixed blessing if the contrast brings with it a discomforting release of tension. In such instances, temporary side effects may spill over and affect the daily life of the meditator and signs of tension-release, perhaps tears or feelings of anger, may occur *between* meditation sessions. When this happens it is an indication that some backlog of tension and emotional stress is being released before a better emotional balance is achieved through meditation. Almost always these somewhat inconvenient side effects disappear when meditation becomes established.

A problem that occasionally arises during the adjustment period is that if a person is very tired, if he or she has been deprived of sleep or rest for a considerable length of time before learning to meditate, or if they have been overworked or overtense, the chances are that commencing meditation may lead to a temporary state where they start "making up for lost time." At this point, the need to rest may be so strong that the person finds themself becoming inefficient. Usually the condition clears up on its own after a few weeks without the meditator having to do anything about it, but sometimes it may require adjustment of meditation time or even temporary suspension of meditation.

An interesting example of this occurred in my own life. When I first learned meditation, I found myself so unusually relaxed that this often resulted in physical weakness. I was continually drowsy and slipped into naps even when I was trying to keep up with my work. At one point during this time, it was necessary to correct about eighty exam papers within two days, yet I found that no matter how hard I tried, I was unable to mobilize the concentration I needed for this task. Because the papers had to be corrected, I went against my TM instructor's advice and stopped meditating entirely for a day and a half in order to regain the alertness necessary to correct the papers. This worked well. I was able to do the work and then return to meditation when I was finished with it.

After the first three weeks (which turned out to be the end of my particular adjustment period) this problem disappeared and I have never had this trouble since. I can now meditate regularly for twenty minutes twice a day and never feel any blurring of my alertness. If anything, I am more alert and efficient than before.

Practically speaking, the best way to handle such rapid stress-release is to reduce radically the amount of meditation time and do so *without delay*. Whenever we have made such a time adjustment with a trainee, almost without exception, it has proved to be helpful. Meditating for shortened periods of time under such conditions, or perhaps only once a day, usually changes meditation back into a thoroughly satisfactory experience.

Reducing Meditation Time

In teaching CSM we frequently reduce a trainee's meditation time from twenty minutes to ten minutes and sometimes to five minutes or less when this is necessary. We even do so after the very first session if the person has experienced severe discomfort during meditation. This reduction is undertaken as quickly as possible without waiting to see if the strong side effects go away on their own. If a person who is experiencing unpleasant tension-release is allowed to go on too long, he or she will often quit meditation and refuse to go back to it later on. This situation can almost invariably be avoided if the adjustment is made rapidly. Such a person will then be able to reinstate longer meditation times later on, increasing the time little by little, until they discover a time which is satisfactory for their permanent meditation schedule.

If we need to assign a meditation time under five minutes, we sometimes suggest that the person practice these shortened meditation periods more frequently, perhaps five or six times a day, although it is unusual to have to reduce the time by this much. Most people show only mild, easily manageable tension-release effects, even when commencing meditation.

Fortunately most of us have a built-in safety mechanism. Most people do not continue to do things that are causing them discomfort or which may threaten their emotional adjustment. This tendency usually acts as a brake to prevent more serious difficulties arising from tension-release. Occasionally a person will fail to listen to the wisdom of his or her own inner self and remain rigidly with a fifteen- or twenty-minute twice-daily schedule in the face of mounting side effects which are not responding to this regime. This can cause a number of complications which we will presently consider. It is precisely at this point that a meditator should feel free to skip meditations if this feels right to do, cut back to once a day or once every other day, or temporarily stop meditating altogether—whichever maneuver corrects the situation. Each meditator must learn to listen to their own inner wisdom as to what duration is best for them under such circumstances.

Some of the useful effects of cutting down meditation time are illustrated by a friend of mine, an extremely competent administrator handling a position of considerable responsibility, to whom I had taught CSM. She experienced a very fulfilling first meditation, but within two days she was complaining that her meditations were leaving her "too vulnerable." On one occasion when she was interrupted by the sound of the telephone, she was so startled that she found herself nauseous and trembling afterward and telephoned me to ask what to do. I suggested that she return to her room, be sure to silence the phone this time, and continue meditating for another fifteen minutes. This was to help her "take the charge off" the disturbing interruptions, and in fact it did so.

Her anxiety and nausea disappeared and she once more felt tranquil.

Two days later, however, she reported that meditation was now causing her to lose efficiency in a distressing manner. While she felt comfortable and unusually rested during the day, she was making "lazy errors" in her work, something uncharacteristic for her. She found herself taking twice as long to accomplish certain administrative tasks which would ordinarily be simple for her to do.

When we talked this over, we both had the impression that while letting up a bit from her regular pace might be a good idea for her in the long run, during the initial "adjustment period" it seemed to be taking too extreme a form. Since she felt it was genuinely interfering with her work, she had begun to resist doing her meditations. I suggested that she cut her meditation time down to ten minutes twice daily. When she did this, her inefficiency cleared up. She was no longer slowed down to a point where she could not work and she continued to derive relaxation from meditation.

This anecdote points up the fact that it is important for anyone practicing the simple Westernized forms of meditation to realize that no time interval is necessarily "correct" for these techniques. Twenty-minute sessions for example are simply one possibility.

Progressive Change

As time goes on and a person has been meditating for months or years, patterns of tension-release, if still evident, have usually undergone considerable change from the way they were initially. If they were prominent at first, they will probably have lessened, giving way to milder and more manageable side effects, or to none.

Some of the observations that the autogenic training researchers have made on these types of change over time are interesting. They noticed that people who at first had many unpleasant feelings and images during their relaxation sessions reported that these side effects were modified as the months or years passed. Eventually they had very few unpleasant experiences or none at all, while healthy, positive images or feelings grew in frequency.

Though emotional experiences were more frequent in the earlier phases of relaxation, these became less with time. Disagreeable bodily symptoms during relaxation also lessened while good feelings of bodily well-being increased. "Aggressive" and "destructive" feelings during their sessions of autogenic training were very prominent in certain types of patients during the first few months of their relaxation sessions. These usually began to diminish with time, with the sessions eventually evoking largely positive feelings.

It is interesting that the autogenic researchers also observed a tendency for trainees to see dark, "dangerous," or morbid colors during relaxation sessions *at first*, but after the person had been regularly practicing relaxation, these tended to change to more agreeable, lighter shades of color. In general, people who had practiced autogenic training over a period of years showed a gradual lessening of *all* kinds of stress-release together with an increase in positive experiences during relaxation.

These changes are exactly the same as those we commonly see in meditators. During his meditations, one TM meditator used to see a series of faces which continuously dissolved into new and different faces with different expressions. In the first few weeks following learning meditation, the faces were threatening and disturbing. They were angry, florid, distorted, almost inhuman with rage—he describes them as "Satanic" in countenance. As he continued to meditate, however, over time the character of the faces began to change. Eventually, the florid coloring and Satanic look had disappeared and the "pinched expressions" on the face and "narrow, beady eyes" were gone. Now the faces had greater softness. They were lighter and more natural in color. The skin was smoother, had become unwrinkled, and the frightening look was changed into a look of composure, peace, and gentleness—a look that brought him comfort.

At the same time this man's family noticed that the uncontrolled outbursts of anger which he had always shown had disappeared. He had become much more easygoing, understanding, and co-operative. His best qualities seemed to have come to the fore. He himself was able to recognize that the change in the faces must have reflected some deep inner change and release of tension in himself. Eventually, after he had been meditating for about two years, the faces rarely appeared any more. Now he saw rural scenes, quiet cottages, fences, lawns, and villages during meditation.

The Resolution of Tension-Release

If a person interrupts meditation prematurely because he or she suddenly feels restless (a rather common side effect during meditation) this restlessness is often carried over into daily life instead of dissolving in the quiet of the meditative state. This can be disappointing if they had hoped to come out of meditation quiet, calm, and soothed.

In general, the best way to handle such an uncomfortable side effect is to remain meditating, recognize that the effect is normal, and continue to bring your attention periodically back to the focus of meditation. Most often the side effect disappears on its own when treated in this fashion.

Sometimes the meditator may find that he or she is still releasing tension when the time for meditation is up. When this happens there is often a feeling that the meditation session is "incomplete" and that something is still unresolved. If the meditator then ends meditation abruptly, irritability and lingering tension of greater or lesser intensity may be experienced afterward. If the meditator strongly feels the need to remain longer to "work" through some tension-release in meditation, then it is better to stay on with the meditation (another five or ten minutes at most) until the process feels completed.

It seems that there are many ways in which the meditator signals to him or herself that disturbing or stressful material has been "neutralized" and the meditation session is, in a sense, ready to terminate. Autogenic training researchers have noticed this phenomenon and studied it carefully.[6] Often the relaxed person will visualize a calm, peaceful atmosphere, perhaps a beautiful sunset or "falling asleep in affectionate arms." If these follow a fairly disturbing session, they seem to indicate a resolution of the tension state.

Other terminating experiences take the form of spontaneous sleepiness, yawning, or a disappearance of all imagery. Or the person may find that an increasing number of positive thoughts and images are entering their mind, ones that are more peaceful, less active, and less stress-related. At this time feelings of warmth may increase or the person may visualize light shades of uniform colors such as light blue, turquoise blue, pale gray, silvery tones, or light yellow. She or he may even see a whiteness or a blankness or an empty space, and sometimes reports a "blinding white light," which resembles certain so-called enlightenment experiences reported by mystics.[7] The fact that in numerous records of autogenic training, this sudden impression of blinding light was found to occur only after highly stressful material had been neutralized and "handled" during the relaxation session, suggests that this is a very positive sign indicating a peaceful inner resolution of disturbing material. Anyone experiencing the "white light" during meditation should probably be reassured by these observations and may want to notice for him or herself whether the brilliant light did in fact signal the same sort of positive resolution. Some meditators also report that aqua or "electric" blue light has these same implications for them. Whatever the specific manifestations, a feeling of completeness and a sense of relief are typical of the end of a period of stress-release.

Techniques for Handling Persistent Side Effects

Very occasionally, side effects from tension-release refuse to go away, persisting after the session. If this happens there are some effective techniques for dealing with it.

The first deals with *physical* side effects. Let us say that stress-release takes the form of a physical symptom, perhaps a localized pain in the back of the head. If it is a pain that first appeared during meditation (an indication that it is probably due to tension-release) and refuses to leave by the end of the session, one strategy is to stop whatever meditative focus you ordinarily concentrate upon and turn your attention lightly onto the area of pain itself, absorbing yourself entirely in it. You are not trying to get rid of the pain or fighting against it in any way, but simply using it as a meditational focus, as you might use a mantra.

This way you will come to know the pain minutely and sensitively. You will "fuse" with it, rather than opposing it as though it were an outside force, and by so doing change the situation. As you come more into harmony with the pain, it may spontaneously dissolve without any effort on your part. Strange as it may seem, I have yet to see this device fail, and I recommend it for any persistent physical side effect of meditation.

Emotional side effects, such as uncontrollable crying, which continue after the session, may need to be handled differently. Usually such release phenomena have their own timetable. A "crying jag," for example, may be beneficial if allowed to play itself out and will usually self-terminate.

If anxiety which is stirred up during meditation continues afterward, an effective tactic is to take a few long, slow breaths, letting the air flow downward deeply into your lungs until it "feels" as though it had reached and permeated your entire abdomen. After this, very slowly exhale your breath until the last air seeps out. If you wish, you can even imagine that the air is flowing downward throughout your whole body as you breathe in, and that it is flowing out through the soles of your feet as you breathe out.

Deep breathing exercises such as these, perhaps coupled with some simple physical exercises such as Yoga stretches,† are usually effective in handling an upsurge of anxiety. It is also useful to talk over any uncomfortable thoughts or feelings which may have surfaced during meditation with a person you trust. The experience

† The basic Yoga "postures" (or stretches) are widely taught today in community health facilities, YMCAs, YWCAs, and other local organizations, and in a number of good instruction books.

of sharing these discomforting sensations with another can sometimes lead to important insights and considerable relief.

If none of these tactics are effective, then you need a temporary rest from meditating and should suspend meditation for five days. This is an excellent strategy for helping stress-release to right itself. When this interval is up, return to mediating, slowly at first, perhaps starting with only ten minutes once a day and only gradually increasing meditation time as it feels comfortable to do so. Feel free to back off and shorten your meditation time again if necessary or even to take another rest from it. Your own flexibility and good judgment should be the yardstick.

Temporary Setbacks

Something which causes difficulty in a small number of cases is the fact that certain symptoms which may have been present before learning to meditate may temporarily *worsen* after the person learns to meditate. Usually these symptoms will then get better and disappear as the meditator continues with daily practice. Irritability, tension headaches, or other undesirable conditions related to stress, occasionally show this "paradoxical" effect.

A striking instance of this was a patient of mine whom I referred to a TM center for training‡ because his severe tension headaches had not improved during psychotherapy. He found meditation to be a very gratifying experience but during the first week after he began to meditate his headaches became worse than ever. They came more often than usual and continued through his meditation sessions.

His meditation instructor explained to him that this was "normalizing," to be expected, and that it would probably straighten out in the near future when some of the initial tension had been drained off. This is, in fact, what happened. The second week after learning to meditate, his tension headaches were much less frequent. By the third week they had lessened to a point where he had fewer headaches than before learning to meditate.

‡ Before teaching CSM, I regularly referred patients for training in TM.

After one month, they had all but disappeared and now, as long as he regularly maintains his meditation, he rarely experiences a tension headache.

In the example just given, the TM instructor's advice to stay with the meditation until the symptoms lessened, was effective. Sometimes, however, this advice is inappropriate. Dr. Leon Otis of the Stanford Research Institute tells of five subjects, three of whom were TM meditators, and two of whom had learned another form of mantra meditation in his laboratory, who, after commencing meditation, suffered a reoccurrence of serious psychosomatic symptoms which had previously been under control.[8] These included a bleeding ulcer (under control for the previous five years), a reoccurrence of depression requiring psychiatric care and medication, extreme agitation that resulted in the termination of employment, and other distressing symptoms.

Dr. Arnold Lazarus also reports some incidents where learning TM precipitated psychiatric problems.[9] A thirty-four-year-old woman patient made a serious suicidal attempt following a weekend training course in TM; several patients alleged that TM increased their feelings of depression; and some agitated individuals reported that meditating with TM tended to heighten their already existent tension and restlessness. Dr. Robert Woolfolk also reports a case in which a schizophrenic breakdown seemed to have been precipitated by TM.[10] Lazarus concludes on the basis of evidence in the field of relaxation that relaxation training (including mediation) is not for everyone, but when properly applied to selected cases by informed practitioners, it can overcome many facets of stress, tension, and anxiety. In my own psychotherapeutic work, I have seen several TM meditators in whom tension-related physical symptoms or a latent emotional illness apparently became aggravated after commencing meditation. While these people are the extreme exceptions, they are a cause for concern.

It is interesting that this kind of symptom aggravation has been so well managed in autogenic training, a relaxation method which, in its more than fifty years of existence, has trained thousands of patients in hospitals and medical clinics, some of them people who were seriously ill and presumably vulnerable to the least disturbances in their delicate adjustment. I suspect the reason for this relaxation technique's excellent record is twofold:

1. Autogenic trainees are initially taught to do the exercises *only for very brief periods of time*. No more than thirty to sixty seconds are allowed for each Standard Training Exercise until the trainee becomes proficient in its use and until all side effects of tension-release are brought under control.

2. Trained teachers work to *adjust* the technique carefully to suit each trainee's requirements.

CSM employs some of these same safeguards, and it is interesting that among the more than 1,500 people who have learned CSM to date, we have seen no symptom reoccurrences, emotional breakdowns, or other unfortunate occurrences following the learning of meditation. While there is always the possibility that something untoward might happen on some future occasion, I believe we have avoided such difficulties so far because, if anything, we err on the side of *under*meditation. We immediately reduce meditation time at the first sign of an emerging difficulty, rather than risk any buildup of stress in a meditator. We also emphasize careful adjustment of the meditative technique to suit individual requirements.

While these may seem obvious precautions, they contrast with much of TM practice. TM teachers are trained to uphold the "purity" of their technique at all times, which means that the individual teacher has little leeway to vary the technique to suit special circumstances. The teachers are reluctant to reduce meditation time (although they will sometimes do so) because they have strong feelings about the "proper" times for meditation. The assumption is that TM by itself will automatically handle any problem if the person keeps meditating faithfully for fifteen to twenty minutes twice daily, and in fact this is usually what happens. In those occasional instances where this does not work, the TM teacher may then try to handle the problem of stress-release by instructing the meditator to practice Yoga breathing exercises or certain Yoga postures before meditation. This may be useful in some cases but not in all. If the TM teacher notices continued distress in the meditator which has not dissipated after some days or weeks of meditating-plus-exercise, he or she may then reduce meditation time to fifteen minutes, but will not lower it below ten minutes even if the side effects are serious. At present writing, IMS also considers brief meditations of three to five minutes to be ineffective and not "meditation." In addition they will not permit the trainee to change the mantra which has been assigned to him or her even if he reacts strongly against this sound.*

TM teachers' relative inflexibility in these matters may seem surprising to some people but can be understood if we consider the authoritarian nature of the World Plan Organization. What "Maharishi says" is unhesitatingly accepted as truth by every TM teacher and advice from the top is followed without questioning. This leaves little room for individual decision on any teacher's part, and therefore meditators' problems are handled by adhering to rules.

For this reason, although tension-release is not a serious problem for most meditators, those who practice Westernized meditative techniques should recognize the importance of learning to regulate their own meditation if this becomes necessary. In my opinion, most of the unfortunate complications reported from practicing meditation need never occur if a radical adjustment downward in meditation time is undertaken promptly enough. As indicated, however, this should only be done if distinctly disagreeable side effects continue unabated for one or more meditation sessions, and if returning to the mantra (or other meditational device) has proven ineffective in dealing with them. Each person will judge this for her or himself by trusting in the wisdom of their own inner selves to know what is correct for *them* in terms of how much meditation is beneficial. Handled with common sense, meditation can then become a highly useful means for self-development.

* We will discuss the problem of changing mantras when we come to consider the meaning of the mantra in Chapter 10.

7

How to Use Meditation Under Stress

When meditation is practiced on a regular daily basis, this usually results in certain advantages for the meditator. Evidence suggests that it is the person who rarely misses having at least one full meditation per day who reaps the most benefits in the long run. But what about the short run? Can the selective use of meditation during times of momentary stress be useful?

Various schools of meditation differ on the answer to this question, but if we ask meditators themselves, we find that most of them have at one time or another tried meditating at some specific moment to overcome a particular difficulty, and they report that meditation is surprisingly effective for such purposes.

Since there have not been any systematic studies conducted on what we might call the "strategic" use of meditation, we will consider reports from meditators who have invented their own ways of using meditation to help them through life crises, large and small. There are, by now, enough of these reports to give us useful information.

Mini-meditations

Many meditators to whom I have taught CSM have reported that they effectively use very brief meditations at strategic points during the day. These meditative experiences may not be more than a minute or two in length and might be termed "mini-meditations." One patient of mine who works under extreme pressure at her job, says she repeats her mantra silently to herself for a minute or so during work whenever her job becomes particularly tense. This causes an "immense calm" to descend over her and she then feels "balanced."

I have myself used mini-meditations. Once when I was caught in a traffic jam in the Lincoln Tunnel outside New York City, I found myself becoming extremely tense. The tunnel was filled with highly irritating fumes and the drivers were honking. As the moments ticked by, I was increasingly uncertain whether the traffic jam would clear up or whether we were in for hours of waiting. To counteract my rising anxiety about this, I began repeating my mantra. While thinking the mantra, I kept my eyes open, watching the other cars ahead of me. This seemed more reassuring than closing my eyes in the face of what I felt to be a situation where there might be danger. Within less than a minute this mini-meditation brought me a sense of calm and reassurance. I was now able to look at the whole problem with good-natured optimism, and to wait easily through the next fifteen minutes until the traffic began to move again.

Mini-meditations are also sometimes useful to increase the effectiveness of one's regular meditations. A TM meditator who suffers from hypertension recently told me that his two scheduled meditations of the day, although very relaxing for him, had nevertheless been unable to hold in check an extreme buildup of tension during working hours. When faced with decisions at the office, he would feel his blood pressure rising to a high pitch and could do nothing about it. Eventually he discovered that this undesirable rise in tension could be reversed by taking time out to meditate for five minutes whenever he recognized that he was heading into trouble. These mini-meditations, scattered throughout his day, took the edge off his tension buildups and made a marked difference in his ability to handle the stress of work with a relaxed attitude. He describes this strategy as "worth more than any tranquilizer I have ever known." It might be valuable to try this method with other meditators suffering from high blood pressure. Perhaps by teaching them to use mini-meditations in addition to their regular meditation sessions, the effectiveness of meditation for combating hypertension might be improved.

Limitations

While it is sometimes extremely useful, mini-meditation must obviously be used sparingly. If a person practicing mantra meditation were, for example, to think their mantra every time any difficulty arose, the mantra might become connected in their mind with the idea of *trouble*. Conceivably it might then begin to exert a disturbing rather than a quieting influence when they went to use it for meditation.

This problem was expressed clearly by a traveler I met on a plane with whom I was discussing meditation. She explained that she had a special "emergency" mantra which she used only when she found herself in tense, threatening situations (one of which, for her, was riding on a plane!). While this emergency mantra seemed to be extremely effective in calming her when she found herself in a tense situation, if she used it when she was in a *calm* situation, it had the opposite effect: then it would remind her of unpleasant emotions associated with flying, or some other intensely anxiety-provoking experience, and she would find herself becoming "up tight." Ironically, her regular TM mantra could not help her in moments of emergency, being entirely connected in her mind with a quiet, peaceful non-urgent state. She therefore was careful to use her emergency mantra only when she was *already* extremely anxious.

This woman's experience makes sense if we view the anxiety as what psychologists call a "conditioned response" to her emergency mantra—a response which has become linked with the mantra because at one time it occurred *simultaneously* with it, under conditions which were sufficiently arousing to cause the two to become associated. The result is that the mantra now tends to *evoke* anxiety when used at a neutral time. Ordinarily we try to avoid a coupling of the mantra with tension. This is probably why

TM teachers advise their pupils never to use their mantras strategically to counteract anxiety. As indicated by the examples above, however, meditation *can* be used for such purposes, provided that the meditator selects a separate emergency mantra and uses *it* for stressful occasions, as did the anxious plane traveler, and if he or she is aware of the possible dangers of overusing the mantra (or other meditational device) for such purposes.

Meditations under highly stressful circumstances *are* usually mini-meditations. The nature of a threatening situation demands that we keep our attention focused on the external world, which means that deep and prolonged meditation is out of the question. This is also why many people will keep their eyes either fully or partially open during a mini-meditation. When we feel ourselves in danger, we instinctively glance around us and keep a sharp watch over our environment. Closing our eyes when we feel threatened may make us more anxious because it gives us a feeling of being unprotected and vulnerable.

Other relaxation techniques can also be used strategically. A young singer who had studied autogenic training is reported to have discovered by chance that during her relaxation exercises, she could sing very fine, high notes which she had not been able to achieve otherwise. She then decided to try inducing a state of autogenic relaxation during her singing practice, and found she could do so by repeating only one portion of her autogenic formula. Eventually this young woman was able to master alto passages when singing in actual stage performances by thinking this formula just before she commenced the aria.[1]

The relaxation literature also tells of an eleven-year-old boy, failing badly in his class work, who was encouraged to practice his autogenic relaxation exercises for several minutes between classes. Each time after he did so, he felt refreshed and it was easier for him to participate in class work during the following hour.[2]

In another instance, a golfer who had noticed after eight weeks of autogenic training that his swing had definitely improved, decided to try to increase his efficiency even more by repeating part of his relaxation formula to himself just before hitting the ball. When he did this he had the distinct impression that the relaxation exercise dissolved disturbing tensions in his shoulders and added to the precision of his golf technique.[3]

Preparatory Meditation

Meditating when we are right in the midst of a stress situation is different from meditating *ahead of time* when a stressful situation is anticipated. When anticipating certain types of difficulty, a full deep meditation rather than a mini-meditation may be preferable—a full twenty minutes for meditators who are used to meditating for this amount of time.

A teen-age patient of mine who was a TM meditator was extremely nervous about her forthcoming performance in a school play. After talking it over with me, she decided to try meditating for a complete twenty-minute session about half an hour before the performance on each of the days she was to appear. When she did this, to her surprise she found it an extremely effective strategy. She felt calmer and less self-conscious on the stage when she had meditated beforehand.

At the American Conservatory Theater in San Francisco, meditation is regularly used as part of the training program and the company reports that the relationship between actors, and their overall performance, are improved when a cast meditates together before a play. In this connection, I remember how soothing it was for me to meditate just before a TV appearance. Both the director and the cameraman, as well as myself, were meditators, and we held a group meditation just before the TV cameras began to click. We had the impression that it affected the show in a very positive manner.

Meditation and Exam Anxiety

An interesting use of preparatory meditation has been reported by students who find this a useful technique before taking an examination. It seems to be a very effective way to lessen exam anxiety, providing the meditator is familiar enough with his or her own reactions to be able to gauge how soon before the examination it is best for them to meditate. Getting to the examination room early and sitting quietly in the corner meditating may be an excellent way to enter an exam for certain students. The student will emerge from his or her meditation relaxed and with an improved perspective on the forthcoming test. For a person who tends to feel drowsy following meditation, however, meditating directly before an exam would be a poor idea since motivation to achieve could be lowered in this manner and so could alertness. She or he might also emerge from meditation lacking the degree of aggressiveness needed to tackle the examination successfully. For such people meditating about an hour before an exam, instead of in the exam room, would be much better.

Recently I conducted an experiment with students at Princeton who were facing their final examination. Many of them had indicated some anxiety about this exam since it constituted a large portion of their final grade. I decided to try to counteract their exam anxiety by leading the class in a mini-meditation (three minutes in length) just before I handed out the test booklets. I showed them a simple zazen breathing method which I knew would be relatively easy for them to master even if they were not experienced meditators, and purposely kept the meditation time brief in order not to induce sleepiness or *over*-relaxation in the students.

Although the class was initially a bit startled at the announcement of the meditation (for which they had not been prepared), they entered readily into the spirit of it. In an anonymous questionnaire turned in after the exam, over 80 per cent of the students reported that the meditation had been helpful in relaxing them during the examination, and the majority of these students said they would like to institute group meditations before other exams at the university. About 20 per cent reported having felt annoyed at having to stop to meditate when they had been "all psyched up" for the exam, but none reported that it had harmed their subsequent performance.

Presurgical Meditation

An important potential use for strategic meditation is in preparing for surgery. While I do not know of any systematic study in this area, I have used mini-meditations myself prior to dental surgery and know several other people who have also done so.

The period of waiting in the office before being escorted to the dental chair affords a good opportunity to apply strategic mini-meditation unobtrusively. When I do this it calms me immensely and I am much better prepared for the dentistry. On one occasion I followed this preparatory meditation with mini-meditations during the time the dentist was actually working on my teeth. Since this was a stressful situation, I kept my eyes open, and during the prolonged (hour and a half) dental session, I allowed mini-meditations to come and go naturally. This was the most relaxing dental session I had ever experienced and it was surprisingly pain-free.

On other occasions I have not found it possible to meditate while in the dentist's chair and if I do not feel like meditating at such times, I never force it. I have not been able to identify the reason why mini-meditation sometimes comes naturally during the actual dentistry and at other times is unwanted by me. This may have something to do with the hour of the day, or perhaps it is due to some difference in my physical or emotional state at the time.

Meditation to Counteract Phobias

An interesting use of preparatory meditation has been reported by a behavioral psychologist, Leoné Boudreau.[4] A college student who had come for treatment complained of a host of incapacitating fears. He feared enclosed places, elevators, "being alone," and examinations. He was so frightened by these situations, in fact, that he had been attempting to avoid them at all costs since the age of thirteen. This of course hampered him considerably on many levels. In addition, the physical symptoms of anxiety which he experienced during his attacks of panic contributed to a strong fear of becoming "mentally ill."

This student was first treated by "systematic desensitization," the therapy in which the patient is instructed in methods of deep relaxation such as progressive (muscle) relaxation, or visualizing a calm, peaceful scene. The situations that he fears are then introduced to him, one by one (usually in verbal terms) in manageable steps. Only when he is finally able to remain calm and relaxed throughout the presentation of one step is he allowed to proceed to the next more anxiety-provoking visualization, until finally he can remain calm even when visualizing the most intense of images involving his most feared situation.

This method is frequently effective in reducing phobias which hang on even after the original emotional cause has been removed. In the case of this particular student, however, though both muscle relaxation and "calm scenes" were used for systematic desensitization, the treatment had no effect on his particular phobias.

His therapist then introduced him to an even more stringent form of treatment called "mass desensitization," where the patient is instructed to practice his desensitization sessions for three hours continuously on three consecutive days. Although sometimes this intensive approach works when a simple, milder method has failed, this student continued to show no improvement in his severe symptoms.

At this point the student happened to mention that he had once learned TM and occasionally practiced it. Feeling that there was nothing to lose by trying an experiment, the therapist suggested that each day the student imagine vividly that he was in one of the situations that particularly frightened him. As soon as he had imagined his phobic scene clearly, he was to follow these imaginings immediately by one half hour of meditation. He was also instructed that should he find himself actually *in* one of his fear-provoking situations, he was immediately to stop whatever he was doing and meditate for a half hour.

The student co-operated with this plan and the results were surprising. Unlike the other techniques for desensitization, meditation was almost immediately effective. Shortly after he began to use TM to deal with his fears the patient showed marked improvement. Within one month his need to avoid enclosed places, being alone, and elevators, had all but disappeared. What is more, since his tension level had decreased when he was in these situations, he now no longer experienced his abnormal physical sensations and this reassured him as to his physical and mental state.

This promising result suggests that meditation may be useful in treating phobias and other similar conditions. Using it this way might, however, be comparable to using the mantra in an emergency. Conceivably it could be overdone.

Meditating Athletes

Probably the most widely publicized use of meditation for strategic purposes has been for athletics. A number of athletes report that they use meditation to prepare them for athletic contests. Since they are increasingly doing so, it seems worth investigating what elements of meditation make it particularly useful for people engaged in sports.

Meditation, as we have seen, tends to reduce anxiety levels, making the meditator calmer, less worried, and more quietly self-confident—obviously useful attributes for an athlete who is about to enter a contest. Relaxation and ease of mind can be helpful in almost any undertaking, but in sports it is important that the person not be so relaxed that he stops caring whether or not he wins the contest, a point which will be discussed later.

A student of mine at Princeton, Andy Rimol, became interested in this subject. Captain of the university's basketball team, he claimed that meditating had greatly improved his game. According to his report, after he started meditating with TM in his sophomore year, his stamina increased markedly and he was easily able to undertake extra sessions in basketball on the same day without feeling fatigue. He also reported that his co-ordination in the game improved.

Because he was so personally impressed by the effects of meditation on his athletic prowess, Rimol decided to conduct a research study in our laboratory to measure the perceptual-motor co-ordination of meditators and nonmeditators by comparing their performances. He also planned to compare two different groups of meditators, those who would be allowed to meditate just before the perceptual-motor task and those who would not.

Blasdall's Star Tracers

Before Rimol commenced his study, however, another researcher, Blasdall, had compared the performance of regular TM meditators with that of nonmeditators on the Mirror Star Tracing Task, a rather difficult and sometimes quite frustrating puzzlelike test where the subject is handed a pencil and asked to trace a design of a star by looking at it in the mirror only.[5] This means, in effect, making your hand move backward, mirror-image fashion. Before being asked to perform this task, the meditators meditated for twenty minutes while the nonmeditators simply rested for twenty minutes with their eyes closed. This way both groups were in a rested state when they undertook the Star Tracing Task. As the experimenter had predicted, the meditators performed significantly better in this task than the nonmeditators.

Although this was certainly a promising start, Blasdall's study had left open certain questions. For example, how do we know that the meditators would not have done better than the nonmeditators in the Star Tracing Task if they had just walked into the experimental laboratory "cold," without being allowed to meditate first? In other words, maybe it is possible that people who have been meditating for a long time simply have better co-ordination—perhaps the *immediate* meditation before the task had absolutely nothing to do with Blasdall's results. Obviously this question is important when considering the value of a strategic use of meditation for athletics.

Rimol's Labyrinth Players

Rimol reasoned that meditation might have both long-term *and* immediate effects on perceptual-motor performances.[6] Based on his own experiences and those of other athletes whom he knew, he felt that regular meditation did improve co-ordination skills in general, but his own experience had taught him that meditating prior to an important basketball game also helped him do better in that *specific* game than if he had neglected to meditate beforehand. The challenge was to design an experiment which would test both these possibilities at once.

He chose three groups of male college students as the subjects in his experiment. The first two groups included students who had been regularly practicing TM for five months or more before the study started. The third group had never practiced TM or any other kind of meditation.

To measure the subjects' motor skills, Rimol chose to use a rather demanding game—the "labyrinth game." It consists of a movable board fastened in place in a box. Two controlling hand dials on either side of the box can manipulate the board so it tilts forward, backward, or toward either side, and the player is allowed to use both hands at once to tilt the board. The board has a numbered path with sixty holes scattered along it, the goal of the game being to get a round metal ball from the start (hole 1) to the finish (hole 60). The score is the number by the hole where the ball finally falls in. What makes the game difficult is that even the smallest error results in the ball falling into one of the holes. Needless to say, all subjects were carefully screened beforehand to make sure they had never played this game before—practice gives a player a distinct advantage.

All Rimol's subjects were given a five-minute practice session and then were asked to try to make "as high a score as possible." After this, each group underwent a specific activity for twenty minutes. Half of the meditators were asked to lie down on the couch and rest with their eyes closed but *not* to meditate, the other half were asked to sit and meditate. The nonmeditators were also asked to lie on the couch and rest with their eyes closed for twenty minutes. After the twenty minutes were up, all subjects were given another formal "test," in which they once again tried to do their best.

The first question which interested Rimol was whether or not meditators would do better than nonmeditators in the pretrials before any of the subjects had either rested or meditated. Would they show any *long-term* effects of meditation on their motor skills?

The results were clear-cut on this question. The meditators did score significantly higher on this unfamiliar perceptual-motor task than did the nonmeditators right from the start. As a group they were superior in their co-ordination as measured by this particular task.

The next question was whether meditators who had been allowed to *meditate* between the first and second tests would show more improvement from first to second, than meditators who had not meditated between taking the two tests but had only rested— or than the nonmeditating "control" group. Again, the results were clear.

All three groups of subjects naturally improved somewhat on the second testing. This was to be expected since playing at any game for a while helps one improve through practice. The most interesting finding was that the meditators who had meditated between the two tests did significantly better on the second test than either the meditators who had simply rested or the nonmeditators. In fact, the meditators who had not been allowed to meditate between the two trials did *not* improve on their final test any more than the nonmeditators had! There appeared to be an immediate short-term effect of meditation on this perceptual-motor task. This suggested that the strategic use of meditation directly before the task at hand may be particularly important to persons engaged in special skills.

Unanswered Questions

Though meditation seems to affect perceptual and motor performance, there are some important things which we do not know about this process. How *many* weeks or months, for instance, must a person have been practicing meditation before its influence can be seen on his motor skills? Can someone who has been meditating for two weeks do as well in an athletic contest as someone who has been meditating for three months? Or as a person who has been meditating for a year?

We also do not know whether the immediate influence of a meditation session on motor performance depends upon the subject being an experienced meditator. Is it possible for a subject who has never meditated before in his life to get the same benefit out of a meditation experience if he is taught how to do it "right on the spot," as someone might get who is experienced at meditating and has been doing it for some time? My experience in teaching a class how to meditate just before their final exam suggests that prior knowledge of meditation may not be necessary to obtain good short-term results, and a study by psychologists Daniel Goleman and Gary Schwartz at Harvard showed that even novices who had learned to meditate for the first time that day in the lab, were less anxious after a stress-inducing film and recovered more quickly from it than nonmeditators, although they did not show as marked a recovery as did experienced meditators.[7]

One final question important for athletes who might want to learn meditation is—how *long* do the benefits of a meditation session last? In other words, if meditation improves motor skills and perception, how long does that improvement hold up? When does it begin to dwindle and taper off? In practical terms, how far ahead of a game should an athlete meditate to get the best results from his meditation?

Rimol thinks this varies with the individual. He personally finds that if he meditates just before a game, he tends to feel so "mellow" he no longer cares much about defeating the other team; he just feels "warm and friendly" toward them. For this reason, he makes it a practice to meditate an hour and a half ahead of time when he plans to play in a game. This enables him to increase his efficiency while at the same time letting a competitive state of mind build up in him again. On the other hand, Bill Walton, the basketball star of the Portland Trail Blazers, finds that he is more energetic and aggressive if he meditates immediately before the commencement of a game. Obviously, such individual differences must be determined by trial and error and athletes discover for themselves just what timing they should follow for their strategic meditations if they are going to use this technique to obtain the best results.

These various strands of information suggest that the strategic use of meditation in the field of athletics is well worth investigating. Despite the need for more research, the results are promising enough so that individual athletes can feel secure in trying out for themselves the manner in which they may use meditation for this purpose. This advice applies in general to all the other strategic uses of meditation as well. Used with discretion and good common sense, the possibilities are wide for applying meditation to many specific situations in one's life.

Extra Meditation

Another important use of meditation does not depend upon mini-meditations or preparatory meditations, but relies upon increasing the *number* of meditations in any one day.

Meditations per day can be increased effectively under certain circumstances, provided the person proceeds with caution. IMS, for instance, advises TM initiates that they can meditate as often as they wish under two sets of circumstances—if they are sick or confined to bed or if the meditator is a pregnant woman. Clearly they recognize the strategic value of extra meditation under particular circumstances. I would like, however, to expand on the list of situations for which it may be appropriate.

Meditating When Ill

Meditating as often as one wishes when ill can be very useful for certain persons. A friend of mine, to whom I taught CSM about a year ago, recently had some abdominal surgery. When she was lying in the hospital immediately following surgery and under heavy medication for pain, she remembered being instructed that when ill, she could meditate as often as possible. Actually, she had not been meditating regularly before she went into the hospital, but suddenly felt strongly that she wanted to do so, and proceeded to meditate about five or six times a day during her stay in the hospital.

The meditation had a "startling" effect on her. A pain-killer was unnecessary after her first few postoperative hours and she required no sleeping medication while in the hospital. Her doctor reported that her progress was so rapid that he wanted to know what special "magic" she had used to accomplish this. She told him that she had been meditating and although initially skeptical, he finally commented that he was so impressed with the way she had responded to the surgery and particularly to her lack of need for sedative drugs that, "whatever you are doing, it must be right."

But what about IMS advice to TMers that they add extra meditations when sick, *only* if they are so ill that they cannot get out of bed? No doubt this advice serves the purpose of preventing overmeditation, but the distinction between being bedridden or not, is to me an arbitrary one. The belief that extra meditations are indicated in one case and not in the other is peculiar to IMS and is certainly not supported by scientific research. I know of several instances where patients who were ill but *not* confined to bed added meditations to their day to cope with their illness and said that the results were excellent. A colleague tells me, for example, that extra meditation sessions helped him recover from a recent severe virus much more quickly than usual, although he never went to bed during the entire time.

Despite such glowing reports, people's impressions that meditation has helped them cope with an illness better are not scientific proof that meditation actually does help recovery. For this, a controlled study would have to be carried out with one group of persons having a known illness referred for meditation training and another group of persons with the same illness not trained to meditate. Records could then be kept as to which group recovered more rapidly. The only carefully controlled research in these areas to date has studied hypertensive and asthmatic patients. This will be discussed later, when we come to consider the relationship of meditation to stress-related illness.

A discussion of the strategic use of meditation when ill is not complete without making note of the fact that not everybody is able to meditate when they are ill. Certainly not all people can meditate during all types of illnesses. I have known several people to report that when they had the flu they were so weak that even though bedridden, they could not "summon up the energy" to meditate. If they tried to meditate it did not "take," no matter how long they stayed with it. Eventually they had to abandon any attempt until they felt better. Interestingly, Yoga scriptures advise against meditating when one has fever, quite possibly a reflection of long experience with some of these difficulties.

The inability of some people to meditate when weak or feverish highlights the fact that although meditation is considered a relaxation technique, a person must possess a certain minimum amount of available energy to meditate. Some, my husband and myself included, have at time commented that we were, at a particular moment, too exhausted to meditate. We were so tired that the kind of alert-relaxed involvement that meditation requires was not possible. Rather than being comforting, it would become unpleasant and a strain.

As in so many other things concerning meditation, this is a highly individual matter. Some people report that meditation acts as a stimulant at times when they feel exhausted. I suspect that some of us may tend to use meditation as a calming agent while others may use it more as an energizer. This is not to say that we have a choice over the way we use meditation, but rather that our systems may have different requirements and thus make different use of this highly versatile technique.

Meditation During Prolonged Emotional Stress

Those of us who teach CSM find that additional meditations may be necessary when a person is under a special emotional stress such as the illness of a loved one, financial crises, or other conditions where a continued strain must be faced. Unlike the occasional use of mini-meditations to cope with a specific situation, this involves the scheduling of extra *regular* meditations over a period of time. Obviously this is a more serious matter than an occasional mini-meditation and should be handled with careful attention to its effects. Properly used, however, it can be extremely effective.

A patient of mine, a CSM meditator recently faced a family emergency in which his wife was rushed to the hospital acutely ill. During her stay there, he put in many days of emotional strain waiting for her recovery. At the same time the pressure of serious decisions about the family's future and the total care of the children were weighing on him. During this period he found himself spontaneously meditating five or six times daily. Without this intense program of meditation, he says, he does not believe he could have endured the strain of this crisis. With it he managed well, made sound decisions, and was able to plan constructively for his wife's eventual return home and subsequent recovery.

In teaching CSM, we have noticed that when a person is in a state of continuing stress, his or her *first* meditation of the day may seem almost futile, a mere "drop in the bucket" so to speak. Under such conditions they report that this first meditation has merely "scratched the surface," seeming only to "skim off" the uppermost layer of tension but no more. If the meditator then waits the regular half-day before meditating again, so much tension may have accumulated that they may experience the same thing with the second meditation; it too will seem to skim the surface.

If, however, the first meditation of the day is followed only one hour or an hour and a half later by another full meditation, this second meditation may have quite a different effect. It is as if the first meditation prepares the ground, and this closely spaced second one is then able to "take hold" and may have a deep therapeutic effect. The final and third meditation, usually coming in the late afternoon or in the evening, will also be more effective under these circumstances. In this way the entire day may be affected because of the double morning meditations.

At times I have advised patients under unusually severe stress to do two "double meditations" (that is, a pair of meditations separated by only an hour or an hour and a half) twice a day. These four strategically placed meditations each day during a time of intense emotional stress often work extremely well, as in the case of the man described above.

It is important, however, to watch how such extra meditations are affecting one's behavior, whether or not they lower alertness or result in any undue amount of tension-release. If so, they should be reduced. It is also important to discontinue the extra meditations once the emotional crisis is resolved, so that overmeditating will not develop into a habit.

Alternating Meditation with Rest

A striking instance of the use of extra meditations to handle an emotional crisis was reported to me by a psychologist colleague. He found himself in a severe panic because of certain distressing incidents which, while obviously upsetting, could have been better tolerated at another time in his life. He was experiencing sinking sensations, loss of identity, loss of control, and an eerie sense of unreality. These extreme reactions probably had, at least in part, some physical basis but this was not clear at the time and it was obvious that some extreme measure had to be employed to break the rising panic.

Since he ordinarily meditates regularly with TM and is familiar with the strategic use of meditation, he decided to try meditation to quell his panic. He first withdrew from all stimulation into a darkened room and meditated for twenty minutes, after which he lay down on his bed, half sleeping and half resting. He set his alarm clock, roused himself once more after an hour, and meditated again for twenty minutes. He continued to do this the entire day—remaining in a quiet darkened room and alternating meditation with complete rest on an hourly schedule. As the day proceeded, he experienced immense relief as though he were being "pulled out of a black pit" and as though "pieces of a picture puzzle were being put together."

Although this meditation strategy did not cure his basic condition, which involved some hormonal changes of middle age which later required medical treatment, change of diet, and some psychotherapy, it did serve as an excellent emergency measure. In effect, it reversed what was a potentially dangerous psychiatric condition so well that it is a method worth considering under extreme conditions. Clearly if such a radical measure is used, it should be discontinued once the severe condition is brought under control.

Meditation Under Catastrophic Circumstances

We do not yet know how people use meditation when under extreme duress involving a threat to their lives—as, for instance, when stranded in a lifeboat at sea, imprisoned in enemy territory, or facing other catastrophic situations. Systematic reports of such uses of meditation have not as yet been collected. It seems very much to the point, however, to consider some of the reports of persons who have used other relaxation techniques which, in effect, evoke a meditative mood, in order to comfort themselves and increase their strength and endurance under extreme conditions.

Several reports from autogenic trainees who used this technique to handle various catastrophes are reported in scientific journals and books. All of these people were caught in situations where self-protection and survival assumed paramount importance. For all of them, the use of the relaxation technique had an important effect on both their minds and bodies and helped to support them so that they did not "go to pieces." Instead, their egos were often strengthened under the adverse conditions.

These reports range from isolated instances of persons who found their relaxation training helpful when they were being menaced by the Gestapo, to groups of soldiers in a POW camp where no medical assistance was available, to soldiers facing dangerous battle situations and political prisoners in solitary confinement or during interrogation.

A particularly impressive example of the strategic use of a relaxation technique is the story of a middle-aged German Jewish woman who happened to have learned autogenic training when she was a young girl in Berlin during World War II.[8] While hiding from the Gestapo, this woman at one point lived "illegally" for two and a half years, hiding wherever she could in order not to allow the authorities to know that she still existed. She was always under immense danger, suffering continual anxiety and degradation.

During the air raids, when she had to stay alone upstairs in an apartment and often in complete darkness, she experienced her most difficult ordeals. It was then that her relaxation training proved to be crucial. "How else would I have been able to stand this recurring terror?" she writes. "I was not only afraid of being hit by a bomb, but even more so, of the possibility I would get hurt and thus endanger the people who gave me shelter to save me from the Gestapo. As soon as the air raid sirens started, terrible feelings of anxiety developed. However, with the [relaxation] exercises, I could reduce these feelings to a relatively tolerable level, and somehow keep them away from me. I managed to remain calm and almost without fear until the attack was right close by." At this point her relaxation training did not help any more, but as the attack moved further on, "I quickly regained my inner calm with the exercises. . . ." This woman was convinced that it was in part due to her relaxation training that she managed to get through those years of terror and that she finally emerged with relatively little psychological damage. An exhaustive depletion of vitality did not occur, she said, because she was able to compensate for the repeated severe buildup of tension by inducing the comforting relaxation.

It is particularly interesting to note the limitations of relaxation training in this woman's account. The point at which its effectiveness seemed to break down was in the face of imminent threat to life—the height of the bombings. In these moments the self-protective impulse to flee (which of course could not be acted upon under these circumstances) took over and the survival instinct became overwhelming.

What is also interesting is the fact that resuming the relaxation exercises again as the bombing receded helped her to handle her excess anxiety in such a way that restablization could occur. As this woman indicated, the use of the relaxation exercises somehow prevented deeply disorganizing effects of these repeated traumas on her personality. This is an impressive account and there is certainly no reason to suppose that persons well trained in meditation, which is similar in many respects to autogenic training, could not achieve much the same results if they entered a meditative state under similar circumstances.

Relaxation Under Physical Stress

In another interesting account of the strategic use of relaxation, a physician, H. Lindemann, has reported the manner in which he used his relaxation training while he was alone for seventy-two days in a one-man kayak-type boat crossing the Atlantic.[9] He would use frequent *short* periods of autogenic relaxation (similar to mini-meditations) to economize his energy, constantly promoting recuperation from stress. He claims that this helped him cope decisively with problems of fatigue and sleep while on this grueling journey.

Relaxation exercises coupled with self-suggestions were also effective in reducing his periodically recurring hallucinations. From time to time to would "see" such things as a food store inviting him to buy food and then would experience a sudden powerful urge to jump overboard in order to get to the store. By quietly entering the relaxed state and repeating to himself that these hallucinations were *not* real, he was able to regain his equilibrium. His training also helped him overcome depressive states and desperate situations such as he faced after capsizing, by combining the relaxation with repeated suggestions to himself such as "I am going to make it . . . my muscles can hold on . . . I am going to make it."

Meditation and Self-Suggestion

Autogenic training is so structured that it can, when necessary, incorporate into its procedures various specific self-suggestions if these seem advisable. This feature seems to lend itself particularly well to dealing with emergencies such as those described by Lindemann.

We do not yet know if a meditative state can be put to a similar use. It seems entirely plausible, however, that such a phrase as "I am going to make it" could be substituted for the repetition of a mantra. When repeated under emergency conditions it might fit into the rhythmic pattern already familiar to the meditator, established by long practice of repeating the mantra, and in all probability should be experienced as both comforting and reassuring. It is not inconceivable therefore that self-suggestion could be incorporated, when strategically necessary, into an existing meditative framework. At least, exploration of such a possibility should be undertaken.

As the examples in this chapter illustrate, one of the most important factors about meditation which makes it of potential use in stressful circumstances is the fact that it does not depend upon any outside person or force. It therefore seems particularly useful for people who face situations where they may be physically or emotionally at the mercy of some uncontrollable external threat. Using meditation strategically under such conditions could not only be an important contribution—it might be a lifesaving one.

8

Some Intriguing Rhythms

Some teachers of meditation suggest meditating at specific times of day in order to get the greatest benefits from this practice. IMS, for example, advises morning and late afternoon meditation and devout Hindus meditate at sunrise and sunset. To find out what scientific evidence there is that meditating at one time of day is more effective than meditating at another, we need to consider our body rhythms and how they work.

Bodily Cycles

Human beings, like all other animals, and like the primordial oceans from which we sprang, are subject to cyclic highs and lows, so that we are literally a different person from one hour to another. On thousands of scores, we all change physically and emotionally in response to daily, monthly, and yearly rhythms. We are aware of some of these rhythms—as when our hunger increases, our energy ebbs or flows, or we feel drowsy or wakeful—but we may be totally unaware of other changes in us, such as body temperature, which also take place in a cyclical manner.

The body temperature of human beings regularly varies from a low point in the small hours of the morning (whether we are awake or asleep) to a high point in the afternoon. This occurs in every person who is active by day and sleeps by night and is such a persistent rhythm that even enforced inactivity over a long period of time cannot alter it except under very unusual conditions —and then only partially.[1] Despite a regular daily fluctuation of one to two degrees in the body's temperature, however, we do not ordinarily recognize this change while it is occurring. In the same way, liver and kidney functions, brain chemistry, blood sugar levels, blood hormone levels, and a host of other bodily processes differ markedly from hour to hour. Even sensitivity to taste and smell is different in the morning from the way it is in the evening, as is the effectiveness of our memory, ability to learn, and capacity to make fine discriminations. Some of these changes may determine our resistance to stress at different times of the day. Pain tolerance can vary according to the hour, and allergies may follow a "timetable," peaking at one time of the day and almost disappearing at another.

Daily highs and lows in adrenal hormone levels are closely related to the way we cope with stress. As Gay Luce points out, a certain dose of amphetamines can kill 77.6 per cent of a group of animals when given at one time of day but the identical dose will kill only 6 per cent of these animals when administered at another time of day.[2] The animals' times of high resistance to these drugs correspond to the level of adrenal hormones in their blood. Similarly, a medicine administered to a person at one hour of the day may have a different effect from the same medicine administered at another hour, a fact now beginning to be recognized by physicians.

Morning vs. Evening Meditation

Since we are not the same person from hour to hour, is meditation a different experience for us, depending upon what time of day we enter into it?

While there is not an answer to these questions based on experimentation, many people report sharp differences between their morning and evening meditations. One graphic example of this is my husband, who says that his morning meditation is like a vibrant muscle massage with a thousand invisible and gentle fingers kneading his whole body in rhythmic fashion, from his toes to his head. This is both invigorating and relaxing for him—a welcome waking-up-to-the-day. In the late afternoon, however, the very idea of these massage-like pulsations is unpleasant. His meditations at that time take on a soothing, quiet, siesta-like quality, serving to waft him away gently from the cares and pressures of the day. During his second meditation, he describes sensation as being at a minimum and mental quiet and drifting as the primary experience. Similarly, a colleague reports that his morning meditations tend to involve an awareness of the practical matters which must be handled in the day ahead; his later meditations are more self-pleasing "fantasy-trips."

Meditation "Readiness"

Most people experience certain moments during the day when they feel like meditating and other moments when they feel resistant to the idea. If they *force* themselves to meditate when they are not in the mood (something which may be hard to do) they report that their meditation tends to be superficial, restless, or "not really meditative." They are likely to experience many organized thoughts during such a session and be less aware of their mantra or other meditational device. Instead, they may find themselves making plans or engaging in other typical "unmeditative" preoccupations. They feel as though they were on the surface of the experience. Oddly enough, they may be relaxed following such a meditative session, despite its seeming superficiality. Because of this, an argument might be made for forcing oneself to meditate at some regular hour each day, no matter how one feels about doing it.

Unfortunately, there is no easy answer to the question of whether or not we should be highly disciplined about meditation. Although making a routine of any habit is an advantage, forcing ourselves to meditate "against the grain" can lead to just the kind of effortful striving that meditation is designed to counteract. The question seems to be whether we can hope to gain freedom by donning chains—even if the chains are said to be for our own good. I have talked with a number of people for whom meditation became an emotional stress because it was approached in too rigid a manner. For the kind of person who makes everything into a chore, meditation can all too easily fit into this mold, and this is clearly a disadvantage. If a basically permissive form of meditation is made into a virtual enslavement, it is not surprising that the meditator often escapes the whole process by abandoning it.

One of the main tasks when teaching meditation is to help a new meditator assume an easy, relaxed attitude toward the meditation process itself—not simple to accomplish of course if he or she happens to have a compulsive personality. As a general rule, I advise new meditators that it is better to skip a meditation altogether on a given day than to force it. It is the person who understands their own rhythms and respects their own wish *not* to meditate, as well as *to* meditate, who will be most likely to stay with the practice and use it as a genuine growth experience.

One of my successfully meditating trainees put it very well: "I've never really pushed myself into a meditation," she said. "I've never forced myself to do it when I had a feeling of 'ugh, it's the last thing I want,' and for that reason, I've always come out of meditation smiling and with a lovely feeling of being refreshed and peaceful." Some people, however, will postpone meditation *indefinitely* because they "aren't in the right mood yet." This is a different matter. I will discuss such blocks to continuing meditation later when we come to consider the problems which may arise in adjusting to the changes meditators find in themselves.

Yoga Scheduling

The fact that we feel more receptive to the idea of meditation at certain moments of the day may be obvious, but the exact pattern that meditation-readiness follows (if indeed there *is* a pattern) is not clear.

The ancient discipline of *Swar Yoga* (literally, "unification through breath") proposes a unique method for identifying recurring periods in the day when meditation is said to be suitable. According to Yogic belief, the "correct" times for meditation correspond to those moments of the day when a person finds himself breathing predominantly through his *left* nostril. This can be easily ascertained by blocking each nostril in turn with the pressure of a finger. The nasal passage through which the air passes more freely is the dominant nostril.

When one nostril is dominant, the other is recessive, with a switch in nostril dominance generally taking place (in most people) at the end of every hour or hour and a half. The yogis believe that the left nostril concentrates energy in the *right* side of the body and brain, causing the person to be more "passive," "emotional," "introverted," and "feminine" in outlook.[3] According to Swar Yoga texts, meditation should be practiced only when the left nostril is dominant (i.e., when the right side of the body and brain are considered to be active). If one tries to meditate when the right nostril dominates, the meditation session is said to be relatively ineffective and the person to feel restless and have many distracting thoughts.

This Yogic belief relates to what neurophysiologists are presently learning about the functions of the two cerebral hemispheres of the brain. The *left* hemisphere (controlling the right side of the body) has been found to control verbal activity and logical, sequential, practical thinking; while the *right* hemisphere (controlling the left side of the body) has been found to control space perception, musical awareness, and the intuitive, holistic types of thought which characterize meditative and artistic states of mind.

Yoga theory concerning variations in meditation readiness with nostril dominance, has points of correspondence with the reports of those meditators who contend that they find themselves quite unable to meditate at certain times of day but ripe for it at others. As yet no experiments have been carried out to test this Yogic belief. It would certainly be simple to have a group of meditators check nostril dominance before meditating and then record their "depth" of meditation. If there is truth in the Yoga belief, it might have considerable practical application, since if nostril dominance happens to be "incorrect" for meditation at a particular time, it can be *voluntarily* switched by lying down for several minutes on the opposite side of the body from the nostril one wishes to clear. Gravity draining the sinuses produces the desired nostril dominance.

The Basic Ultradian Rhythm

There is evidence from a different field which may supply additional clues about meditation readiness. Scientists concerned with the rhythmical nature of biological processes have identified a short, 90- to 100-minute cycle of rest and activity which seems to repeat itself throughout the day and which conceivably may relate to meditation readiness (although this possibility has not been studied). This cycle is called the *ultradian rhythm*, from the Latin words *ultra*, meaning "beyond," and *dies* meaning "day." The word literally means "outside the limits of our daily rhythm," in this case signifying a shorter time span than the twenty-four-hour day.

It was not until the 1950s that the scientific world learned about such rest/activity cycles. At this time it was discovered that one phase of sleep was anything but "peaceful" in the ordinary sense of the word, for it was accompanied by physiological changes indicating a very excited state. One of these was a rapid, spasmodic darting of the eyes beneath the lids which occurred in bursts during this time, giving the state its name of Rapid Eye Movement (REM) sleep. REM sleep, which turned out to be the time during which most of our elaborate vivid dreaming occurs, was found to recur throughout the night roughly every 90 to 100 minutes in adults and every 60 minutes in infants.

No sooner had this sleep cycle been discovered when Dr. Nathaniel Kleitman, co-discoverer of REM sleep, noticed that human infants showed a regular 60-minute rest/activity cycle during *wakefulness* as well.[4] On the basis of this he speculated that rhythmic changes in level of activation during the day may occur in a similar manner in adults. Perhaps rest and activity regularly alternate in persons of all ages, "around the clock."

Exploring a Daydream Cycle

In 1966, my husband, Dr. Harmon S. Ephron, and I were involved in research on the functions of REM sleep. Working with theories involving the need for periodic stimulation of the brain during sleep, we were impressed by the unceasing alternation of quiet and active states during the night. Could it be that the same kind of alternation between restful and active states continues throughout the day (as Kleitman suggested) but that during the day the state of inner stimulation (we called it "endogenous afferentation")[5] manifests itself in periods of heightened *day-dreaming*?

To find out about this we conducted a preliminary study with a colleague co-operative enough to carry around a small portable tape recorder strapped to his shoulders for fifteen hours as he went about his daily chores in a vacation cabin. During this time he whispered into the microphone every thought, no matter how seemingly trivial, that he could identify as passing through his mind that day. The only time he ceased talking was when he slept.

This pilot study resulted in a sketchy but consistent pattern. We saw that our colleague had shown peaks of daydreaming roughly every 80 to 110 minutes during the day and that these daydreaming sessions seemed to alternate with periods of outwardly directed thinking of a more practical, logical nature.

Unknown to us then, however, this experiment was to be repeated with more sophisticated research methods several years later by other researchers. But prior to this, several lines of research had been slowly converging, all of them pointing to the existence of other kinds of daytime rhythms which also have a periodicity of about 90 to 100 minutes.

The Oral Activity Cycle

In 1922, a Japanese scientist by the name of Toni Wada had conducted an unusual experiment. In order to study the timing of stomach contractions (supposed to be indications of hunger or readiness to eat) she had confined a group of subjects to bed for a whole day to measure these contractions. This she did by inserting recording balloons into their stomachs, which were then inflated slightly with air. In this way she was able to measure the quantity of air pressure within the balloon and since the more forcefully the stomach contracted, the more it pushed air out of the balloon, she could obtain indications of stomach muscle activity. Recording these contractions, Wada found that they recurred with considerable regularity every 90 to 100 minutes throughout the day.[6]

Forty years later, two psychoanalysts involved in sleep research uncovered some evidence consistent with Wada's. Drs. Stanley Freidman and Charles Fisher of Mt. Sinai Hospital in New York City became interested in the question of whether or not "oral" (mouth-oriented) activities might recur in roughly the same manner during the day as REM periods do during the night.[7] According to psychoanalytic theory, night dreaming often serves to discharge "oral" drives. If peaks of nighttime dreaming recur every ninety minutes, they reasoned, perhaps this periodic "drive discharge" might occur with the same regularity in the daytime.

To test this possibility, Freidman and Fisher decided to investigate people's tendencies to put things in their mouths. Would this tendency show a regular rise and fall throughout the day similar to the rise and fall Wada had found for stomach contractions? If so, would these fluctuations recur on a schedule similar to that of the REM periods at night?

To explore this, the experimenters created a comfortable den where each volunteer was asked to spend a number of hours in isolation. The den contained a refrigerator stocked with food, an electric pot with a continually fresh and tempting supply of coffee, and books, magazines, and cigarettes. The subjects were allowed to read, write, or sketch during this time, but were kept isolated from other distractions and from each other.

Observing these subjects through a one-way mirror, the experimenters were able to record every object each person put into his mouth, every time he did so, and the exact time of day this was done. When these activities were later transferred to a time chart, the researchers saw a pattern emerge.

The intensity of oral (mouth-oriented) activity reached a peak about every ninety-six minutes, at which time there was a much greater tendency for the subjects to reach for food in the refrigerator, take a cigarette, sip coffee, or whatever. This was followed by the gradual subsiding of oral activities until the next spurt of "orality," which took place about 90 to 100 minutes later. Clearly "oral" activities were recurring regularly despite the fact that the subjects themselves were unaware of any such changes in their behavior.

Apparently Freidman and Fisher had identified a fundamental bodily rhythm. Since their experiment, animals have been shown to have a similar periodic waxing and waning of hunger during the day. A group of cats allowed free feeding have shown bursts of eating activity every fifteen to thirty minutes—a waking cycle that corresponds exactly with the typical *cat* REM cycle of fifteen to thirty minutes.[8] Other researchers have found that brain waves and muscle tone in monkeys recur around the clock in an ultradian rhythm similar to the *monkey* REM cycle at night.[9]

The Daydream Cycle Revisited

On the basis of the findings of the Mount Sinai group, two sleep researchers, Drs. Daniel F. Kripke and David Sonnenschein at the University of California, began to wonder if in man, waking dreams (that is, daydreams) might occur in cycles similar to REM cycles.[10] To find out, these researchers placed their subjects alone for ten hours in a comfortable room with no clocks, books, or other distractions and every five minutes during this confinement, a whistle was blown as a signal to the subject to write down a brief description of whatever he had been thinking about during the previous five-minute interval. During this experiment electrodes were taped to various parts of the participant's head and near his eyes so that both his brain waves and eye movements could be continuously recorded.

Since the subjects had little else to do under these isolated circumstances, as might be expected they reported a good many fairly extensive daydreams. But they also spent considerable time thinking about problems, looking around, and moving around the room, enough so that two types of thoughts were fairly recognizable: organized, practical thinking on the one hand and extended reverie states on the other.

Analyzing the results of this experiment, Kripke and Sonnenschein found that daydreaming did indeed follow a 90- to 100-minute cycle, as they had anticipated it might. At the peak of this cycle the subjects tended to have very emotional, sometimes even bizarre thoughts and images, while at the cycle's low point they thought about everyday problems and tended to make plans for the future, or they organized their lives by simply observing their immediate surroundings.

The experimenters next wondered whether these same ultradian rhythms would exist in a more natural environment. That is essentially the same question we had sought to answer when we asked our colleague to walk around recording his thoughts while engaged in his natural, everyday activities.

Kripke and Sonnenschein conducted the second part of their experiment by asking volunteers to carry small cassette tape recorders with them as they went about their daily routine. As the subject moved about, a timer connected to his belt activated a buzzer every ten minutes, signaling him to dictate a summary of his thoughts for the previous ten-minute interval.

In a naturalistic study such as this, we would not expect subjects to have intense daydreams as often as under abnormal laboratory isolation conditions, but the researchers found that the 90- to 100-minute rhythm of daydreams persisted nonetheless. Apparently then, this ultradian rhythm is strong enough to continue *despite* distractions from the environment.

An Ultradian Rhythm for Meditation?

Although the implications of these studies for the scheduling of meditation have not as yet been explored, laboratory experiments to test the possibility that meditation readiness, like daydreaming, fluctuates in an ultradian rhythm, would not be difficult to conduct. Perhaps with future experimentation, we may find that the meditative mood, like the reverie state, tends to recur about every ninety minutes. If this is the case, we might then want to ask some further questions.

If a person were to meditate when he happened to be on the *outward* swing of his ultradian cycle (moving into his period of *activity*) what would happen? Would this make him more resistant to meditation? Would it reduce the effectiveness of his meditation? Could such mistaken timing make a meditation *entirely* ineffective in certain instances, or perhaps even cause it to be an unpleasant experience?

In the other direction, we might wonder whether co-ordinating the timing of a meditation session with maximum *inward* swing of the ninety-minute cycle—those times when we naturally become ruminative, imaginative, and physically quieter—might help us to realize the deepest possibilities of meditation.

While only careful research can answer these questions, in the meantime, observation of large numbers of meditators suggests that perhaps we intuitively observe our ultradian rhythms through our spontaneous choice of times to meditate, *without realizing we are doing so.* Many of us naturally vary our meditation time on any particular day. We may have been thinking of meditating for half an hour or so, but it is only at some particular moment that we find ourselves actually making an active effort to do so. Are we in this manner perhaps instinctively timing our meditations to coincide with the inward swings of our own ultradian rhythms?

Until experimental answers to these questions are forthcoming, each of us has to discover, by trial and error, our own best hours for meditating each day. This we can do through respecting our feelings of readiness (or unreadiness) to undertake meditation at any particular moment of the day. We should, however, undertake such a self-experiment without, if possible, destroying the routine nature of our meditation. It is still a good plan to establish a regular meditation time for ourselves each day, and then vary it only if we feel *strongly*, on any particular day, that we are not ready for meditation at that time. This way both regularity and flexibility will be insured.

There is obvious value in making meditation as much of a set routine as is genuinely comfortable. Linking times for meditation with some already established habit such as getting out of bed in the morning or traveling to or from work on a bus or subway, or connecting it with any other regular event in our lives, can be a help in doing so, since this increases the regularity of our meditation in an easy, natural manner.

Despite the desirability of routine, however, evidence points to the fact that such strategies are really useful in the long run only if the regular time of day selected genuinely *feels comfortable*. It is logical that meditation, which leads us back to ourselves, should be conducted in harmony with the tidal ebb and flow of our energy and moods. This way it can remain a gentle process, an interlude when we are kind to ourselves.

Influences of External Rhythms

The relationship of our internal rhythms to meditation is one side of this question, but there is another side that is equally intriguing: the effects of *external* rhythms upon this practice. Do changes in the earth's atmosphere or in the cosmos perhaps make certain *clock* times (that is, actual hours of the day) more appropriate for meditating than others?

Recent research shows that our inner production schedule is closely co-ordinated with the wider rhythms of nature that determine sleep and activity each day. The light/darkness cycle, the lunar cycle, changes in electromagnetic fields and other geophysical events—all these continually interact with our own in-built rhythms, forming part of a co-ordinated, oscillating system.

Solar Rhythms

As we increasingly recognize man's interrelationship with his environment, it is clear that the human being is intricately co-ordinated with the rhythms of the universe. Sunlight, for instance, a fundamental influence in our lives, appears to synchronize us with the rhythms of our planet.* As Michel Gauquelin has pointed out, life on earth is profoundly affected by the sun because the earth resides in a very real sense within the "atmosphere" of the sun.[11] Not only can solar eruptions ("sunspots") interfere with electricity on earth, causing fade-outs in radio reception and accounting for intense geomagnetic storms that affect our weather conditions, but living things as widely different as fiddler crabs, chick embryos within eggs, and dry grain seeds have been shown to respond with incredible precision to the presence or absence of sunlight and to its varying intensities.[12]

While the normal response of plants and animals to the daily arrival of the sun has been impressively documented, one need only sit quietly in a garden in the early morning hours to experience the transformation that accompanies the approach of the sun. The isolated chirpings and warbles of the first birds, the intermittent moaning of the mourning doves, the distant whirr of the grasshoppers, gradually swell in predawn to an oratorio as the sun approaches the horizon—and when it finally swings into sight, sweeping the land with its rays, the birds sound triumph, enveloping us. Daytime has brought new birth.

The Sun's Influence on the Body

It is interesting that in *biometeorology*, a new branch of science which seeks to explore the influence of cosmic forces upon human and animal life, researchers have documented, among other things, some of the unusual responses of organisms to the daily arrival of the sun. Particularly important from the point of view of considering best hours for meditation, may be certain preliminary experiments performed in 1938 by a Japanese physican, Maki Takata, which suggest a little-known relationship between human blood serum and the sun.[13]

Takata, who is renowned for developing a test for the flocculation of the blood (this is the blood's propensity to curdle into

* The lunar influence is also important but it seems to have a greater daily influence on nocturnal animals than it does on humans, who are *diurnal* (i.e., active during daylight hours).

small fluffy lumps when a chemical reagent is added to it in a test tube) found, by chance, that the "blood flocculation indexes" of large numbers of Japanese people rose at times when sunspots were directing a concentrated beam of waves and particles toward the earth. The meaning of these changes in the blood serum with exposure to sunlight could not be determined, but Takata later demonstrated that this flocculation index regularly reaches an extreme low point in the early pre-waking hours of the morning. It then shows a sudden dramatic rise beginning about twenty minutes before sunrise which continues at a somewhat reduced pace for about half an hour *following* sunrise.

Going a step further, Takata then took subjects up in a plane to an extremely high altitude, where the "atmospheric shield" against solar radiation is much thinner. As he had expected, he found that these subjects' blood flocculation indexes rose sharply as the plane rose into the less shielded atmosphere. With greater exposure to solar radiation, the blood showed more marked changes, supporting the idea that the sun was involved in these changes in a very direct fashion.

Takata's findings underline the importance of the great solar synchronizer in our lives. It is perhaps not surprising, therefore, that through the ages human beings have considered the moments of sunrise and sunset as having powerful, even mysterious properties, and that they have often linked religious practices and meditations with these times of day.

Primitive peoples, naturally rising before dawn, have often greeted the newborn morning sun with special ceremonies and worship. Until very recently, in fact, sunrise and sunset controlled most of humanity's waking life.

Even today, Hindus still awaken in the very early hours of the morning and perform prescribed purifications which include meditation and worship. Failure to meditate in the early morning hours is actually listed as one of the "fourteen failings," and Sanskrit scriptures refer to predawn as *Brahma Mahoorta* (time of pure consciousness) or *Amrit Bela* (time of the nectar of life).

In similar fashion, Moslems chant morning prayers at day's commencement and pious Jews, rising to pray in a meditation-like state, are instructed to wait until there is "sunlight in the sky" to begin actual prayer. Sunrise prayer and meditations are also used as special spiritual exercises in Christian, Buddhist, and other monasteries.

Down through history the meditative mood, manifested in rituals, prayers, or forms of meditation, has been prescribed to coincide with the rising and the setting sun. Countless observers in diverse areas of the world have found sunrise a time when they are moved to a sense of profound wonder and meaning. To a lesser degree sunset has been considered an hour for contemplation, meditation, prayer, or solemn ritual. The rise and decline of the sun, it seems, deeply affects our life and our moods.

Does this mean that meditation is most beneficial if it is co-ordinated with the natural cycles of light and darkness?

The belief that it should be probably cannot be separated from the total view of life subscribed to by people who consider *all* activities in relationship to the natural cycles of earth, sun, moon, and universe. This point of view is particularly true of Yogic philosophy, where man, who is seen as part of the cosmos, is said to reflect the whole of which he is a part, and thus to contain within him the pulsations and rhythms of the entire universe.

From this follows the concept that ill health and emotional distress result from disharmony between man and the natural forces about him. When man is out of tune with the cosmos, he is thought to be like a fine instrument unco-ordinated with other instruments in an orchestra. The notes he strikes are discordant, and the world appears to him as harsh and threatening, because he is now paced differently from it, having broken contact with his roots.

In the Yogic system, as in many other spiritual disciplines, meditation is viewed as a means of re-establishing the unity between man and nature. It is thought to bring the individual pulsations of the human being into synchrony with the larger pulsations of the cosmos. For this reason Yogic tradition prescribes meditation at those times of day when the meditator can best synchronize his or her daily life with these wider cycles.

It may be that there is wisdom in such a concept, but unfortunately it has not as yet been tested in the laboratory. Folk beliefs, even if they are repeated the world over, are not prone to attract research interest or funding and may never obtain scientific verification for reasons that have little to do with their potential value. Hopefully this attitude will change with respect to the meditative traditions, so that controlled experimentation can contribute to our understanding of whether pervasive cosmic influences such as the solar and lunar cycles affect meditation readiness.

Instructions to Meditate Morning and Afternoon

These ancient belief systems are the source of the instructions given in certain Westernized forms of meditation such as TM, to meditate each day "in the morning before breakfast and in the late afternoon before dinner." Such instructions obviously differ somewhat from the original traditions since they have been tailored to fit Western life but their derivation from ancient belief is obvious.

In the process of transposition to fit the needs of industrialized society, however, they may have lost some of their original meaning. It may be persuasively argued, for example, that we should pay attention to the natural cycles of light and dark because the actual moment of sunrise may have deep physical, emotional, and spiritual significance for man. It is somewhat less convincing, however, to say that just before one takes coffee and orange juice, or just before one commutes to work, is necessarily the time when a person will be in greater communion with cosmic rhythms. Similarly, since "late afternoon before supper" is not usually the time of the actual setting of the sun in temperate climates, does it make sense to look upon it as reflecting any "correct" time to meditate? If we are not going to observe the ancient traditions in their original form, is there any point in observing them at all? There is, unfortunately, no direct experimental evidence relating to these matters and we must rely at present on the reports of meditating persons.

In my contacts with large numbers of people practicing the

simpler Westernized forms of meditation, I have not yet seen harm arising if a meditator has had to vary their daily meditation schedule so that it deviated from a strict "before breakfast, before dinner" ritual. For thousands of Westerners who use practical forms of meditation, to have the first meditation of the day late in the morning, or even at lunch hour, may be completely satisfactory.

In the same manner, meditating late in the evening or just before retiring for the night can be extremely useful for those people who find this to be their only available uninterrupted time in the day. Such variations in routine may, in fact, make the difference between a person being able to fit in two meditations a day or not being able to do so. In light of this, feeling comfortable with such variations is extremely important.

Perhaps we can clarify this matter by making a distinction between those times of day when meditation is *best*, that is, when meditating brings maximum benefit, and those times when it is perhaps not *best*, but when it is nevertheless still possible to do quite successfully.

Adrenal Hormones and Morning Meditation

There is some evidence that suggests that there may be inherent wisdom in a "before breakfast" meditation, if we are seeking an *ideal* time for our first meditation of the day. Human adrenal hormone secretion has been shown regularly to reach its peak in the hours between 4 and 8 A.M. Secretion of these hormones is related to stress, with adrenal hormones released in the bloodstream in high concentrations at times when the organism is facing intense stress, apparently in order to help the body cope. While it has not been demonstrated in man that *emotional* susceptibility is directly related to concentration of adrenal hormones, researchers have reason to suspect this may be the case.

At the Hartford Institute of Living, Dr. Charles Stroebel and his co-workers observed monkeys to find out what time of day the monkeys showed the strongest fear responses and physical vulnerability.[14] They wanted to know whether the peak hour for fear would coincide with the peak levels of adrenal hormones in the bloodstream. They found that the monkeys responded with the most distress to danger signals in the environment in the *early morning hours*, just before and just after awakening from sleep—the exact same hours, in fact, when their adrenal hormone levels were at their peak. At this time, too, they were the most vulnerable to physical distress.

Exploring this question further, this same group of researchers studied the manner in which rats responded to frightening stimuli at different times of day. Rats differ from monkeys in that they sleep during the day and are active at night. Like the monkeys, however, the rats reacted with most fear when their adrenal hormones were at their peak, which for them was just before and after awakening from their long resting period. At other times of the day, when these rats were showing their lowest concentrations of adrenal hormones, they actually took twice as long to react fearfully to the experimenters' warning signal.

If this cyclic emotional instability and physical vulnerability exists in human beings too, linking up with our peak hours of adrenal hormone concentration, then the hours between 4 and 8 A.M. should logically be the most vulnerable ones of the day for us. While we have as yet no direct evidence that human beings are actually more emotionally unstable at this point than during the rest of the day, we do have some indirect evidence—the fact that the greatest concentration of Rapid Eye Movement (REM) sleep of the night and therefore the highest concentration of dreaming takes place during these same early morning hours.

REM Sleep as Stress State

As we have seen, REM sleep is a highly activated type of sleep and some researchers have viewed it as a time of stress. During REM the slow brain waves seen on the EEG in the quiescent sleep stage are replaced by a rapid, irregular, desynchronized pattern remarkably similar to that of the most alert wakefulness. Physiological changes indicating a highly excited state are also seen at this time. Heart rate, respiration, and systolic blood pressure all show marked irregularity during REM with no discernible pattern appearing to govern their erratic fluctuations. In human males, penile erection is a regular accompaniment of the REM state. Paradoxically, muscle tone in head and neck virtually disappears during this state with the head and neck becoming limp, but the sleeper may make sudden thrashing movements or twist or turn quickly from side to side. It is during REM that the ulcer patient is most apt to have his nighttime ulcer attack, cardiac patients tend to experience heart attacks, and when a number of other illnesses affected directly or indirectly by stress seem to be aggravated. The REM state is generally a time of heightened physical vulnerability.

It is therefore interesting to find that REM sleep and hormone levels may be closely interconnected. Studying the levels of blood hydrocortisone (an adrenal hormone) throughout the night, Dr. Elliott Weitzman of Albert Einstein Medical College noticed that this hormone did not seep steadily into the bloodstream of his human subjects during the night, as might be expected.[15] Instead, it seemed to increase in "puffs," which were usually timed very closely with REM sleep. This suggested to Weitzman that REM periods and the secretion of adrenal hormones are related. Perhaps the increasing turmoil of the early morning sleep state does indeed reflect a generally unstable condition in man at this time.

From the standpoint of meditation, these studies suggest that meditating in the early morning hours might help a person to start his or her day in a more harmonious manner. Meditation presumably is a peaceful and stabilizing influence which could be useful in counteracting this period of particular vulnerability.

While all this suggests that there *may* be an objective reason for having one's first meditation of the day before eight in the morning, the findings could also be interpreted in another manner.

We might reason, for example, that since it is at the end of their daily resting period when human beings and lower animals alike show their lowest resistance to any kinds of stress, then *whatever* time we wake up (even if we are relatively *late* sleepers) we may well need a period of quiet stabilizing before we are fully ready to face the additional strains of daily living. There may therefore be considerable wisdom in the suggestion to meditate first thing in the morning, even if our waking hour happens to be later than 8 A.M. Certainly it seems appropriate to make one's morning rituals as gentle and supportive as possible.

Varying the Morning Hour

In many cases, however, we have to allow practicality to determine our choice of hour for meditation. While this may seem rather obvious advice, I have known a number of people who have discontinued the practice of meditation simply because they could not find a comfortable way to fit a before breakfast morning meditation into their schedule (or a late afternoon one) and erroneously believed that if they were not able to schedule meditations into their lives *in this manner and no other*, then meditation could not work for them.

The reports of large numbers of meditators indicate, however, that practical forms of meditation appear to be highly effective for most people on almost any reasonable schedule. A number of meditators who have said they cannot fit in their first meditation of the day until their luncheon break, have reported benefits from this practice equal to those of almost any pre-breakfast meditator I know.

For the sake of expediency, I have even advised some housewives with young children to schedule their first meditation of the day in the midafternoon, when the baby is taking its nap. This is often the first hour of the day when these women are genuinely free from chores long enough to meditate. Of course the later the hour one does the first meditation, the later the hour the second meditation will have to be for the proper spacing if one is going to observe a spacing rule—i.e., that meditations should ordinarily be spaced no closer than four hours apart.

This rule, emphasized by IMS, seems to be sensible advice since it allows for a healthy alternation of meditation with one's active life. Again, however, the usefulness of putting a fairly sizable amount of time between meditations has not been experimentally tested and it is even conceivable that this assumption may be incorrect.

The Late Afternoon and Bedtime Meditation

There seem to be certain practical advantages in having one's second meditation late in the afternoon *if* that can be conveniently arranged. Late afternoon meditation appears to serve an important function by breaking the day in half. Many people report that meditating at this time is an excellent way of "washing away" the accumulated tensions of the day, giving the meditator a "second wind" for the evening hours, clearly an advantage for many. Deciding whether to meditate in the late afternoon, however, inevitably raises the important question of whether or not it is possible to meditate late in the evening.

There are respectable precedents for late evening meditation. Many religions have prescribed prayer and meditation in the evening hours and the "darkest hour of the night" (midway between sunset and sunrise) is advised by Hindu scriptures as the time to meditate when faced with an insoluble problem.[16] If, say the ancient texts, one meditates upon a candle flame (the practice of tratak) at the darkest hour for forty consecutive nights, then the answer to the problem will be found. The belief that meditation is suitable for night hours is widespread and influences many present-day teachers of meditation. Richard Hittelman, for example, writes that sunrise, sunset, and *before retiring* are excellent times for practicing meditation.[17]

Curiously, IMS feels differently about this, standing firmly by their belief that meditation at night, if it is not actually harmful, is certainly unwise. They teach that it will so charge the meditator with energy that she or he may be unable to sleep afterward. This is a reasonable assumption, of course, *if* one is the type of person who does become suffused with energy following meditation and cannot sleep after it.

Our research shows, however, that most of the people who have tried meditating just before retiring at night find it very useful and *not* stimulating. We recently distributed a questionnaire on meditation habits which was returned by 86 CSM meditators and 34 TM meditators—a total of 120 respondents. It included a question on whether the meditator had ever tried meditating late at night and, if so, whether he or she had been able to go to sleep afterward. Two thirds of the CSM meditators said they had tried meditating late at night (this is permitted in the CSM teaching) and of those who had tried it, 90 per cent reported that they were able to sleep easily afterward while 10 per cent said that meditation had made them so energetic they could not sleep. By contrast, only two of the thirty-four TM meditators had tried meditating late at night. Both had found it possible to sleep easily afterward but had never repeated the experiment.

From a practical point of view, it seems wise for each person to discover for him or herself, by trial and error, just where they stand in this matter. If you find that you are one of the minority of people who react with renewed energy after a late-evening meditation, then you should obviously not meditate late at night, unless you are studying for an exam or need to be alert and energetic during the night hours for other reasons. It is not wise to experiment with late evening meditation before your three-week adjustment period is up, however, since one's reactions after first learning to meditate are often not typical. It is also useful to check on your ability to meditate late at night once or twice a year. Some people who are "energizers" for the first few months or even for the first year after learning to meditate find that after they have been practicing meditation for a while they are able to meditate late at night very comfortably.

It is also a good idea not to meditate *lying down* in bed because of the need to keep meditation separate from one's ordinary sleep-producing cues. Some meditators in our survey, however, reported that they successfully meditate just before going to sleep at night by sitting propped up in bed against a pillow; and a few apparently do meditate actually lying down, either morning or evening, and find it helpful. Again, this is a matter of determining the individual's responses.

One other objection is sometimes raised by TM teachers about presleep meditation. They feel that using it will eventually make the meditator come to depend upon meditation to bring on sleep, obviously an undesirable occurrence. You might, so the argument goes, eventually train yourself so well to link up meditation and sleep that if, by chance, you do *not* meditate on a particular night, you could not get to sleep at all.

While this sounds reasonable from a theoretical point of view, I have not known anyone to report having had such an experience. None of those people who meditate just prior to sleep have indicated that they are unable to go to sleep on occasions when they may have forgotten or been unable to meditate at bedtime. Clearly this is a subject for further experimentation, preferably in a sleep laboratory.

Where We Stand on Timing

Perhaps this question of the correct hour for meditation can be summed up by saying that no matter what the needs of one's schedule, personality characteristics will in all probability place certain limitations on what each particular meditator can do successfully. Since, however, it is possible to fit meditation time into even an unusual daily schedule and still derive benefit from it, I suggest to meditators that they try to find out how much changing around of their hour of meditation they personally can tolerate. There will be times when even the most conventional meditator may miss a late afternoon meditation. Those people who know they can meditate successfully at bedtime can easily make up the missed afternoon session at night, still achieving their two meditations of the day.

The cardinal principle, with respect to timing, seems to be that to be effective, meditation should be comfortable, fit into our lifestyle and be feasible. While conceivably we may be able to attain the maximum benefit from it by scheduling it at certain hours of the day rather than others (though this has not as yet been proven), it is better to meditate comfortably and well at another time of day than to give up meditation entirely because you cannot fit it into certain time slots. Meditation at other times of the day may not accomplish certain things, but it may do *other* jobs for us extremely well.

The "Mystery" of the Mantra*

Do different mantras have different effects on personality? Are people ever assigned the "wrong" mantra by mistake? Why do TM teachers select a secret mantra for their trainees? What happens if someone reveals his or her mantra to another person?

These are some of the most frequently asked questions about meditation, testimony to the fact that Westerners are obtaining much of their current knowledge of meditation from publicity dealing with TM. As we look at the mantra with an eye to clarifying its meaning and its uses, some light may be shed on the TM claims too.

As we have seen, mantra meditation is by no means the *only* effective form of meditation. As Robert Ornstein puts it, "Almost any process or object seems useable and has probably been used. The specific object used for meditation is much less important than the maintaining of the object as the single focus of awareness during a long period of time. . . ."[1] Nevertheless, mantra

---

* The word "mantram" is sometimes mistakenly believed by Westerners to be the singular, and "mantra," the plural of this word. "Mantram" is actually the neuter form in Sanskrit, is considered quite rare, and today is used primarily in southern India. When using Sanskrit nouns in English, the convention is to take the *stem* form from the Sanskrit (rather than one of the singular forms) to use as the English singular, and simply to add an *s* to form the plural. The Sanskrit stem form is "mántra." Its English plural is therefore "mántras," although in common English usage we have dropped the acute accent. Essentially, this is all one needs to know to use the word correctly in English.

meditation, as opposed to other forms, is particularly popular at the present time; even Benson's method makes use of the mantra "one." We shall therefore look first at its basic premise—that sound can affect the emotions, the thinking, and even the physical well-being of human beings.

Impact of Sound

Obviously certain sounds have different effects from other ones. We respond differently to a Mozart sonata than to a rock concert. Some proper names seem soft and pleasing to us; others seem harsh and unpleasant. While our responses may be partly due to past experiences (our personal associations to different sounds) there are good reasons to suppose that we also have innate responses to certain sounds.

Most people react with comfort and relaxation to the sound of a bubbling brook, or to gentle rainfall on a wooden roof; and they tend to respond with discomfort and tension to the sound of a trip-hammer (even at a distance where its loudness is not a factor), or the sound of chalk scraped against a blackboard. Even subhuman organisms respond differently to different sounds. The use of certain types of music to stimulate the growth of plants, for example, is no longer viewed as merely a pleasant folk tale. Many colleges of agriculture are now teaching their students to use music to foster the growth of healthy crops based on the results of experiments in this area.[2]

Actually the concept that specific mantras have specific effects does not presuppose any mysterious process. Since various sounds elicit different responses, it is logical to suppose that repeating one particular kind of sound to ourselves might have a somewhat different effect on us than repeating another one.

I have mentioned the modern Westernized technique of meditation developed by Dr. Herbert Benson, the Harvard cardiologist. Consider Benson's choice of the sound which he asks his trainees to repeat during their meditation: the word "one." While he chose this word because it was "euphonious" and did not have "sharp" sounds (he considered the next number up the scale with such a pleasing quality to be "nine"), the word is interestingly close to the Sanskrit mantra "Om," which is traditionally considered to have powerful effects. Most of the other leading Sanskrit mantras also end in a resonant nasal sound—in "n," "m," or "ng" —sounds that tend to reverberate within the head even when we are merely *thinking* them.

Recent research suggests that we may be producing movements in the small muscles of the middle ear when we "think" in sound. When Dr. Howard Roffwarg and his associates at Montefiore Hospital in New York City studied the middle ear muscles of sleeping subjects, they found that activity in these muscles tended to occur during dream sequences involving sounds, and not to occur when there had been no imagined experience of sound in a subject's dream.[3] If muscles within our auditory apparatus can respond to an imagined sound in a dream just as they do to "real" sound, then the emotional impact of imagined sounds may be quite similar to that of real ones.

If you wish to conduct an experiment of your own to find out the effects of using different sounds as "mantras," it is instructive to try Benson's method of meditation using two words. To do this, sit comfortably in a quiet room, close your eyes, and begin mentally repeating the sound "one" to yourself on every out-breath. The sequence goes like this: breathe in—breathe out— "one" . . . breathe in—breathe out—"one" . . . Keep repeating this sequence in your mind for about two minutes and then substitute mental repetition of the word "two" on each out-breath.

You will probably find a difference in your responses to the two sounds, how great a one depending upon your sensitivity to specific sounds and your own preferences. If you intend to perform this experiment, it is probably a good idea to do it before reading further, however. The following discussion might influence your observations.

In an informal test of these two sounds, many people reported that thinking "two" involves a slight, almost imperceptible twist of the tongue which has been trained to reach toward the front of the hard palate for the "t" sound. Thinking "two" also made some people's stomach muscles tense slightly and it was often described as being somewhat sharp and abrupt in sound as opposed to being gradual, lingering, and resonant (the qualities most often attributed to "one"). The sound "two" was more often felt as being light, superficial, and at times even somewhat annoying, while many people felt the sound "one" to be calm and steadying, giving them a sense of being "pulled together" or centered. Those who found "two" an abrupt sound, sometimes found themselves becoming *restless* rather than quieted by their meditation.

Despite this, in trying this experiment some of you probably discovered that you respond with greater calm to the word "two." What calms one person may excite another, and the other way around—another reason why meditational devices should be selected with the aim of suiting them to the individual.

You may also have noticed *associations* to these two words affecting your reactions. Mental associations to the word "one" are quite significant for English-speaking people. "One" implies unity and completeness. It is the word for "singular" and also the word for "all," the phrase "one world" meaning not so much a *single* world as a *unified* one. The word "one" seems in fact to imply both individuality and totality at once, a concept which may be seen by some as having metaphysical implications. Repeating the word "one" can affect the meditator, then, not only because of its sound but because it evokes the thought of being "pulled together" into one unified being. "Two," on the other hand, has no such connotations for most people. In fact its associations in the English language are rather meager, although for any particular individual it may hold very meaningful *personal* associations.

Our mental associations to a word can even have an effect on our reaction to it if the sound is in an unfamiliar language such as Sanskrit. Certain TM mantras, for example (depending upon how they are pronounced), sound like two short English words put together, and some meditators (myself included) will often visualize these English words when they repeat their mantra mentally. Such responses are of course likely to fade after a while— many meditators indicate that their mantras recede in their minds into a vague, pulsating beat rather than being identifiable as a *word* when they are having a particularly deep and restful meditation. On our recent meditation questionnaire, 45 per cent of the CSM and TM meditators reported that they "hear" the mantra as a *word* only "occasionally or never."

The Effects of Specific Sounds

This kind of consideration leads to the possibility of some interesting experiments. We could, for example, make some predictions on the basis of what we have so far informally observed about the response to different sounds using Benson's method. One such prediction might run as follows: "For *most* people repeating the sound 'one' is more soothing than repeating the sound 'two.' " Then, in scientific fashion we could proceed to test this assumption, an elaboration and formalization of the experiment you have just performed for yourself.

At Princeton, researcher Douglas Moltz and I set out to investigate the effects of word sounds on mood in a more formal way.[4] We began with the simplest component of words—single syllables without specific identifiable meanings in English—sounds such as "wys," "grik," "rahm," "noi," and others. From a large pool of such nonsense syllables, a group of colleagues selected five sounds which seemed to them to be extremely "soothing"; another five which seemed extremely "jarring"; and five more which seemed neutral in their effects. Their choices were used to make a list of fifteen nonsense syllables.

Next we presented this list to each of 100 subjects. These people were asked to repeat mentally each one of the fifteen sounds to themselves and rate it on a seven-point graded scale which ran from "extremely soothing" to "extremely jarring." When they had done this we found a very high agreement among subjects' ratings. Two sounds were rated extremely high on the "soothing" end of the scale by the overwhelming majority of subjects; only three out of 100 raters reported any negative reactions to them at all. In the same way, two other sounds were rated as "jarring" so often that only two subjects had any positive feelings about them. One other sound was rated "neutral" the majority of the time.

We therefore had no difficulty in selecting the three sounds which had received the most extreme ratings. These were used for Part 2 of the experiment. At this stage of our investigation we asked thirty students who had never meditated before (and who had not taken part in the first part of the study) to repeat each sound silently for a period of five minutes, and at the end of each such period to fill out an adjective checklist describing their mood *while they were thinking that particular sound.* They had also filled out these checklists before the commencement of the experiment. We were testing the possibility that certain word-sounds have differential effects on mood and the contention of the meditative traditions that particular mantras have *particular* effects.

We had anticipated that possibly some of the sounds might be more soothing than others but were unprepared for the results, which showed that changes in mood varied in a much more selective fashion than that. For example, only one sound (LŌM) caused anger and hostility to decrease significantly in our subjects, while another sound (GRIK) caused an angry, irritable mood to *increase* significantly. Repeating the sound GRIK also *decreased* depression and dejection.† This last finding agrees with a well-known clinical observation, namely, that if a depressed person becomes angry at someone or something other than him or herself, then their depression often vanishes.‡ Other findings were that the sound LŌM decreased "sluggish" feelings, and the sound NOI lessened feelings of being "worn out" (both fatigue-related moods), while GRIK had no effect at all on fatigue or inertia. In the same way, NOI and GRIK lessened feelings of depression and dejection, while LŌM had no effect on depression. NOI was the only one of the three sounds that decreased tension and anxiety, but all of the sounds were equally effective in reducing a feeling of "vigor" and "activity" (perhaps *any* sound will quiet people down).

It seems then as though sounds may have very specialized

† The findings reported here for this experiment reached statistical significance. Other mood variables which were not affected to a significant degree by repeating these sounds, are not reported.
‡ Psychoanalytic theory explains this by saying that one of the causes of depression is anger turned inward against the self. If this anger is redirected *outward* again (where it can now be coped with) then the depression lifts.

effects on people who repeat them, even when they are not pronounced out loud but only "thought." If the results of this experiment are borne out by future studies, it is possible that someday we may be able to predict accurately the effects of sounds on moods—something potentially useful for therapeutic purposes. Conceivably different mantras might be used selectively for lightening depressions; soothing an irritated patient; counteracting fatigue; lowering anxiety; releasing creativity; increasing energy; or any number of other purposes. Specific assignment of mantras to obtain special effects to suit individual needs has been practiced for thousands of years by masters working with the ancient meditative traditions, with claims of remarkable success. Perhaps we are on the verge of being able to apply this ancient art of the guru in a scientific manner, on the basis of laboratory experimentation.

If future studies also show that simple nonsense syllables have specific effects on mood, then researchers may want to go a step further and design experiments to find out whether some of the traditional Sanskrit mantras, whose long-term effects can be predicted by teachers, are more effective for certain purposes than other, more "prosaic" everyday sounds. This may well be the case, because these ancient mantras were selected and refined through a trial-and-error process lasting for thousands of years.

If we were to find that Sanskrit and other ancient mantras are indeed more effective than ordinary words for certain purposes, we can visualize researchers working to identify the particular consonants and vowels and the combinations of these, or the particular pitch and length of beat, which gives the mantra the effect it has. Only through experiments such as these will we be in a position to make fully effective use of mantra meditation on a scientific basis. In the interim, we will still have to resort to what is largely a trial-and-error process in assigning mantras to individuals, and must be alert to the reaction of each person to the particular mantra assigned to them—or which they have chosen, as the case may be.

Even clinical evidence, however, suggests that the choice of a specific mantra for therapeutic or self-development purposes should not be viewed as meaningless.* I was recently consulted by a TM meditator who had been unable to establish a satisfactory adjustment to her meditation, despite the fact that she had returned repeatedly for "checking" from her TM teacher. Eventually she had abandoned TM because she found it "almost unbearable" to sit for twenty minutes repeating a mantra which, she stated, she had found "extremely unpleasant" from the first. Because her antipathy to her mantra was so great, it seemed possible that this might have been one of the reasons she had had so much difficulty. The obvious first move was for her to select a new mantra. I therefore presented her with a list of sixteen CSM mantras and suggested she select one of these or make up one of her own.

She responded with enthusiasm, readily chose a new mantra from the list, and commenced using it. As soon as she did this she was able to resume meditation regularly and to her surprise her meditation was now experienced as extremely relaxing, helpful, and enjoyable. While she said her former TM mantra had always appeared as an unpleasant image "hanging somewhere over in the left of my visual field," her self-selected mantra had an entirely different and very calming effect on her.

I have known of three other instances where TM meditators who had reacted adversely to the mantras assigned to them by IMS, felt comfortable for the first time in meditation when they themselves selected other mantras. These instances do not, of course, prove that the original TM mantras were necessarily "wrong" for them. It could be the *freedom to choose* which was the crucial factor here. No longer feeling locked in to a situation which for one reason or another they resented, these people may now have felt free for the first time to enjoy meditation. On the other hand, as our preliminary research on the effects of specific nonsense sounds suggests, it may be that some mantras, including some specially assigned TM mantras, strike some people as genuinely unpleasant and therefore make them tense rather than relaxed. Since such problems as these could be researched in the

* Selection of specific mantras for *spiritual* growth, of central importance to the meditative traditions, obviously rests on different considerations and is not the subject of this book.

laboratory, almost unquestionably we will soon be learning more —probably much more—about the mantra and its use in meditation. Until then, our own intuition about what is "good" for us may be the best guide we have.

The choice of the mantra certainly need not be a mysterious or secret process. On the basis of our study on the effects of sound on mood, and my own experience teaching meditation, it would seem that there are very specific objective criteria which can be applied in selecting a mantra, and I would strongly doubt that there is any such thing as the "right" mantra for any one person. Our work suggests that there are more likely to be a number of different mantras which can be beneficial for each person and that the one which is finally chosen may need to be determined by the specific changes that the person seeks to bring about in him or herself. There are also likely to be a number of mantras which might be more neutral in their effects on the same individual, and still others which might be irritating, possibly even tension-producing for them.

The TM Mantras

What then should we think of the TM claim that by a special secret process their teachers are able to assign a mantra which perfectly suits each trainee?

First let us consider the manner in which the TM mantras are assigned. According to TM teachers who have been willing to discuss the subject† openly, there are 16 TM mantras which are regularly used. These mantras are assigned to TM trainees on the basis of age. Age eighteen to nineteen, for example, usually receives the mantra "Ieng," age twenty to twenty-one the mantra "Ien," and so forth. This fact is often confirmed by students who typically exchange their mantras with each other, despite instruc-

† Part of sworn testimony by TM teachers in the pending New Jersey trial of the *Coalition for Religious Integrity* vs. *The World Plan Organization*, seeking to forbid the teaching of TM/SCI in the New Jersey school system on the allegation that such teaching is in violation of the American constitutional separation of church and state.

tions to the contrary. At one time, a group of Princeton students reported to me that they all seemed to have been assigned the same, or nearly the same, TM mantra, which they pronounced variously as "Iam," "Ima," or "Ieng." These students apparently fell within the same TM age group with respect to mantra assignment.

Several of the TM mantras are what are technically known to Yoga practitioners as *bija* mantras. Bija means "seed." The idea is that there are certain basic thought forms that are eternal (they exist before any language). They are described as living, *conscious* sound powers, equivalent to deities.[5] The sound "Om" is considered to be the universal sound from which all other mantras spring. It is the very essence of sound, and from it emerge the powerful bija mantras that themselves are the seeds of other mantras. The bija mantras are believed to be very powerful sounds that vibrate the various *chakras* (energy centers) of the body if intoned correctly, but otherwise to be no more effective than any other slogan repeated to catch the attention. According to Shyam Bhatnagar, a *pranava* (sound) therapist and lecturer in Swar Yoga‡; "A mantra can lose effectiveness when we are not sensitive to its more subtle sounds and therefore cannot accurately reproduce them. When intoned under *proper* conditions, a mantra can awaken the dormant energy of an individual, his unique wave pattern, his bija. Recognizing this unique pattern in a disciple, the guru must draw on his own direct realization of the mantra in order to intone the exact frequency which will ignite the intrinsic power coiled up in that mantra and in that individual."[6]

Proper use of mantra, according to Yogic tradition, rests on a number of conditions which cannot readily be met in Western life. Each mantra is traditionally analyzed by the guru who dispenses it according to the sounds used in producing it and the parts of the body the particular sounds are designed to vibrate. The sound frequencies at which the mantra is transmitted will then determine whether higher or lower stages of a particular en-

‡ Swar Yoga is an ancient system of centering which, through breath control, is believed to maintain equilibrium between the right and left hemispheres of the brain.

ergy center (or chakra) will be affected. Yoga tradition stresses the fact that this process depends for its effectiveness on the *tonality* of the teacher's voice when imparting the mantra, as well as the pupil's ability to reproduce that tone (either aloud or in his mind). The "instantaneous effect" which a mantra correctly pronounced is thought to produce depends on the master's skill. An exact and even inspired intoning of the mantra is apparently required to get "life" into the sound.

Whatever "secret" there is in the mantra therefore seems to lie in how it is chanted (actually it is almost sung). The word alone is considered to be barren, much like a musical notation which remains mechanical and empty until enlivened by the interpretation of a musician. Just as the notes of the scale played by a beginner on the violin differ from those same notes played by Isaac Stern, so the effect of the mantra differs according to whether it is conveyed by a well-meaning neophyte or by a person who, with many years of practice, has mastered the particular sound to be produced.

Such a skill is said to be rare even in India. While there are many students of the *Mantra Shastras* (Hindu scriptures describing the mantras) who understand their use, very few of them are thought to know how to *intone* these mantras properly. Even an expert will learn to pronounce only ten to twenty of them in a lifetime. Since there is no notation system which conveys their pronunciation, the "notation" remains in each guru's head, passed down over the generations by word of mouth.

A close relationship between master and pupil forms the basis for the assignment of a mantra by a guru to suit his particular student at a particular stage in the student's spiritual development. The mantra may later be changed a number of times to correspond to the student's advancing inner growth. Since a mantra is assigned only after careful examination of the disciple and an exhaustive study of his condition, it is difficult to see how such a process could be duplicated by relying on such general information as a person's age to determine the choice of a mantra. As any psychologist knows, deep character traits are not revealed by asking such questions as age, occupation, and state of health, almost the entire extent of the questionnaire which prospective TM meditators are asked to fill out. Furthermore, the TM method of assigning mantras does not seem to take into account any of the effects of sound on mood such as are suggested by the recent Princeton study. People in the same age group may be depressed, hostile, tense, easily fatigable, or present any number of other special characteristics which differentiate them one from another. Should a depressed individual receive the same mantra as a hostile one just because they are in the same age group? Our study suggests that perhaps they should not.

The Mantra in India

The Sanskrit word mantra means "thought form." By implication mantra is the very language given by the sage Manu, the lawgiver in the ancient Indian tradition.[7] Mantras represent the nature of deities and in the traditional sense cannot be separated from them. Thus the power of the deity resides in its name. The name or the formula of the deity (mantra) becomes a means through which a connection is established between the worshiper and the deity. It is the power of the mantra which brings down the deity and makes it enter the image.[8]

Mantras are not, however, a rare commodity. According to some Indian sources, there exist millions of Sanskrit mantras and 700,000 mantras alone are said to be contained in the great *Shastra* (encyclopedia) of authenticated knowledge* known as *Mantra Maharanava* (literally, "ocean of mantras"). Mantras are listed as well in other texts to which the gurus turn when selecting an appropriate one for their disciples. The pamphlets containing these lists are described as being so vast, in fact, that when piled up they reach from floor to ceiling and even the "small" version of the encyclopedia (called *Mantra Mahodidi*) contains several thousand Sanskrit mantras.

A mantra may be one syllable, as in the case of the mantra

---

* Mantras whose specific effects are known are said to have been "authenticated" by practitioners over a period of several thousand years.

"Om," or it may consist of many verses from the Vedic scriptures; sometimes with as many as sixty or more syllables. In Tantric tradition it may be a hundred and ten syllables of prose or poetry.[9]

Mantras are dispensed by holy men in India to eager recipients for every possible purpose. There are mantras to be used for illness or physical discomfort. There are special mantras for business contingencies or for bringing wealth and blessings. There are mantras to facilitate the learning of mathematics and others to increase the ability to "read" minds. There are mantras for social uses, and mantras for love, courtship, and marriage. There are even mantras for use in sorcery, together with talismans, secret rituals, and other paraphernalia for casting spells.

The essential use of mantra, however, predates all of these uses. It is the source from which the more mundane uses of mantra have sprung. "Mantra," in its pure sense, is "primordial sound," associated with the Ultimate Reality (*Brahman*) itself. "The world was created by the utterance of the proper sounds, and it is maintained by the repetition of the proper sound. . . ."[10] Therefore, by uttering mantras like "AUM" one "creates the universe." A point worth noting about Indian mantras is that a mantra *chanted out loud* is generally considered to be more powerful in its effects than one which is simply repeated mentally.† The exception to this rule is said to occur in the case of a few people with extremely high concentration resulting from years of arduous training in meditation. These people are supposed to be able to achieve extraordinary effects by silently repeating their mantras, effects even "higher" than those obtained by chanting them out loud. Such an achievement is considered extremely rare, however, and certainly not attainable by someone learning a simple Westernized centering technique for the first time. From the traditional Indian point of view, we might question the overriting importance which IMS attributes to its special mantras, which are *never* chanted out loud after the first few minutes of the TM initiation ceremony.

† The writing of the mantra over and over again in its original Sanskrit characters is also considered a highly effective technique for centering in the Yoga tradition.

The Admonition of Secrecy

TM meditators are told to keep their mantra absolutely secret. What happens if they do not follow this advice?

As usual in this area, the answer to this question has not been experimentally determined, but we do have some practical information which may shed light on it. A number of people, against their TM teachers' advice to the contrary, voluntarily share their TM mantras with others. Despite their disclosures, those who have reported that they have shared knowledge of their mantras in this fashion have seen no loss in the effectiveness of these mantras. They still meditated with the same kind of beneficial results as before. In none of these instances, however, did any of these people go around *chatting* about their mantra or using the word in everyday conversation or treating it lightly. I think this fact is important.

There are some very sound psychological reasons for reserving the mantra as a special sound to be used only for meditation as much as this is conveniently possible to do. The mantra is used to bring about a deep sense of inner peace and in this way becomes what psychologists refer to as a "conditioned stimulus" for relaxation. That is, it becomes a personal signal which automatically brings about a certain kind of deeply relaxed state because it has been associated with that relaxed state in the past. This is a very effective method for insuring that future meditations will be productive.

There are ways, however, that one can "extinguish" a conditioned response—render it ineffective. One way is to repeat the response frequently under different sorts of conditions than the ones you desire to bring about. If, for example, your mantra was "Om" and you went about saying to your family, "Please pass me the *Om*-vegetables"; "May I have some *Om*-pie?"; and "Let's go to an *Om*-movie!", all throughout the day (particularly if you used the word in a casual and superficial tone, not intended to deepen your awareness of the mantra), then you might find that "Om" was beginning to lose its special significance for you—it would no longer be an effective "signal" to turn inward.

Another reason for not telling one's mantra to a casual acquaintance or talking about it under conditions which are not genuinely serious or respectful is its highly personal nature. If we have a special mantra that has been assigned to *us* alone (or which *we* have selected) it eventually becomes a part of ourselves. It may even symbolize our own identity. For some people, to refrain from sharing this special word with others can therefore be an extremely important step toward independence. Such people may have always felt compelled to "share" everything they think or do with others. Their mantra now becomes one part of themselves that they can clearly call their own.

Ancient Views on Revealing the Mantra

As for the traditional Indian stand on the secrecy of the mantra, this depends on the use to which the particular mantra is put. Many mantras are freely divulged in India—but these do not include the bija mantras, which are used specifically to "unlock the potential of the different chakras." Bija mantras are dispensed according to a precise diagnostic procedure by means of which the guru is said to determine where the blocks in the chakric centers lie and which particular mantra can best be used to open them. Some gurus advise their pupil not to reveal the particular bija mantra they are presently working with because if they were to do so their enemies might learn of their weak points and so be able to take advantage of them. Obviously such a consideration cannot be considered necessary in the West, where almost no one knows about chakras. It is therefore hard to imagine that this might be the logical basis for TM secrecy.

There is, however, a special type of master-pupil relationship which is cemented in India by the giving of a "devotional" or "guru" mantra. This guru mantra insures the discipleship. It is considered to bind master and pupil together forever, being almost in the nature of a spiritual "marriage contract." A guru mantra must be kept secret at all times, it is never to be known by anyone save the master and pupil. Just as a married person would not lend his or her wedding ring to a friend, so the guru mantra is traditionally kept secret. If it is revealed, then master and pupil are "divorced," their spiritual bond broken. It would seem that if TM is following any Indian tradition in its admonition of secrecy, it is the concept of the "devotional" or "guru" mantra.

One other occasion demands that a mantra be kept secret, but it too is scarcely applicable to Western life. Certain specific mantras are sometimes given in India with the express purpose of conferring "powers" upon the recipient (such as the ability to read others' minds, etc.). If the recipient reveals such a mantra to another person, then part of this new power is said to be shared with the other person. For selfish reasons, therefore, people receiving such "power" mantras will usually not reveal them. It would seem that TM mantras are not intended to confer powers of this sort and so this reasoning cannot explain the TM call to secrecy.

We are left, therefore, with the educated guess that the TM mantras are probably considered by TM's founder, "Maharishi" Mahesh Yogi, to be guru mantras and that their secrecy may be considered a sign of a devotional bond between teacher and student, forged during the TM initiation ceremony. Whether such secret practices—however firmly rooted they may be in traditional practices—are relevant for Westerners learning meditation, is an open question.

As for my own position on the secrecy of the mantra, when I teach CSM I advise trainees not to tell their mantra to others often, if at all. It is best, I suggest, not to use it as an everyday word, and, if possible, not even to say it out loud to oneself. In short, it should be kept as a "special" word for "turning inward" —not for any mysterious reasons, but because this is sound psychology.

Music and Chanting

Many forms of meditation make use of sound to create the meditative mood, the sound of the mantra is but one of them.

The human voice chanting and the sound of bells, instruments, or special types of music, are also frequently used to invoke the meditative mood. Sound seems to have a profound effect on both mind and body and its use for altering states of consciousness is well known. Music therapy is frequently used in the West to change mood, and in the East music has been used to effect profound changes in the way one experiences one's self and surroundings. The more far-reaching changes, however, do not rely on melody. As Ornstein points out, in the Middle and Far East melody plays a much less central role in music than it does in the West.[11] Instead, it is the tonal qualities of the music that are emphasized in these traditions. Long-drawn-out vibrating sounds may be produced to stimulate that part of the brain which responds to music in its most unstructured form as *sound*, with less emphasis on the sequence or patterning of notes.

Shyam Bhatnagar, an Indian sound therapist, has developed a unique means of using an ancient stringed instrument, the tamboura, together with mantra chanting, which he interweaves with the vibrations of this instrument for pranava (sound therapy). The unusual sounds produced in this manner are used to affect consciousness. The tamboura produces long, sustained tones, overtones, and sympathetic resonances, and its ever changing patterns of rhythm and harmony create powerful waves of sound which are believed to stimulate the various chakric (energy) centers in the body. Whatever the precise method by which they act upon it, there can be little doubt in the mind of a listener that this sound often alters consciousness, producing a profoundly meditative mood. The vibrations of voice with instrument can bring about a deep sense of relaxation and many people feel refreshed and energized afterward. One meditator described the sound as "a sense of choirs and organ music resonating through vast spaces . . . when hearing it an almost ancient mood flows through you."

According to Bhatnagar, the use of music *during* one's own personal repetition of the mantra should be discouraged, however, because attention to the two different sources of sound—inner and outer—can conflict with one another. Despite the fact that this practice is traditionally frowned upon, 12 per cent of the meditators who answered our meditation questionnaire said that they occasionally use music in this manner and find it useful, although none of those questioned used music *regularly* with meditation.

Most people do not find it satisfactory to use music along with the repetition of the mantra. When I listen to recordings of Bhatnagar's tamboura vibrations, I cannot repeat my mantra at the same time—the effects of the music are too strong. The use of music with meditation appears to have its main value as a means of preparing for meditation.

We are left, therefore, with a group of facts. Some of them are contradictory, some in agreement—all are in need of more systematic research. Since sound seems to have a distinct impact on human beings, the choice of a specific mantra may be more important than previously recognized in the West, but exactly in what way, we are only beginning to discover, and the bulk of such effects are still unknown. This means that a suitable selection method for matching a specific mantra to a particular trainee has not yet been developed on a scientific basis. In its absence, our own inner wisdom as to which sounds "feel" right for us to repeat mentally, seems our best guide when undertaking any method of meditation.

A Few Nagging Questions

There are a number of instructions on how to practice meditation which many people take for granted simply because they were given by their meditation teachers. Some of these are questionable. What do we really know, for example, about such things as postures for meditation, about suiting a particular meditation technique to a certain person, or about the meaning (and perhaps the value?) of temporary vacations from meditation?

Correct Postures for Meditating

It is often said that the lotus position is the ideal one for meditation even though it is certainly not easy for many Westerners. However, while it is the prescribed posture for persons studying *advanced* forms of meditation (often with the aim of furthering spiritual development), unless someone has been carefully trained in Yoga or Zen, it is usually more satisfactory for most to meditate sitting in a chair.

Even in a chair, however, the question of posture in meditation remains important. An uncomfortable sitting position can distract a meditator so that it cancels out the benefits of meditation. Some chair-sitting meditators complain, for example, that their head involuntarily drops forward when they go into a deeper meditation state, which in turn pulls on the neck muscles and can increase an already existing back or neck problem. This can quite effectively spoil a meditation. For such a person one solution may be to sit in a chair with a high enough back so that their head can rest comfortably against it when meditating, or if they like to sit on the floor, leaning back against the wall may be a good solution. TM teachers, however, feel that one should not support the head because this may encourage sleep; teachers of zazen feel that one should not lean against walls or backs of chairs[1]; and writers on Yoga meditation advise their followers not to lean back against the furniture while meditating because it is "important to your health."[2] People who have tried supporting their neck because they felt they *needed* it, however, have not reported that this made their meditation any less effective or that they felt in any way more sleepy. Once again, this seems to be an individual matter as far as practical meditation is concerned.

As for meditating lying down, this position is associated with sleep and for many of us dropping off to sleep is an automatic response to lying down quietly with eyes closed. Nevertheless, the classic Yoga posture, *salvasana*, which clearly evokes a meditative mood, is performed lying on the back, as are many of the autogenic training exercises. Baba Ram Dass, for example, advises his students to lie down for certain meditations if reclining does not lead to sleep.[3] It is therefore certainly possible to consider lying down when meditating if this becomes necessary. This is important to realize, because an occasional person finds that meditating while lying down, or partially lying down with head and back just slightly propped up, is for him or her the *only* feasible position. The people who feel they *must* meditate this way seem the least apt to fall asleep during meditation when lying down. Perhaps such a person is intuitively aware of certain physiological or psychological needs which make lying flat his or her best position.

As indicated, this advice refers only to the practical forms of meditation. Spiritual meditation always requires a certain prescribed posture, usually the lotus position or some variation of it, and the very process of mastering it becomes a form of meditation for the devotee. Since so many of the great meditative traditions insist on the importance of the proper grounding of the person in the pyramidal shape before "true" meditation can be said to take place, it is possible that certain deep states can only be obtained this way.

The practical meditator, however, should decide for her or himself what goals are appropriate for meditative practice and select the form and level of the discipline that best suit these aims. An average tennis player has no need for a four-hour workout every day if they simply want to play on weekends with friends. A tennis pro, on the other hand, may have to practice more than this, and this practice will be highly specific and designed to overcome special problems. Meditation postures follow the same rules —they must be more rigorous and exacting the higher one sets one's sights in terms of personal and/or spiritual development. In the *practical* forms of meditation there are many options with regard to the best position. Ultimately each meditator must decide for him or herself which is most suitable.

Vacations from Meditation

In our previously referred to meditation questionnaire, one of the questions asked was whether the meditator had ever taken a "vacation" from meditation. If so, for how long and were they later able to resume meditating regularly?

More than half of the meditators who answered reported having temporarily stopped meditating at some point—the longer they had been meditating the more apt the meditator was to have taken time off. Sometimes these "vacations" were only a day, a few days, or a week in length; sometimes several months or longer. In a few cases they involved stopping meditation for a year or more. The people involved had all spontaneously resumed meditation afterward, and most of them said they were able to be fairly regular in their practice of meditation after the vacation. Occasionally, though, they reported having had difficulty resuming the practice because they felt "guilty" for having stopped.

Just why people feel they need these breaks from meditation is an interesting question. There may be a number of different reasons why they occur and why at times they may even be helpful.

Certain people are aware of why they temporarily stop meditating. A patient of mine who stopped for three months was in the process of dissolving a marriage which had ended two years before, but which only now she had the strength to terminate legally. During this period of her life she stopped meditating, although she considered the practice extremely valuable to her and one of the contributing factors in her decision to make a new life for herself. She reported that meditation had increased her sense of independence and her wish to be entirely on her own. Since it was not yet feasible to put these positive plans into *action*, the meditation sessions during this interim period left her with a painful sense of frustration. To avoid this frustration, she simply abandoned meditation temporarily. She said that the knowledge that meditation was still "there," however, should she really need it, gave her security.

Other people stop meditating temporarily because another activity is substituting for the meditation. Some vacationers, for example, find that meditating in natural surroundings is an exalting experience, but others find the opposite. For the latter, the breathing of fragrant mountain air, the sound of a brook whispering through a pine forest, the smell of the sea, or other experiences which naturally bring about the meditative mood, are so compelling that they find themselves no longer using formal meditations while on their holiday, but will usually resume regular meditation on their return to "civilization."

Similarly, at certain points during their artistic work, some people will find so much excitement in the act of creation that they may temporarily forget to meditate or may feel that meditation slows down their intense creative drive. Such people may stop meditating during the height of their productivity. A number of creative people, however, report the opposite, as we shall see when we consider meditation's contributions to the creative process. For these people, meditation seems to enhance their work, freeing and strengthening their creative drive. Clearly this is an individual matter, sometimes not even predictable for the same person from one project to the next.

An occasional meditator may also stop temporarily because he or she finds that when under heavy stress, meditation *increases* their anxiety, rather than calming them down. As one student puts it:

> At times I have stopped meditating when I've been particularly stressed—when I'm under too much stress TM is very annoying —it intensifies the stress so I cannot meditate.

Stopping is usually the only solution for these people at this point. Reducing meditation time under such circumstances seems to do little good. Closely related to this reaction is the one described by a CSM meditator who found that when she was under severe emotional stress due to the impending death of a parent, her meditations lost their value for her. She now could not fit meditation comfortably into her pressured schedule and was finding herself becoming irritated and tense during meditation instead of calmer. In order to avoid what is known as "counterconditioning," whereby meditation might become a "signal" for tensing up, she stopped meditating entirely during this period. After her parent's death and following a period of mourning, this woman was able to resume meditating with the same beneficial results she had originally obtained.

Many of the same reasons that lead people to stop meditating *entirely* cause others to take vacations from it. Various blocks to meditating, foremost among which is guilt at allowing oneself to have pleasure, can result in frequent intermittent breaks from meditation. When this happens it is usually the reflection of an internal struggle; a wish to meditate and enjoy the benefits of this practice is counterbalanced by an equally strong need to escape from meditation and the anxiety or guilt it entails. The solution is "on-again, off-again" meditation. The person meditates until too much guilt accumulates, takes a vacation from it until the guilt subsides, and then starts again with a temporary feeling of well-being—until guilt builds up once more.

Other people may stop not because of any deep-seated problems, but rather to establish a sense of independence in relation to the practice. They have a need to prove to themselves that they are not rigidly controlled by the routine of meditation but that they can freely elect to practice it. A student expresses this clearly:

> Sometimes TM becomes too much of a routine—too confining—too restrictive—so on occasion I have stopped for a few days.

For the fairly sizable number of people who occasionally stop meditation in order to establish their sense of independence from the practice, these breaks often are effective and do establish the meditator's autonomy. Under such circumstances, the vacation can be considered to have been a healthy move. Essentially we should never meditate because we have to, but because we want to. If we have to stop meditating temporarily to make this point clear to ourselves, then that is a wise decision.

Some people may have to take more radical steps to restore power to their technique however. Shifting temporarily or even permanently to a different type of meditation may be for them the only answer to this problem. Even if we use a different meditational technique only occasionally as a change of pace, it may "recharge" our original technique, lending it "new life." Many people have a strong emotional attachment to the meditational device they were originally taught to use. This is understandable, for the device can become in time an intimate reflection of our deeper self. We therefore usually gravitate naturally back to it when it is sufficiently enlivened so that its effectiveness has been restored. The process is like that of recharging a battery which has run down. There is no need to throw away the battery, but sometimes a special process is required to make it work again.

Another constructive reason for vacations from meditation is a phenomenon which is recognized by educators. If someone studies a subject such as a foreign language for a number of months, and then stops studying it or even thinking about it, it is not unusual to find on a test taken several months later, that the person has an even better grasp of the subject than he or she did directly after the period of intense conscious effort. The implications of this are that some form of learning has been going on during the "rest" period. By stopping the active process of forcing ourselves to learn, we sometimes allow learning to consolidate, to become a natural part of us; something which would not happen if we were to keep our "nose to the grindstone" all the time. Do people continue to develop from meditation even during those intervals when they may not be actively practicing it?

This does not seem to be the case with the physical results obtained. When hypertensive subjects who have reduced their blood pressure through meditation stop meditating, their blood pressure gradually starts to rise again, showing that the effects of meditation are wearing off. This process can only be reversed by resuming meditation.

On a psychological level, however, it is not at all certain that the effects wear off in this manner. Some evidence suggests that the meditative attitude may continue as an important part of one's life, even if one takes a vacation from meditation. Meditators who are not currently meditating will report that they nevertheless find themselves spontaneously entering meditative moods during the day when formerly they might have been tense and overdirected in their attitudes. Meditation can change the way a person lives their life in a rather fundamental respect, a change which is not likely to be easily reversed.

A final reason for vacations from meditation is the fact that any routine, no matter how beneficial, can be wearing after a while. We sometimes need a vacation from the best things or the most important people in our lives. Time spent away from them can result in our being all the more enthusiastic about them when we return. Perhaps this is so with meditation. Most people come back to meditation after their "time off" apparently no worse for the experience and sometimes with a newfound sense of freedom about their meditation.

Certainly, given the frequency of vacations from meditation in the general population of meditators, no one needs to feel guilty for taking some time off or feel that because she or he has done so, they are a "failure" at meditation. Guilt about such a vacation can make for serious difficulties, even if the vacation itself does not, because the guilt makes the meditator define him or herself as a failure. This in turn is likely to make them hostile to the entire endeavor of meditation. It is those people who cannot forgive themselves for taking a vacation from the practice who are most likely to stop meditating permanently following their vacation.

Suiting the Technique to the Person

While the permissive forms of practical meditation "work" for a surprising number of people, some people are unable to adapt to them. Permissive meditations such as TM or CSM may be too "free" for these people. If so, practicing them may increase their anxiety level, rather than reduce it. Not everyone wants or needs maximum flexibility in a meditative technique. On a questionnaire given out at Princeton University on meditation practices, college students gave interesting opinions when asked to evaluate various meditation and relaxation techniques:

> Zazen meditation was very interesting. I think it provided a necessary alternative to TM. Sometimes TM is too free and open—a more rigorous meditation is necessary.

> My meditation technique (CSM) may not have been as effective for me since I am an ordered, logical individual who may have needed a more structured method.

> I think progressive relaxation suits my character better [than CSM]. I'm a fairly nervous person and progressive relaxation does more to relax me on a physical level.

Clearly the wrong meditation technique can make difficulty. One patient of mine was unable even to talk about learning TM without becoming anxious. Many of her friends were practicing TM successfully and although she "wanted" to learn it, she had an obsessive fear of losing control during meditation. Since she was unable to contemplate going to the TM center, I decided to try teaching her an abbreviated version of CSM. Despite my attempts to teach her in a quiet, nonforcing manner, however, she was unable to meditate without becoming *more* anxious than she was before trying and was particularly worried about meditating "incorrectly."

We did not try meditation again until a year had passed and she had shown considerable progress in her adjustment to many aspects of life. Since she still kept saying that she longed to be able to "meditate," I decided to teach her Benson's method—the meditator using Benson's method or any of the other breath meditations can always tell whether they are doing it "correctly."

Teaching her this method turned out to be quite effective. She preferred Benson's to a more open-ended approach, although she could not practice even this form of meditation for longer than three minutes and ended up using it only for "mini-meditations" when she felt tense.

While the art of suiting the meditative technique to a particular person in his or her present stage of development is as yet unexplored, it may well be one of the most important areas for future investigation.

Atmosphere of Instruction

To be taught to meditate by a person who takes the experience seriously is essential. The meditation teacher gives the trainee "permission" to contact his or her own self deeply; the act of instructing a person in meditation is therefore in a sense to sanction an inner rebirth. For this reason, the actual moment of learning meditation is frequently deeply meaningful. It is a milestone in the person's life and even the appropriateness of some form of simple ceremony is often intuitively recognized.

The spirit of meditation can certainly not be conveyed by describing the outer trappings of the practice. Meditation is not the devices used to foster it, it is a way of being. Unfortunately, however, some people are taught how to "meditate" in an offhand manner by roommates, friends, or family members. "All you have to do is just sit down and keep saying this word over and over to yourself in your mind," they may be told, or other similar easy phrases. While sometimes the instructions they get in this manner are even technically correct, they do not teach the person how to meditate. Glibness in teaching meditation fails to convey the spirit of the practice. The meditation experience may therefore be shallow, boring, or even make the new meditator feel ridiculous. If it does, this person may never meditate again.

Because it relies upon the evocation of a particular mood, over the ages meditation has been transferred from person to person with an attitude of quiet respect; a *feeling* as well as a technique has been transmitted. This process can be looked at as a long procession of people stretching back through time into antiquity. We might imagine each of these people holding a small lighted candle with which, in turn, this person can reach out to ignite the candle of a new learner. The process continues over the centuries until, at a particular moment, someone leans forward and ignites the candle flame within you—and you, too, become a meditator—an endless procession of humanity sharing with humanity down through time.

To teach meditation without recognition of this profoundly human element is, I suspect, to leave out a vital part of the practice. Even if meditation is taught in a book or by recording, this should be done with respect and concern for the new meditator and a sense of genuinely sharing an experience with him or her. Every attempt should be made to convey the spirit as well as the technical aspects of the practice. Meditation imparted mechanically, casually, jokingly, as a parlor game, or in a too impersonally conducted experiment, is cold by contrast.* It is something like the presumed test-tube baby of the future. All contingencies may have been taken care of in a practical sense but this baby will never have been bathed in the waters of the womb or have known the comfort of any other heartbeat than its own.

* I have mentioned the strategic teaching of a meditation exercise to a class before an exam. Such simple centering exercises as these do not constitute the "teaching" of meditation unless the instructor specifically indicates he or she expects those learning it to be able to adopt it as a regular practice. If so, the instructor should teach it quite differently with careful follow-up instructions about meditation routine, possible side effects, ways of adjusting the meditative process to suit the trainee, and so forth. The instructor also should prepare the trainees more carefully for their first meditation and offer them a fuller, more emotionally satisfying initial experience.

Meditation is therefore a delicate process. Managed correctly it may lead toward self-realization. Handled carelessly or without proper flexibility it may be ineffective, perhaps even detrimental to those who learn it. The way in which practical meditation, when properly managed, *does* contribute to personal growth is the next area we will discuss.

III

Meditation
And Personal Growth

A New Partnership

In the 1950s and 1960s, middle-class Americans became aware that while they were relatively well situated with regard to material benefits, something of fundamental importance seemed to be lacking in the way they led their lives. This something has been variously defined as love, creativity, meaning, personal growth, self-fulfillment, or spiritual values. Whatever the term used, it is clear that such values would formerly have been considered quite beside the point for psychotherapy. The psychotherapist was someone whose job it was to "cure" a patient of an illness. Now, however, there are an increasing number of mental health practitioners who view their role quite differently, taking what has been called a "humanistic" approach to psychotherapy.

This newer approach lays emphasis upon self-fulfillment. It sees people as longing to realize their full human potential and as ultimately striving to do so if given the least opportunity. It emphasizes the importance of individuality. Each person, by virtue of his or her own particular background and experience, is treated as unique and important. It accords a central role to *values*; people are not seen as biological machines but as thinking, feeling, judging human beings capable of directing their own destinies. It is essential that each person gain a clear sense of self-identity, discover who they are and who they want to become, so that their potential may be fully developed.

The humanistic approach is positive in nature. Despite the violence, cruelty, and horror that humankind has perpetrated throughout history—the undeniable capacity of man for evil *as well as* good—he is not seen as necessarily evil. While he may sometimes operate almost totally in terms of his negative potentials, he still retains the possibility for realizing his positive capacities as well.

Such a viewpoint has an impact upon the way psychotherapy is approached. The humanistic psychotherapist focuses on helping the patient to perceive him or herself as they really are, to accept their weaknesses and strengths, to be fully themselves. If they learn to do this, they will then drop their defenses and be open to experience; they will "live" in the true sense of the word. The result is a new attention to the creative and healthy side of human nature—a contrast to psychotherapy's former emphasis on personality disturbance and repair.

This approach is not only appropriate for treating disturbed individuals, but deals with the failure of "normal" people to realize their potentialities as well. It addresses itself to the great mass of human beings who feel alienated and at odds with their own nature. It seeks to help people be themselves, more fully and joyfully —to live their lives with meaning.

In this aim meditation and humanistic psychotherapy cross paths. Meditation, working on its own level, helps the self grow naturally without impediment, to flower in its own way and at its own pace. It can be therapeutic in that it often serves to counteract specific psychological or physical problems, yet it fosters a more pervasive change than the mere absence of symptoms. Recognizing this, some psychotherapists are finding meditation a powerful ally in their work with people and a new and exciting partnership is being born.

The Hartford Experience

I first became interested in the possibilities of using meditation with psychotherapeutic patients in 1972. At this time, the Wallace-Benson studies were beginning to appear in the scientific journals. Perhaps, I thought, this technique could be of help to people with incapacitating anxiety. It looked promising, and a working relationship between meditation and the mental health professions seemed a possibility.

Others in the psychiatric field were also sharing my curiosity. The venerable Hartford Institute of Living, one of the oldest and most prestigious psychiatric hospitals in the country, decided at that time to launch a three-year research study on the effects of TM on hospitalized psychiatric patients.

Originally, Dr. Bernard Glueck, Director of Research, and Dr. Charles Stroebel, Chief of the Institute's Psychophysiology Lab, had set out to compare three groups of patients to find out which of several types of relaxation training would be most useful in advancing the progress of psychotherapy: TM, alpha biofeedback, or progressive relaxation. All three techniques looked promising because they had the advantage that once learned, they could be self-administered, something particularly useful for psychiatric patients, who are often prone to expect hospital authorities to provide them with a "cure." The investigators felt that if these patients were able to do something for themselves to improve their own state of mind, this in itself might prove therapeutic.

While the original plan was to compare three groups, as so often happens in scientific research, the plan did not work out. Soon after the studies started, subjects began dropping out of the biofeedback and progressive relaxation groups in large numbers and the statistical value of the study was being negated. The alpha biofeedback subjects reported having difficulty in making practical use of their alpha state or even in understanding its purpose. Patients who had learned progressive relaxation almost unanimously reported that they found this process both tedious and dull. In contrast to both these groups, almost all of the patients who had learned to meditate continued to do so regularly. They generally enjoyed the practice and recommended it to their friends in the hospital. In fact a long waiting list developed to learn meditation.

The loss of these two comparison groups posed a problem for the researchers. To whom could they compare their meditation subjects? The solution they decided on was to match up each meditator with a "twin control" chosen from the hospital population at large. The twin control was another patient of the same sex, roughly the same age, and with a similar personality profile as the meditator. Both groups of subjects were to be evaluated on a number of levels.

The evaluation procedures were extensive. One was a periodic readministration of the Minnesota Multiphasic Personality Inventory (MMPI), a personal self-report form which the patients filled out to indicate the degree and type of emotional disturbance they were experiencing. In addition, each patient in the study kept a daily record of the quality of their sleep, moods, and eating habits. There were also objective measurements of change: brain wave recordings and other physiological measurements, nurses' daily computerized reports, psychotherapists' progress reports, and hospital records.

Studying the first group of meditating patients to be discharged from the hospital, the researchers looked at the records showing their psychiatric condition at the time of discharge. The condition of the meditators had improved significantly more than had that of all the other hospital patients discharged that year. They had also improved more than the group of "twin controls."[1]

While these are the only statistical findings released as yet, the research team has informally noted other changes. The meditating patients often required lighter dosages of tranquilizing drugs and other forms of psychotropic medication after commencing meditation. A number of patients who had difficulty sleeping reported that their sleep had improved. In many instances, their sleeping medications could be reduced or entirely eliminated several weeks after they commenced to meditate.

A preliminary look at the MMPI results showed encouraging changes in the way patients reported their own condition after they had been meditating for a while. The average scores of the meditating patients on the MMPI seemed to show a steadily improving psychiatric condition. These self-reports were also supported by the nursing notes that suggested that with the practice of meditation, anxiety, depression, and unacceptable behavior on the wards tended to decrease.

Despite this encouraging report from Hartford, I needed more specific information before feeling ready to recommend meditation to my patients. I wanted to know which kinds of psychiatric disturbances are likely to respond to meditation; what, if any, are the undesirable side effects of this practice; if there is any type of patient for whom meditation may prove dangerous. To find out the answers to these questions, I traveled to Hartford to consult with the research team at the Institute, and while there I had an opportunity to observe the effects of meditation on hospitalized patients.

Meditation was being used in the Hartford experiment with all types of psychiatric patients. The researchers had even taught a number of schizophrenic patients to meditate successfully, with beneficial results. Dr. Glueck talked about one schizophrenic woman who was so ill and whose thinking was so confused that they initially doubted she could learn to repeat the mantra or understand the purpose of meditation. With careful attention from specially trained teachers, however, this woman had been able to learn the technique and was now showing excellent improvement. I also had an opportunity to talk with a teen-age paranoid schizophrenic boy who was having his brain waves monitored as a routine part of the study. He was definitely pleased with his meditation and told me that he was feeling "less paranoid" since he had commenced meditating.

The researchers showed me the brain wave recordings of psychotically depressed patients who had learned to meditate. They had even taught meditation to two patients who had suffered serious brain injury as a result of accidents. While meditation obviously could not cure the physical damage these patients had sustained, it was helping them adjust to their altered brain functioning. They were now less anxious, more co-operative, and easier to get along with than they had formerly been.

I discovered that the Institute's program for teaching meditation was quite different from that typically used outside of the hospital. Two TM teachers, who were full-time members of the hospital staff, were on the premises at all times, spending as much time as necessary with each new patient learning the technique.

The teachers checked the patients' meditation practice *every day* for the first three weeks, meeting with them individually. They also met with them as a group once a week. After the first three weeks, the patients were usually left on their own to meditate (except for the required group meetings), but at any time of day or night, if a meditating patient had a question about meditation or any anxiety in connection with it, a TM teacher was available on short notice.

Obviously this is the best arrangement for a psychiatric program using meditation, but it raises certain questions. Is it possible that some of the improvements found in these patients were due to the fact that they had someone (their TM teacher) who was deeply interested in them during their stay at the hospital, someone willing to guide them and give them extra attention? In other words, could the special attention by the TM teachers have created a placebo effect?

The researchers doubt this, pointing to the fact that the improvements these people showed were sustained well beyond the time when most placebo effects fade. Two years after the commencement of the study, a questionnaire was sent out by the staff to all patients who had originally learned meditation. Of those who responded (about 70 per cent of those contacted), 68 per cent reported that they were still meditating and obtaining good results from the practice. All of the people in the follow-up study had been discharged from the hospital and were now living at home. Encouragement by the hospital TM teachers was therefore not a factor at this point.

To my many questions about possible undesirable side effects of meditation, the researchers replied that they had found no unfavorable effects of meditation on the patients in their study, possibly because of these special instruction methods and precautionary procedures. A few patients who had dropped out near the beginning of the study had indicated that as a result of having learned to meditate, some of their thinking was "clearing up" so rapidly that they feared they might lose all their familiar defenses if they continued. They were apparently not prepared emotionally for such rapid change, a problem which, as we shall see, others have noticed in their patients as well.

The research team was also acquainted with occasional difficulties which arose from the use of TM in the community outside the hospital. In all those cases which they had investigated, the trouble seemed to have been caused by the fact that the person involved had been using meditation incorrectly. Excessive *over*-meditation seemed to be the major cause of damaging side effects.

In general, the Hartford researchers felt that it appeared that most seriously ill psychiatric inpatients *could* learn to meditate successfully, provided adequate attention was given to the various problems that may arise during the first several weeks of meditating.

The final results of the three-year Hartford study are not presently available. Although the data is complete, most of it has not been analyzed. The study will, however, not be continued at this particular hospital, at least not using TM. Dr. John Donnelley, psychiatrist-in-chief of the Hartford Institute of Living, has recently stated that since TM depends on teaching its users a secret mantra, it "violates the ethics of medicine and cannot be tested scientifically."[2] His comment echoes some of the objections which are familiar to us, namely that research on TM is seriously hampered by IMS's refusal to reveal certain pertinent information to researchers. The termination of the TM studies at Hartford is indicative of a trend which may accelerate in the next few years— a trend away from the limited TM studies of the past toward a broader scientific approach.

Reducing Anxiety

Anxiety is not only a driving force behind most severe psychiatric conditions, but one of the chief stumbling blocks to their effective treatment. The highly anxious person is frequently afraid to talk about the very things which are most important for him or her to face. Unmitigated anxiety leading to panic is so painful an emotion that it is usually avoided at all costs, even if the costs be the undermining of the patient's psychiatric treatment. Any auxiliary therapy that can lessen anxiety is therefore of help, the reason why tranquilizers are so widely prescribed.

In observing patients who are meditating, my psychotherapist colleagues and I have noticed that anxiety becomes less in a majority of them as they continue in their practice of meditation. They worry less about their jobs, their families, and a host of anticipated dangers which formerly paralyzed their initiative. They seem "protected" or "cushioned" from these strains.

As their anxiety lessens, these people also tend to be more relaxed and proficient at handling many tasks. This increased "coping ability" is different from that which we usually see in patients taking tranquilizers or anti-depressants. Drugs may restore a patient to feeling more "normal"—"I feel like my old self since I've been taking my tranquilizer"—but the drug is not likely to foster personal growth or help the person experience life in a new way. By contrast, after commencing meditation, people often find themselves reacting in ways they have not before. The practice of meditation tends to open up new horizons rather than restoring a former state of affairs. For this reason some psychiatrists familiar with meditation will recommend to a patient that he or she try learning meditation, before prescribing tranquilizers for them.[3]

Another advantage of meditation over drugs is the fact that the meditator does not ordinarily lose alertness or become groggy. People taking high dosages of tranquilizers, on the other hand, often complain that they feel dull or sleepy and their reaction times are typically slowed down. Because of this, people taking these kinds of drugs are regularly cautioned not to use machinery or engage in other activities where quick reflexes are required. By contrast, meditators are frequently more alert, nimble, and aware of their surroundings.

The very fact that meditation is something which the patient can do for him or herself also builds strength and confidence. The person who meditates when anxious and thereby regains a sense of calm, senses that they are in control of their own life and that no drug is doing the work "for them." One lesson of meditation, then, is that one can bring physical and mental processes under *one's own control*, a basic step in coping with anxiety.

Combating Addiction

Whether anxiety causes forms of addiction such as alcoholism or drug dependence is uncertain. These kinds of behavior are often strongly influenced by the stratum of society in which the person grows up, their early home situation, and perhaps certain inherited biological characteristics. If anxiety cannot be said to be the cause, however, it is certainly an effective trigger for severe bouts of addiction.

If meditation reduces anxiety, can it then help to control forms of addiction? This question is worth exploring when we consider the magnitude of addiction in our society and the inadequacy of most of our present treatment methods to deal with it. In 1971 researchers Benson and Wallace sought to find out if meditation might have some effect on drug usage. They studied 1,862 TM teachers-in-training who had been practicing meditation for at least three months and often for longer, in an effort to find out how much marijuana, amphetamines, barbiturates, or hallucinogens (such as LSD) these people were still taking after their considerable amounts of meditation.[4] On an anonymous questionnaire these teacher-trainees reported having all but eliminated drug abuse since commencing meditation, and even moderate use of such drugs was greatly reduced.

Whether this was due to meditation alone is hard to tell, however. TM teachers-in-training belong to a tight-knit community. They live together in resident training centers for many months, undergoing an intensive regime of meditation-plus-instruction. While there, they experience strong group pressure to abandon drugs in favor of meditation; "successful meditators" are thought of as being non-drug takers. However, even if the results Benson and Wallace found were due, in part at least, to a need to conform to group standards, this in itself tells us something important about how drug abuse might be controlled. It suggests that a meaningful social community can exert pressures which may effectively reduce drug intake.

In the six-month period before they started practicing meditation, about 80 per cent of these prospective teachers had used marijuana, and of these, about 28 per cent had been "heavy users" (i.e., were using the drug once a day or more). Six months *after* commencing meditation, only 37 per cent of the teacher-trainees were using marijuana and of these, only 6.5 per cent were still heavy users. Among those trainees who had been meditating for twenty-one months or more, only 12 per cent were still using marijuana and only one individual remained a heavy user. The decrease in the use of LSD was even more marked, and similar results were reported for other hallucinogens, narcotics, amphetamines, and barbiturates.

These seemingly anti-addictive effects of meditation also extended to other areas. In the Benson-Wallace study, the percentage of teacher-trainees who drank hard liquor (either occasionally or often) *before* commencing meditation was 60 per cent. This figure came down to 25 per cent for the group who had been practicing TM for twenty-one months or more.

Much the same kind of results were found for regular cigarette smokers—48 per cent of the teacher-trainees said they had smoked before starting meditation and 25 per cent described themselves as having been "heavy users" (that is, as having smoked one or more packs a day). After twenty-one months of meditating, these percentages had decreased to 16 per cent who were still smoking and only 5.7 per cent who were still "heavy users."

What does this study tell us? Did these results occur because people who were more or less ready to stop taking drugs *anyway* signed up to learn TM (this would leave hard-core drug users out of the picture)? Did the serious drug abusers among the meditators happen to drop out of meditation before the questionnaires were handed out, and so were not included in the study? Do drug abusers in general shy away from becoming TM teachers? Are the people who stay with the practice of meditation the type of people who would be more likely to become drug-free in the first place? In other words, does this study apply to a select group only or are its results typical of the general public?

There are as yet no answers to these questions, but some of my psychotherapist colleagues and myself have seen impressive decreases in the use of drugs in patients who do *not* become TM teachers, and whom we have observed both before and after they learned to meditate. It was, in fact, clinical observations of this sort that led Dr. Mohammad Shafii and his associates at the University of Michigan Medical Center to design a study which attempted to overcome some of the drawbacks of the Benson-Wallace one.

The Michigan group felt it essential to have a "control group," something which the Benson-Wallace study lacked. For this they chose people who used drugs but who were not meditators so that they could find out to what degree *non*meditating people naturally cut down on drug usage over time. Because the Shafii group used this additional experimental safeguard, and because they used regular meditators, not TM teachers, as subjects, the results of their investigation are more informative.

The Shafii study showed a striking reduction in the amount of marijuana the TM group was still using after they had been meditating from one to thirty-nine months.[5] The number of marijuana users was now reduced to nearly one third the original number, while the figures for the control group stayed approximately the same, dipping only slightly.*

As to regular cigarette smoking—a habit which when it is compulsively followed is classified as an addiction—71 per cent of those who had practiced meditation *more than two years* reported a significant decrease in their use of cigarettes, and 57 per cent had totally stopped smoking by that time, while cigarette usage for the control group remained almost the same.[6]

Drinking of alcohol was affected too. Within the first six months after commencing meditation, 40 per cent of the medita-

* As indicated when discussing personality differences between those who do and do not learn meditation in Chapter 4, the TM meditators-to-be in this study had originally been using twice as much marijuana as the control subjects.

tors who had been meditating regularly for more than two years had stopped drinking either beer or wine, while no control subjects had stopped. After three years of meditation the figures were even higher—60 per cent of the meditators had now stopped drinking beer and wine. In addition, 54 per cent of this last group (as against 1 per cent of the control group) had also stopped drinking hard liquor.[7]

These studies suggest that meditation can be effective in preventing certain forms of addiction providing that a person is sufficiently motivated to continue meditating for a long enough period of time. There seems to be a definite relationship between the amount of time a person has been meditating and the effectiveness of this practice in lessening drug consumption—the longer, the better.

Perhaps we have come to the point where we no longer need questionnaire studies that ask people what their drug usage was in the *past*. What we need now is to follow a group from scratch, studying them *before* they start meditating and then again one or two years later. Although such a study would be difficult and expensive to conduct, I suspect there will be attempts to do this in the near future. In the meantime, there are some interesting clinical observations which do extend over time.

I have observed three patients smoke less marijuana after commencing meditation, two patients reduce their use of alcohol, and another two stop smoking cigarettes with little, if any, nicotine withdrawal effects.† This represents a large proportion of my patient population who were heavy drug users since only very few of my patients used drugs heavily to begin with. My clinical observations therefore seem quite consistent with the reduction percentages in the Shafii study..

Interestingly, I have seen one patient *take up* smoking mari-

† I have not seen meditation have any effect on food addiction (overeating) in overweight patients, and little is known about its effects in this area. The single study done to date used TM *teachers* as subjects,[8] not a typical group since almost all of them are vegetarians and engage in much more intensive meditation than the general public. These teachers did normalize their weight while undergoing intensive teacher-training, but this may be due to factors other than the meditation.

juana for the first time after she resumed her regular practice of TM. She claimed that her freedom to use marijuana stemmed from the fact that meditation made her feel less guilty and she could now allow herself to experiment. Her behavior in this respect was part of a more general change. She had been a rigidly conventional woman, afraid of being spontaneous in any way. Now she was branching out into new activities in many areas of her life. She did not, however, develop an addiction to marijuana as a result of her easier attitude toward it. Her interest in it seemed to level off and eventually subsided, and at no point was her use of the drug extensive enough to be considered abnormal in our society.

A questionnaire survey on meditation and drug abuse conducted by Dr. Leon Otis has also indicated that a very small number of the meditators questioned (6 per cent) reported that they *increased* drug use after commencing meditation, although the majority (68 per cent of those who had been meditating for less than two years) reported a sharp *decrease* in the use of drugs.‡[9] It seems, however, that any increase in drug use with meditation, when and if it occurs, is sufficiently rare to be of minor significance compared to the pronounced trend toward decreased use of drugs with meditation.

Why Is Meditation Anti-Addictive?

Since meditation lowers anxiety, it may simultaneously lessen the need to take in an addictive substance to counteract anxiety. This is certainly a possible explanation for the effects of meditation on addiction. It may not be the only explanation for those anti-addictive changes we see with meditation, however.

Dr. Andrew Weil, a physician and drug expert whose report on the effects of marijuana usage is a milestone in this area of experi-

‡ Unfortunately Otis was not able to obtain information on how extensive these drug increases were when they occurred, which specific drugs were involved, whether the increases resulted in *use* or *abuse* of the drugs, or the role that the drug increase may have played in these people's overall emotional adjustment.

mentation, considers drug use an expression of a natural and universal drive to achieve altered states of consciousness—a drive which leads children in every culture to engage in such activities as whirling in circles until they fall to the ground, dizzy yet exhilarated by the new and different form of consciousness they have achieved.[10] According to Weil, the drive to reach such unusual states may be behind the universal use of such drugs as alcohol, tobacco, or caffeine, as well as common mind-altering drugs and even the more powerful opium and morphine derivatives. It does *not*, he feels, explain the *abuse* of such drugs, but only their *use*.

While drugs may satisfy the natural need for altered states of consciousness, Weil feels this need can also be met, perhaps even more satisfactorily, through the use of meditation, chanting, special exercises, and other drugless techniques. A natural "high" is not lost, as when a drug wears off. It is also under one's own control, with the person being aware of his or her own role in bringing about the desired state.

Weil comments that people who begin to move in a spiritual direction in connection with drug experimentation sooner or later look for other methods than drugs for maintaining their experiences:

> One sees many long term drug users give up drugs for meditation. . . . but one does not see any long time meditators give up meditation to become acid heads.* This observation supports the contention that the highs obtainable by means of meditation are better than the highs obtainable through drugs.†[11]

A recent report on meditating patients at the Manhattan Psychiatric Center's Alcoholic Rehabilitation Unit seems to support Weil's theory. CSM was taught to twenty-five alcoholic patients in this unit by trained staff members. The patients were chronic alcohol abusers, classified as being in the most "hopeless" 5 per cent of the alcoholic population with respect to the seriousness

---

* As we have seen, there may be some instances where drug usage has increased with meditation, but we have no indication that such people *gave up* meditation for drugs or that they became "acid heads" or otherwise seriously addicted.

† By "better" Weil does not mean morally preferable, but simply more effective.

of their addiction. These men lived as derelicts when not in the hospital and can be considered one of the least promising groups for any new habit formation such as regular meditation. Their lives are ordinarily haphazard and without any routines at all when they are not in the hospital.

At first these patients showed great resistance to learning meditation; they wanted no part of it. Then two of the patients on the ward rather cautiously agreed to try it. As soon as these two had started, the word spread through the unit that meditation was the "best experience these men had had since they had gone off alcohol." It was considered the only thing available in the hospital that could give them a somewhat similar feeling.

The staff members who taught CSM reported that the reaction of these alcoholic patients to their meditation had a special quality. Rather than simply having a quiet rest during meditation, these people had "trips." Many fantastic images and sensations occurred. Meditation was clearly being welcomed by these patients because it was recognized as a substitute activity. It was, in fact, the only therapy capable of calming them in the absence of alcohol.

As with many other in-hospital treatments, this gain did not continue when the patients were discharged into the community. As soon as these men returned to their previous environment, they typically stopped meditating, started drinking again, and eventually had to be hospitalized once more for alcoholism. When they were rehospitalized, however, many of these patients requested renewal instruction in meditation.

I feel that the interchangeability of different kinds of altered states of consciousness should be carefully studied. People who have been heavy users of hallucinogens before learning meditation will often report quite different experiences during their meditation than people who have never used drugs or who have not used them heavily. As one meditator explained:

> I get these really far out experiences during meditation—but then of course I'm familiar with that kind of experience from my drug trips. If I hadn't learned to handle them without anxiety when tripping, I would probably be very scared now and I imagine I would more or less suppress this kind of experience.

This does not mean that former heavy drug users make the "best" meditators or have the "best" meditative experiences—differences in the degree of positive response to meditation seem to be a purely individual matter—but it does highlight the interrelationship between different types of altered states of consciousness. Experience in one does seem to affect experience in others—different altered states do seem to interact. It has been shown, for example, that subjects who can concentrate well on a simple meditative task, are in general more easily hypnotized than subjects who are highly distractible during meditation. This interchange or linkage between different methods of altering consciousness should be studied further.

Combating Physical Illness

Traditionally, general medicine has been concerned with physical illness while the mental health professions have turned their attention to psychological disturbances. Today, however, it is increasingly obvious that separating these two areas of disturbance is not very meaningful. Any specific disturbance may be *mainly* physical or *mainly* psychological, but it is nevertheless always a response of the *whole* person. Being exhausted or having a bad cold may lower our ability to handle our psychological problems, and being emotionally disturbed may lower resistance to physical disease—human beings are total beings: not "mind," not "body," but both in one.

The approach to illness or disturbances that takes this factor into account is referred to as *psychosomatic*, from the Greek words *psyche* (mind) and *soma* (body). It has been estimated that at least one out of every two persons who seek medical aid suffers from an illness related to emotional stress, and this is probably a conservative estimate. It does not include the complications brought about by emotional upsets that occur during infectious diseases, or those conditions which seem to have a large emotional component but which have not yet been formally proven to be of psychological or emotional origin.

The most well-known psychosomatic illnesses are peptic ulcers, bronchial asthma, high blood pressure, and others in which the undermining effect of continuous emotional tension on body systems has been well documented. It is these illnesses that so far have been studied in relation to meditation, although as yet experimentation in this area is scarce.

We have mentioned Dr. Herbert Benson's work. His interest in this subject commenced when he reasoned that meditation might be effective in combating the "fight or flight" response, a response which releases emergency mechanisms in the body that speed the flow of blood to muscles, thereby preparing the animal either to fight an enemy or run from it.

We need hair-trigger "fight or flight" responses if we live in a jungle, if we are fighting a war, or if we face any other situation involving an immediate threat to survival. Emergency responses are not appropriate, however, for most everyday problems. The tensions that civilized people face often cannot be physically fought or taken flight from. Our "enemies" are all too often such things as holding onto a job, making a success of relationships, becoming financially secure, measuring up to competition, or other social or economic problems. These threats are not solved by summoning up a *physical* fight or flight response. On the contrary, their solution can be seriously hindered by physiological reactions such as a pounding heart, rapid breathing, or spiraling blood pressure.

The fight or flight response, incorrectly used over a period of time, can, in fact, be harmful. When the body repeatedly mobilizes itself for threats *from which there is no escape*, this eventually results in profound changes in the body's functioning which may be damaging to health. One such change results in the blood vessels becoming more constricted and remaining that way. The person with chronic high blood pressure (hypertension) seems to be forever geared for a fight or a flight that he or she *cannot make*. The emergency mechanisms of the body, which were useful under primitive conditions, have now become a disadvantage.

Because of these dangers, Benson reasoned that a technique which might relax the inappropriate fight-flight reaction and allow a natural counter-reaction (he called it the "Relaxation Response") might be an effective way of altering the unhealthy physiology of the hypertensive patient. While the Relaxation Response appears to be as much a part of our inherited equipment as is the fight-flight response, it is not so easily brought about in a high-pressure society that demands that its members move at a fast pace, regularly punch real or imagined time clocks, and constantly measure up to invisible demands.

Benson was impressed when the studies on meditation which he conducted with Wallace showed that a profound state of relaxation could be brought on simply by practicing TM. Later, as we have seen, he was able to demonstrate that the same state of deep physiological relaxation can be induced by using his own form of meditation. To date he has studied the effects of both TM and his own meditation method on more than 100 hypertensive patients.[12]

Some of these patients showed significant and sustained decreases in their blood pressure after about two months of practice; others showed only slight, if any, effects. On the average, the patients' systolic reading (the blood pressure during the contraction of the heart) dropped about ten points and their diastolic reading was down about five points—scarcely dramatic results but in the right direction. Many borderline hypertensive patients (whose blood pressure reading is just on the upper limit of what is considered the normal range) achieved normal blood pressure after they learned to meditate and a few patients were even able to reduce the dosage of anti-hypertension drugs they had been taking.

Benson has emphasized that regular practice was essential in order to maintain these good results. Those hypertensive patients who responded well to meditation were able to keep their blood pressure down only if they continued to meditate regularly. If for any reason they discontinued the practice, the pressure would gradually drift back up again. In these reports, meditation seems like a change in diet which eliminates symptoms *only as long as the diet is faithfully adhered to*. Meditation therefore is a preventive measure rather than a "treatment." It must become a permanent way of life if a person is to gain lasting benefits.

Bronchial asthma is also recognized as a tension-related disease and researchers Honsberger and Wilson reasoned that it too might respond to meditation.[13] When they studied a group of asthmatic patients in the University of California Department of Medicine, they discovered that after beginning the practice of meditation, 94 per cent of these patients showed improvement in their asthma symptoms as determined by measurements of their "airway resistance" (a test of free breath flow). The personal physicians of 52 per cent of them also rated their patients' conditions as "improved," and 74 per cent of the patients themselves reported their *own* condition to be "improved." Another group of asthmatic patients who simply read material about meditation for twenty minutes every day (but did *not* learn to meditate) showed no improvement. These were promising results.

Meditation is also frequently used to combat tension headaches. Meditation has proven effective in three cases I have treated where the patient needed help with this problem. I have also received reports from psychotherapist colleagues on nine additional patients who have learned meditation because they hoped to rid themselves of incapacitating tension headaches. In each of these cases, the headaches improved with meditation and in many instances were eliminated. Once again, continued, regular meditation seems crucial. If these patients stopped meditating, then their headaches returned.

Migraine headaches (very different physiologically from tension headaches) often do *not* respond well to meditation. According to Benson, among seventeen patients suffering from severe migraine headaches studied at Boston's Headache Foundation, only three were helped by the regular practice of TM and one subject was actually "made worse."[14]

Counteracting Insomnia

One of the most common symptoms of anxiety is trouble with sleeping. When we are anxious we are apt to find it difficult to get to sleep or experience sleep as genuinely restful when it comes. We may awaken tired, irritated, and tense rather than refreshed.

Since meditation often serves to reduce anxiety, does it help to overcome sleeping problems?

It does, although it is not clear what the exact effects are. Together with some of my psychotherapist colleagues, I have treated a number of meditating patients with sleep problems and have noticed that these patients more often than not report improvement in sleep habits after commencing meditation. Sometimes the improvement is dramatic. At the Institute of Living, the researchers found that their meditating psychiatric patients required far less sedation as their chronic insomnia was replaced by a normal, restful seven to eight hours of sleep. For a number of these meditating patients, in fact, sleeping medications could be eliminated.[15] This is a striking effect and coincides with our clinical observations. We so often see improvement in the sleep of patients who commence meditation that I now routinely recommend to any patient who has difficulty sleeping that he or she try meditation.

Improvement in sleep is also one of the benefits of meditation reported by a large number of people who learn the technique but are unaware of having sleep problems. Researchers Matthew Silverman and Ernest Hartmann recently sent out a questionnaire to practitioners of TM (these were not insomniacs or people with particular sleep disorders, but an average sampling of meditators). Many of these meditators reported they were sleeping better and needing less sleep after having practiced meditation for at least four months.[16]

When these same researchers studied eight meditators in the sleep laboratory over a four-month period they found that these people could now fall asleep faster than they could before meditating. Since the subjects in this study did not have any particular sleep disturbances to begin with, even before learning to meditate it took them on the average only thirteen and a half minutes to fall asleep—a time so short as to be the envy of all those who experience difficulty in falling asleep! After they had learned to meditate, however, even this modest waiting time was reduced. Now on the average they required only eight and a half minutes to fall asleep.

Only two systematic investigations have been done so far where meditation was used with people who actually suffered from insomnia. At the University of Alberta in Canada, researcher Donald Miskiman found that after commencing meditation, people with insomnia could fall asleep more quickly.[17] These particular subjects had had so much difficulty in falling asleep to begin with that the change was considerable. Before learning TM it had taken these insomnia sufferers on the average about an hour and a quarter to get to sleep at night. After learning to meditate, they fell asleep within fifteen minutes after lying down in bed.

Such results are not confined to TM. Other forms of meditation work equally well. At Rutgers University a research team headed by psychologist Robert Woolfolk compared three groups of severe insomniacs, people who, on the average, took about an hour and a quarter to fall alseep at night and who reported other serious difficulties in sleeping.[18] One group was taught Progressive Relaxation; another, a form of meditation which Woolfolk devised; and the third was not taught any technique.

The technique taught to the meditating subjects was basically the same as the breathing meditation described in Chapter 5. The only difference is that when they had mastered the meditation itself, Woolfolk's subjects were then requested to select some specific mental image to focus upon while repeating this exercise.

At the end of four weeks, when the subjects' daily sleep records were studied, the researchers found that *both* meditation and Progressive Relaxation had been effective. The subjects who had practiced these tasks were now able to fall asleep within about a half hour after going to bed and the whole process was much easier for them. To do-nothing control group's sleep habits had not changed. What was even more encouraging was the fact that a follow-up study done six months later showed that these gains were not only retained but, if anything, improved. Some subjects had by then even further reduced the time it took them to fall asleep.

Meditation, therefore, seems to be effective in dealing with some of the problems that are major concerns for the mental health professions: persistent anxiety, psychosomatic illness, sleep disturbances. But does it go further than this and affect *attitudes*, the traditional cornerstones of psychotherapy? We will discuss this question next.

More Open to Life

Many people conduct an inner dialogue in which they criticize themselves for not behaving "properly" or doing things "well." Psychoanalysts refer to this self-critical faculty of the mind as the *superego*, the side of ourselves that sets itself above the ego. A punishing superego is the same as an over-strict, cruel conscience, while a flexible superego consists of reasonable and healthy standards of behavior. An important change frequently brought about by meditation is the altering of the superego so that it becomes more flexible—the meditator will begin to be more patient and understanding with him or herself:

> During meditation, I do not clutch to *engage*. I do not make an effort to cope. I do not try either to succeed or to fail. . . . Although distant music and memories may uninvitedly flow into my ken, there is no effort to define what I see or hear. . . . In meditation I float rhythmically, effortlessly, almost totally divorced from the nagging of commands and "shoulds". . .[1]

If this newfound self-acceptance begins to affect his or her everyday life and it often does, then the meditator may find themself becoming more tolerant of their own weaknesses, life may be seen in better perspective, and they may become more efficient since their actions are no longer hampered by unproductive self-criticism. Easing of self-blame also makes it easier for the meditator to accept certain thoughts that otherwise might be difficult to face without guilt or anxiety.

Dr. Bernard Glueck has pointed out that when meditating, thoughts may come into awareness that would ordinarily cause a person alarm, but that during meditation the *reactions* to them are different. Distress in the face of this usually anxiety-producing material is markedly reduced or almost absent.[2] I have also noticed similar reactions.

One meditating patient, before getting married, became extremely anxious because, when she was a child, her mother's several disastrous marriages had left an indelible impression on her. During this pre-marriage period in her life, her meditations became filled with mutilating images that were so vivid and realistic they would have horrified her under ordinary circumstances. These images would "whiz by" during the first ten minutes of her meditation and then fade as she "really got into meditating," but at no time did they cause her pain or distress. Because of this experience, she was able to discuss them freely in psychotherapy and as a result to resolve some deep-seated fears.

Another meditator experienced anger during his meditations which ordinarily would have been alarming:

> In meditation today I began to realize, to visualize my anger. It was colossal, unholy, soul-searing. It looked and felt like all the fires of hell fused into one ball of broken china, of crashing glass, of steel mills on a gigantic scale. . . . These images then blended with tornado-smashed cities, with cyclones and hurricanes and battlefields which flooded the universe and hurtled through space with calamitous force. . . . Then something happened. . . . As my meditation went on, a feeling of love seemed to dissolve the pain. . . . Something was set to rest within me.

Resolution of an uncomfortable emotional reaction during meditation is not unusual. When this occurs, the person may feel more emotionally alive outside of meditation too. This can mark the beginning of a new era in the meditator's life, a deeper awareness of who he or she really is.

A Repression Lifts

Closely related to the greater ability to accept emotions calmly when in meditation is the dramatic lifting of repression which sometimes occurs in meditators, permitting long-buried memories to come to the surface. One of the most impressive effects of meditation I have seen involved release of long-repressed, terrifying memories in a woman who had for many years effectively banished them from awareness.

Adele initially came to the guidance clinic for help for her young daughter, who was suffering from severe anxieties which hampered her at school, but she denied the need for any psychotherapy for herself although she was obviously tense. Her voice was high-pitched, her breathing rapid, her speech pressured. She had a chronic heart condition for which she took medication several times a day and she suffered from high blood pressure and a thyroid condition. Soon after her daughter began to be seen for psychiatric treatment, Adele complained that she was unable to cope with the child and entered a mothers' guidance group which I was leading.

When she joined our group she was fearful about whether or not she would "fit in" with the other mothers, and it seemed at first as though she was trying too hard to be liked by them. Because she was so tense, I decided that meditation might be a useful aid to her treatment.

When Adele learned CSM, her immediate response was a powerful one. She reported that during her first meditation she had felt as though she were a bird gliding freely through the skies, experiencing a wonderful sense of freedom as she drifted over the countryside. During this first meditation, too, she spontaneously shifted from using the mantra which she had chosen from the list of CSM mantras, and substituted for it a phrase of her own which suddenly popped into her mind—"inner peace." She continued to use this self-made mantra from then on and found it a most effective calming device.

Some effects of meditation on Adele's life were almost immediate. Within two days of commencing this practice, her heart became slow and regular and she was able to dispense with her heart medication within the first week of learning to meditate and has never returned to it.

During the first few weeks, her meditations involved images of floating and drifting in the sky among nature, flowers, and other peaceful symbols. Soon, however, these pleasant "floating" sensations began to alternate with frightening ones in which she would see atomic explosions or other cataclysmic happenings during her meditation. At this time Adele requested an individual psychotherapy session with me.

Because she seemed unusually tense, I suggested that she and I meditate together. We had been meditating for about ten minutes when the session was interrupted by loud, almost hysterical laughter. Adele explained that she had had a sudden fantasy during meditation: she had imagined she was on a boat with her mother and she had pushed her mother off into the water. It had given her so much pleasure that she could not restrain herself from bursting out laughing.

She confided in me that this fantasy was an "incredible thought" for her and wanted to know if it were "normal" for her to have such thoughts. When I assured her it was normal to have many mixed feelings about a parent, a floodgate opened. Up until this point she had insisted that her parents were "fine and wonderful people—no one could ask for better." Now she revealed that she had been a battered child living in terror of an apparently psychotic mother. One memory after another came to the surface in this session, some of them memories which she had managed to push out of her mind since childhood.

Adele had been born without the sanction of the church of which her mother had been a devout member. Because of this, Adele's mother viewed her daughter as having been born "in sin" and developed a mental illness shortly after the child's birth which lasted during the girl's entire childhood.

The first buried memory to surface during a meditation session was an early childhood incident that Adele had long tried to forget. When she was three years of age, in a fit of rage, her mother had grabbed a dish towel, twisted it around the child's neck, and tried to strangle her. It was only when a neighbor across the alleyway, seeing this attack through the window, rushed to the door to intervene, that her mother, in a daze, had let go.

Another meditation session brought to light a different incident, one which Adele had not recalled for almost thirty years. When she was very young, her father had given her a toy dog as a gift before leaving on one of his all too frequent business trips. She had carried this toy about constantly when he was away and, perhaps because of its comforting presence, cried out, "I'll tell Daddy!" the next time her mother started chasing her in order to catch her and beat her. In retaliation for Adele's "answering back," the mother had dragged her into the cellar of their home, locked the door, and told Adele that if she ever revealed to anyone, especially her father, the mother's beatings, she would push her into the furnace. To illustrate this point, she threw the toy dog in the furnace and forced Adele to watch it burn.

Despite the intense difficulties in her life, Adele had managed to save herself from destruction. As soon as she graduated from high school she joined the armed services, determined to learn effective methods of self-defense such as karate and judo. She did learn how to defend herself, and later worked, married, had several children, and lived a generally constructive life, although her many tension-related illnesses attested to the fact that her traumatic early life was still having its effect on her.

As she began to discuss her mother's mistreatment of her in individual psychotherapy, her meditations became filled with hostile fantasies toward her mother. At one point she vividly pictured an atomic bomb that killed her parents but spared the rest of the population. So many painful memories were beginning to surface during her meditation sessions, in fact, that Adele began to be afraid of meditating, while at the same time she did not want to stop because it was obviously benefiting her heart condition. At this point I advised her to reduce her meditation time to three to five minutes per session to slow up tension-release. This worked well and Adele was soon ready to share her painful memories with the mothers' group in which she participated.

This was an important step. Her mother's childhood threats about the terrible punishments that would follow if she told anyone about her mother's mistreatment were still deeply ingrained in her. When the other women in the group accepted her painful revelations with understanding and support, it was a source of new strength for her. Following this, her attitude toward her own mother began to change. She was now able to accept the fact that her mother had been mentally ill and probably should have been hospitalized during those years—that, in effect, she had not been responsible for her actions. This realization so relieved Adele that she was able to return to meditating for a full twenty minutes twice a day, a schedule she has been able to maintain ever since. Memories now stopped flooding her meditation sessions and they were once more filled with largely pleasant fantasies, with only occasionally a momentary violent scene.

From then on Adele found herself less harassed about many things. When her children started yelling at each other around the house, it no longer upset her. Her compulsive nail-biting stopped. Life-long nightmares receded to almost zero. It was also instructive to see her lose her need to prove to the world that she was "self-sacrificing." She was now easygoing and casual in the mothers' group and had stopped trying to solve everyone else's problems for them. As she worked through her painful relationship to her own mother, she also found herself able to play with her little daughter, for the first time, and to thoroughly enjoy doing so.

Adele says that if she had not had individual psychotherapy sessions along with meditation, she would have been so frightened by the upsurge of painful memories that she would not have been able to continue meditating. I agree that had she not had my support and later the encouragement of the group to help her handle her anger at her mother, she almost certainly would have had to discontinue meditation in order to escape unbearable anxiety. I doubt, however, whether psychotherapy *alone* could have helped Adele resolve these problems as she did. She was initially too fearful of facing the painful areas in her life to have allowed herself to enter individual psychotherapy of the type where free association might have been used to recover repressed memories. Meditation, however, enabled these memories to surface within a remarkably short span of time so they could be constructively dealt with in her therapy.

Sense of Self Increases

As we have indicated, the contribution of meditation to personal growth does not stop with removing symptoms, even such crippling symptoms as the repression of crucial memories or an inability to come to terms with anger in oneself, but reaches further, effecting a change which has to do with the unfolding of a sense of personal worth, a growing awareness of the self. A meditator expresses this in his journal:

> When I meditate I go into myself. I come into myself. I apprehend myself as an entity separate from every other entity, separate from every other thing. I am not my house, nor my car, nor the clothes I wear. I am not the rules I live by nor even the words I say. I am me. How strange! This is what it feels like to be me![3]

The ability to view ourselves as separate from our surroundings is called by psychologists "field independence." This capacity frequently increases with meditation, an important consideration since people who are "field independent" are apt to see themselves more distinctly, more clearly, and in a more sharply detailed fashion. They tend to be inner-directed rather than outer-directed, asking themselves, "How does this feel to *me?*" rather than, "How does this look to *others?*" Those with a less developed sense of identity, who tend to rely on other people to shape their attitudes and judgments, are known as "field dependent."

These aspects of personality are particularly interesting because they have some highly reliable testing instruments available to measure them. One is the Embedded Figures Test, a refined version of those puzzles given to children where they are asked to find the "little pictures" hidden within the larger picture. The more "field independent" a person is, the more rapidly he or she can isolate the little figures from the big one that embraces them.

In the Rod and Frame Test, the person has to perform a *physical* task: straighten a rod viewed in a somewhat tilted frame. People who are more "field dependent" tend to straighten the rod by aligning it so that it is parallel with the vertical edges of the frame; they use *outer* cues when performing their straightening task. Those who are more "field independent" tend to straighten the rod by aligning it with the vertical of *their own body;* they use their own *self* as the reference point. The Embedded Figures and Rod and Frame tests are considered very "stable" measures; the way a person approaches these tasks tends not to change over time once he or she has reached adulthood.

It is all the more interesting, therefore, to discover that these tests often show changes in people who have been meditating. In a study conducted with zazen meditators, for example, researcher Melissa Hines found that her subjects scored significantly higher on the Embedded Figures Test after they had been meditating for ten weeks than they had before learning to meditate.[4]

When psychologist William Linden taught a group of third-grade children from an underprivileged background another form of zazen meditation, he found much the same thing.[5] These children were tested with the Embedded Figures Test before they started meditating and again after a period of thirteen weeks during which they had practiced meditation in school a few minutes each day. At the end of the experiment, their scores showed that they were significantly more "field independent"—a finding of importance to people who are concerned with fostering individuality and independence in young children.

The results using the Rod and Frame Test are impressive because no matter how often a person performs this task, his score will not improve with practice. Using the Rod and Frame Test, the Embedded Figures Test, and a task which measures the tendency to perceive the apparent movement of a spot of light in a darkened room, psychologist Kenneth Pelletier of the University of California School of Medicine tested a group of subjects before they learned TM and again after they had been practicing it for three months.[6] He compared them with control subjects over that same time interval. At the end of this period, the meditators' scores had improved significantly on all three measures, while those of the nonmeditators had not improved at all. Basic perceptual measures such as the Rod and Frame Test and the Embedded Figures Test had therefore changed with meditation.

In a recent Princeton study, researcher David James has shown that field independence as measured by the Embedded Figures Test, can even change over the *short term* if a person meditates during the interval. A group of subjects improved significantly more on scores of field independence after twenty minutes of meditating than another group of subjects who simply rested for twenty minutes.[7] In fact, the scores of the "resters" remained unchanged over this interval. This finding is surprising since it had previously been thought that field independence could not fluctuate on a short-term basis. It suggests a strong immediate influence of meditation on our interaction with the environment.

This seems related to the fact that meditators often report that they have developed a greater sense of their own *identity* since they have been meditating. They tend to sense their personal rights in situations where formerly they might have been unaware of them, or can now withstand social pressures without abandoning their own opinions. They may also find themselves becoming more decisive and expressing ideas more openly.

A patient of mine, Richard O., is a successful professional man who grew up in a home where the family members tended to deny their emotions. They rarely showed anger or sadness, always acting "reasonably." Richard learned to exert a tight control over his own emotions and eventually almost lost awareness of them. Now, more often than not, he could not tell when he was angry or when he was sad, or identify any other strong feeling. He could only reason that maybe he *might* have felt a particular way. One of the few times when genuine feelings were available to him was when he had had some drinks, and drinking was becoming a problem for him. One of the first tasks of psychotherapy was to help Richard get in touch with his own feelings and, among other therapeutic approaches, I suggested that he learn CSM.

On emerging from his initial meditation, Richard said he had felt as though he were "in another world" and would have liked to have stayed there for a long time; in fact, indefinitely. When he phoned me the next day to report on his meditation (a routine procedure) he asked me if he might be allowed to meditate more than twice a day, because he found it such a "pleasant experience." I suggested that he not increase his meditation time because this might release tensions too fast for him to handle comfortably.

After meditating one week, Richard returned for his psychotherapy session already showing changes. He no longer smoked during his session (and has not smoked in a session since), was more relaxed in his posture, and talked about different subjects. Before he had been businesslike and intellectual, speaking in a highly organized fashion about his relationship with his wife. In this session, he talked about himself in a somewhat musing fashion, bringing up thoughts about his childhood and his own inability to enjoy himself or to "play" in life. He seemed to have a new interest in exploring his own reactions and for the first time expressed a desire to use therapy to enrich his own life rather than just as a tool to improve his marriage.

The following week, while traveling on a plane, he was meditating and had the impression that he heard his own voice saying: "Empty yourself of your desires!" This rather mysterious statement was followed by an experience of exaltation and the further words: "I can have a drink or smoke a cigarette if I *want* to—but I don't *have* to." This seemed to him to be a startling revelation, giving him for the first time a feeling that he now had a choice of whether or not to drink.

Richard had always found it extremely difficult to know what his own wishes were. After meditating for about three weeks, he reported an "unusual incident." His children had asked him to stop at a roadside stand to buy ice cream. His usual response to such a request would have been to buy the same ice cream for himself as for the others, not realizing that he, too, might have preference for a particular flavor. This time, however, he found himself saying, "Fine, I'll get you what you want—then I'm going to get *chocolate* ice cream for myself." Seemingly a small thing, this was important: he had sensed his own need and stayed with it.

The experience of a new and convincing sense of self during meditation often forms a base of self-awareness which can be built upon to advantage in psychotherapy. Archimedes, the ancient Greek mathematician and physicist, is reputed to have said: "Give me a place to stand and I will move the world." Certain patients seem unable to move ahead in therapy because they seem to lack a base of self on which to stand in order to produce change. In these cases even deep psychological insights may build on quicksand, as it were. Meditation often makes an important contribution to therapy by building into the person a new, deeply convincing, largely wordless experience of self.

Another meditator illustrates this process. Jack, an intelligent although extremely withdrawn man, had been in psychotherapy of one sort or another for nineteen years. Being meticulous in his habits and extremely responsible, he was able to hold onto various administrative positions for a long period of time, but at home he led the life of an isolate with few friends or relationships. Although he was in his mid-forties he had had virtually no sex life. Jack's relationships were fantasy ones. His life was filled with daydreams of dating attractive women but these were always followed by obsessive worries about how he might, even timidly, approach such women should he meet them.

At his therapists' suggestions, he had attended marathons, encounter groups, group therapy, and even undergone a full course of "systematic desensitization" by a behavior therapist—all to no avail. The behavior therapy had even made his symptoms worse because as he tried to imagine dating in the context of being deeply relaxed, instead of feeling calmer he became more anxious and developed palpitations. His increasing tension made him abandon this form of therapy.

His present therapist suggested to him, almost as a last resort, that he learn CSM. Jack, who usually returned sneering after having tried out some new method that had been suggested to him, agreed to learn it.

Surprisingly, meditation worked. Jack was enthusiastic about it and according to both him and his therapist, it "remade" this man's life in many ways. He was deeply impressed with the technique from the beginning and is now a regular meditator. After beginning meditation, his attitude toward experimenting with relationships changed markedly. He was soon able to try out new forms of relating to others. He has initiated some tentative sexual relationships, and his progress along these lines is continuing.

For years people had been making constructive suggestions to Jack about things he might do to "change his life-style." Some of these suggestions had been daring, some mild; but he had not been able to act on even the simplest of them. As he put it, "Even though I could recognize that their advice was good, there was nobody present in *me* that could respond to it—now there is a *me* to listen, and respond, and move on these things. Meditation has given me a center to myself."

The "center" which Jack refers to seems to be an "inner ear" that is sensitive to his own being. It is a center of the self that can mobilize and begin to take action. The result is that where before he seemed to have no "backbone" or substance, now he has a new assertiveness and for the first time is making progress in his psychotherapy.

Through meditation, people begin to see themselves as self-determining beings, separate from their surroundings. At the same time they also begin to feel more intimately connected with all that surrounds them. An entry in my husband's meditation journal expresses this:

> During meditation I am me, not "you," not your values. I am *me* and my values are reconstituting me. . . . A tree is not a slave, its growth is its own. In meditation I grow as a tree, I live with the sun and the earth, and am my own ten commandments. . . .

Greater Openness to Others

Just as meditation can increase one's sense of individuality and leads to self-assertion, allowing one to feel close to one's self, by the same token it often increases one's sense of closeness to others. As Erich Fromm has pointed out, love of self and love of others are but two aspects of one fundamental capacity for loving.*[8] It is interesting to see meditators become more individualistic and at the same time, more co-operative and friendlier to others than they were formerly. The openness and ease with people which often come with meditation and the increased friendliness and greater tolerance for the weaknesses of others, parallel the easing of the meditator's attitude toward him or herself.

It is a common psychological observation that as self-blame lessens, so does the tendency to blame others.[9] In the same way, if we can experience joy in our own aliveness, we will support the aliveness of others, the reason why psychotherapists begin by helping their patients to accept *themselves*. Relationships with other people seem automatically to improve as this occurs.

Another by-product of growing certainty about one's own identity is that having become the center of their own awareness, meditators may find themselves having less of a need to be the center of attention in a social gathering; it is no longer necessary to prove an identity and self-importance which are now self-evident. This may lead the meditator toward a more natural relationship with other people. He or she may become more genuinely aware of others for their own sake because they are no longer concerned with how they are "coming across." Meditators' families frequently report that they have become "much easier to live with." Their friends often say they are "easier to talk with," "friendlier," or "warmer."

I recall an immediate change of this sort which I noticed in a patient within a few days after she had learned TM. This woman had behaved in a critical, argumentative, and suspicious manner in her treatment sessions with me, but in this hour she was different. Her face was relaxed and more attractive. She looked

* Fromm makes a sharp distinction between self-love and "selfishness." The "selfish" person is said not to love himself, but hate himself. His lack of fondness and care for himself then leaves him empty, frustrated, and anxiously concerned to snatch from life whatever satisfactions he can. This makes him seem to care *too* much for himself, but he is actually making an unsuccessful attempt to cover up and to compensate for his failure to care for his real self, and therefore to be able to care for others. People who have genuine self-love, on the other hand, have the capacity to love both self and others.

directly at me when she spoke. Her speech was quieter. For the first time since she had come into therapy I felt that I was facing a friendly human being, one with whom I could work in a constructive give-and-take fashion.

It was significant that in this session she reported a change in her relationship with her little daughter as well. Since she had commenced meditating, she was finding herself no longer so "hard" on the child and she realized that in the past she had been taking out feelings of anger at her husband on the little girl. Now, she said, she could quietly instruct her daughter without *commanding* her to do things, and the child was responding by becoming more emotionally open with her mother.

Several research studies support these observations on the fortunate changes in human relationships that sometimes occur with meditation. Studying the social effects of teaching TM to high school students, educator Howard Shecter reports that meditating students showed a significant increase in "tolerance" scores on tests of social attitudes given to them before learning TM, and again fourteen weeks after learning it.[10] Along similar lines, researcher David Ballou, studying the effects of meditation on the personality of prisoners, found that when a well-known clinical measure of personality, the MMPI, was administered to two groups of prisoners—one group which was taught TM and the other which did not learn to meditate—the meditators improved significantly on the "social introversion" scale, moving toward the more "socially outgoing" end of the scale, while the scores for the control group remained unchanged.[11]

In another prison study, researchers found that prison records kept on meditating prisoners showed that the number of positive activities these people participated in such as sports, clubs, and education had doubled after they started meditation, while the number of prison-rule violations was reduced. Nonmeditating prisoners, on the other hand, did not change in their behavior over the same period of time.[12]

While such studies need to be carefully evaluated in terms of other possible factors that may have influenced changes in the prisoners—such as the positive attention they may have received from TM instructors or the expectations they held for the technique—the fact that they correspond with what I and other psychotherapist colleagues have seen in patients, suggests that they probably reflect genuine changes in social attitude and relationships with meditation.

As the "case studies" described in this chapter illustrate, the improvements we see in meditating patients are not merely psychiatric ones; that is, meditation does not just result in the solution of an emotional problem, although this can be the case. Equally important is its capacity to expand the ability to live life more fully and to savor the sense of self. For this reason, meditation has many benefits to offer numerous meditators who will never need psychotherapy.

13

The Creative Meditator

When asked whether meditation makes people "more creative" I find it somewhat difficult to respond. The answer is both "yes" and "no." Meditation helps some people develop certain characteristics we identify with creativity; but this does not make them artists, inventors, or creative scientists if they do not have the interest in or ability for this sort of work. Meditation also helps others already in creative fields to develop their abilities further. On the other hand, many meditators who benefit from meditation in other respects, have not become more creative, and some people already doing creative work, do not want to meditate or do not continue meditating if they learn.

The relationship between meditation and creativity is difficult to pin down because "creativity" does not seem to be a single characteristic. It is a combination of character traits or abilities which are only loosely linked and our methods for detecting even *one* of these qualities are not as yet exact. Despite such problems, however, when psychologists Marie Dellas and Eugene Gaier, of the State University of New York, reviewed the literature on creativity they were able to arrive at a composite picture of the "creative person."[1] It sounds surprisingly like someone in a state of meditation.

According to their study, the creative person is capable of an unusually flexible *inwardly directed* awareness which permits a much greater than usual use of "primary process thinking." "Primary process" is the name given by Freud to the laws governing those unconscious processes which operate differently from familiar conscious thought. They are the "stuff that dreams are made of"—a type of thinking using symbolic, often pictorial ways of expressing deeply buried needs and desires. The primary process tends to surface in drowsy states where the mind is unhampered by logical restrictions. It can produce bizarre images: the "absurdities" we sometimes see in dreams, or the strange forms that hallucinations may take.

Creative breakthroughs which have occurred in dreams and other altered states of consciousness where primary process thought is prominent, abound: Robert Louis Stevenson received his inspirations for most of his books from his dreams; the material for Chagall's paintings was taken directly from his dreams; Howe was inspired with the idea of the needle with the hole at the bottom—an insight which enabled him to complete an operable sewing machine—from a dream; a reverie and a dream revealed to Kekulé the structure of the benzine ring, and to Crick the DNA molecule. There are many other examples which illustrate that contact with primary process is an important factor in the creative process. This is significant because meditation encourages primary process thinking. Like the creative person, a meditator drifts from idea to idea and image to image during meditation, unhampered by the restrictions of commands or "shoulds."

Ability to experience primary process thought is not in and of itself an index of creativity, however. This contacting of the unconscious must also be controlled; it needs to be integrated with and regulated by the conscious mind. Apparently it is neither the conscious *nor* the unconscious mode of functioning which is most useful for creativity, but rather the smooth interaction of these two modes which leads to success in creative endeavors.

There is some research which has demonstrated this relationship between meditation and the ability to use primary process thought in a controlled fashion. Psychologist Terry Lesh used the Rorschach inkblot test as a means of measuring the amount of primary process thinking each person was able to use in a constructive manner. The subjects were psychological-counselor trainees who were tested before and again after they had been practicing Zen meditation for a period of four weeks. At the end of this time, the ability to make constructive use of primary process thought had increased in the meditators, but had not changed in the nonmeditating counselor trainees.[2]

In another study, psychiatrist Edward Maupin discovered that the more effectively his subjects handled primary process thought and visual imagery during their meditation, that is, the more comfortably they were able to experience this "free-wheeling" kind of thought without either suppressing it or allowing it to "run away" with them, the more satisfactory they afterward judged their meditation sessions to have been.[3]

Increased openness to experiencing emotion, and the ability to allow oneself to respond to problems on an *intuitive* level, are two additional personality traits which Dellas and Gaier found distinguished creative people from the average. Again, both of these traits are frequently increased by meditation. Many meditation teachers encourage their students to adopt an intuitive approach rather than logical thinking. A Zen archer, flower arranger, painter, or poet is taught to allow their art simply to "happen." They are to respond with a delicately attuned awareness to what is occurring, rather than to impose rational rules on the process. In the same way, a Westerner learning TM is taught not to "clutch" at the mantra, but to allow it to "come to them" in a natural easy manner, without effort or planning.

The *koans* (riddles) used in Zen and the manner in which they are resolved also illustrate the way in which intuitive thinking is employed in meditation. Time after time the Zen student reaches an *intellectual* solution of the riddle, only to have it rejected by his Zen master, until finally an inner crisis is reached. Realizing that intellectual skills are worthless to solve the problem, the student then gives up the fight for a rational solution, "lets go," and is said to "throw himself into the abyss." It is then that "enlightenment" occurs. Solving the koan, therefore, involves the ultimate rejection of the logical, linear intellectual approach in favor of an intuitive grasp of a problem. This "letting go" and "plunging into the abyss" seems to correspond to the "creative leap" which artists must make. Many creators report that much of their production takes place in an "egoless" state similar to that during which a Zen student solves his koan.

Creative people also have access to a relatively unfocused kind of attention which Dellas and Gaier have called "perceptual openness." This is the opposite of our usual ways of perceiving. What we ordinarily notice is almost always strongly limited by certain factors. Among these are our needs of the moment. If we walk down the street when we are hungry we will generally notice many restaurants and grocery stores but few, if any, movie theaters or shoe stores; children selling newspapers will not capture our attention, while those eating ice cream cones will; the smell of a rose garden will go unnoticed while that of a barbecue will seem to fill the air.

In the same way, our *past* experience ordinarily limits what we perceive. When we walk down a particular street every day, in all likelihood we rarely notice the buildings on that street because we are familiar with them. We will, however, generally notice a *new* street, or a new building on a familiar street, immediately. Our perception of the unfamiliar tends to be keen. Because of this selective process, most things with which we come in contact are never fully registered in our consciousness. "We see what we want to see, what we need to see, and by and large, what we expect to see."[4]

A look at the history of certain creative breakthroughs suggests that this tightly programmed, limited mode of perception is not as typical of the successful artist or scientist as it is of the ordinary person. These gifted people's thought tends to seek the unknown and move freely about, unrestricted by narrow goals. Creative people are said to be tolerant of changing situations and easily able to adopt fresh ways of seeing things. They are more "perceptually open" than the rest of us. Because of this they will be aware of many things in their environment that may escape the so-called "normal" person, and they may also be able to remember and make use of this information more effectively.

Art is often an unusual presentation or arrangement of familiar objects in the environment, an ability to "make strange" ordinary objects. This makes it possible to notice them as we would if they were entirely new to us. A Campbell's soup can or a box of Morton's salt is nothing when seen in the kitchen cabinet. If it is not presently needed, it goes unnoticed. Placed in a gallery, however, it becomes something startling. The artist who first puts an ordinary object into a gallery is considered "creative" because he has seen the object as no one has seen it before. The Zen masters would say he has been able to view it with "the eye of the beginner," a valued achievement in the Zen tradition.[5]

Scientific discoveries as well as artistic ones require the ability to view an old problem from a new perspective; as do practical discoveries, those "inventions" we all make when we meet a novel situation with an innovation in our everyday life. Instead of filing away a piece of information into a familiar "cubbyhole" in the mind, the person in the process of inventing allows it to connect mentally with seemingly *unrelated* pieces of information. A wine press, for example, was used over the ages but inspired only thoughts of fragrant flowing liquid and revelry, while printing from wooden blocks was a developed art by the dawn of the fifteenth century—yet these diverse processes had never been connected in anyone's mind. Johann Gutenberg saw a wine harvest in a new light, however. Watching the power of the wine press, it occurred to him that the same steady pressure might be applied by a seal onto paper—the *pressure* could enable printing to take place. This inspired the invention of the printing press.[6] While not all, perhaps not even most, unusual combinations of previously unrelated information turn out to be so useful, when they do they can be trailblazing.

As psychologist Rollo May points out: "Obviously if we are to experience insights from our unconscious, we need to be able to give ourselves to solitude."[7] Meditation can be described as a state of *inner* solitude and, during it, perceptual openness similar to that characterizing the thinking of creative people often seems to occur. The Hindu meditational tradition advocates the opening of the "third eye," seeing more and more from a new vantage point, and the Sufi sect of Persia views meditation as a means of developing an added perceptual organ which is said to enable one to overcome the limitations of the normal perceptual system. In addition, one of the general aims of traditional schools of meditation is a state called "nonattachment," in which one is said to exist "without desires." This state has some similarities to the attitude of creative persons who are not goal-bound, but freer than most people to scan a vast field of impressions without becoming caught up in any one of them.

The opening-up of perceptions through meditation is however more than a momentary thing. It often influences a person's general manner of responding to stimuli, both inner and outer, when he or she is *not* in meditation. As we have seen, yogis and Zen masters failed to habituate to clicks outside of meditation, indicating that they were unusually open to stimuli during their ordinary waking lives.

Even people who have been meditating for a relatively short period of time can experience increased perceptual openness. In a survey conducted as part of our research at Princeton University on the effects of meditation on personality, 73 per cent of the subjects reported that they had improved in "awareness of external and internal environment" after having meditated for three and a half months.

While meditation can affect certain aspects of creativity, it is unlikely that all of the traits which cluster together in the "creative person" are affected by meditation. Some of them seem to be the result of heredity or personality drives so strong and fundamental that they are unlikely to be created or destroyed by any outside intervention. Three important aspects of creativity which do respond to meditation, however, are: productivity, originality, and stamina, or "staying power."

Increased Productivity

Increased productivity often depends on the ability of ideas to flow easily and rapidly. Meditation may bring about such a release of ideas. Within a week after learning to meditate, my husband was able to write a forty-page scientific paper that he had been postponing for six months. In contrast to his previous difficulties with it, his ideas now flowed unhesitatingly, a change he traced to the free-floating thought of meditation, where images and ideas drift unhampered by self-criticism.

Within the first week after learning TM, one of my patients discovered that she could do crossword puzzles with great ease, something she had never been able to do before. Her previous inability to do these puzzles was related to the fact that she had always had difficulty in any situation (such as an examination) where she was required to "switch perspective." She would arrive at an exam having studied the course material thoroughly from *one* viewpoint, only to find herself unable to tackle it from the different perspective required by the test. In the same way, when trying to do a crossword puzzle she used to "get into a rut." Seeing one possibility for a word, she could not abandon this when it did not fit so as to enable herself to scan her memory for other words, a necessity for creative puzzle solving. Meditation, however, seemed to unlock her ability to shift gears mentally. She was now free to reshuffle ideas into new combinations.

The most impressive effect of meditation on blocked productivity which I have witnessed occurred in a college student. Susan was a brilliant young woman and an outstanding scholar, but when she was an undergraduate at Princeton she was so self-critical and perfectionistic that she was unable to write more than a few pages of her Junior Paper (a key requirement at the university) without tearing it up in disgust. Although she had completed research for the project, she faced the equivalent of the familiar "writer's block" in preparing it. Her six months of work resulted in continual frustration and she was in danger of failing her junior year because of this stalemate.

When her visits to the counseling service on campus and my considerable encouragement as her adviser failed to help her, I suggested that she learn meditation. Susan agreed, went to learn TM, and for two weeks after that did not contact me. At the end of this period, she walked into my office and handed me a thirty-five-page typed manuscript, a complete draft of the paper. When I read it I realized it was more than a draft; with little change it was ready to be submitted as a solid piece of research, more than adequately fulfilling her junior independent work requirement.

Susan later told me that the reason she had finally been able to write her research study was that meditation had literally "opened up the floodgates," permitting her ideas to flow. A particularly important aspect of this incident is the continuing effects meditation had on her. She was now able to handle her studies with ease, and began to realize her full academic potential. A year later, she was graduated from Princeton, Phi Beta Kappa, and received Highest Honors.

Aside from anecdotes such as the above, there is some experimental evidence suggesting that meditation may help to increase productivity. In Melissa Hines's study on meditation and creativity mentioned previously, she found that what psychologists call "ideational fluency," a tendency for mental associations to flow easily, rapidly, and productively, can be influenced by meditation. There was a significant increase in ideational fluency in the zazen meditators she studied over the ten-week period, while the control subjects' ideational fluency was unchanged.[8]

Curiously, this improvement in the meditators took place almost entirely in the *last four weeks* of the study. During the first six weeks, there was relatively little improvement. This suggests an accumulative effect of meditation on certain mental processes connected with creativity. Perhaps the *longer* a person has been meditating, the more likely it is that he or she will have personality changes in the direction of increased perceptual openness and ideational fluency. Since a number of people report an almost immediate "opening up" of productivity after beginning meditation, however, it is obviously not necessary for *everyone* to have been meditating a long time for this to occur.

Improved Quality of Creative Work

Some people have reported striking changes in the *nature* of their creative work which they themselves have attributed directly to meditation. Probably the most impressive instance of this is a former patient, Antoni Jurkiewicz. Toni found psychotherapy an exceedingly painful experience. He had been to several therapists before coming to me and during the time that he and I worked together, this sensitive, gifted young man found it so anxiety-provoking to talk about his problems that he would lapse into silence a good portion of the time.

Since Toni showed an interest in drawing and painting, I decided to use art therapy in his treatment. When crayons and a large pad of paper were made available, he readily "drew his feelings" on paper and we were able to discuss them. Sometimes he would alter his drawings to reflect newer, more healthy attitudes toward himself. His artwork was not outstanding however. He was a rather awkward beginner and I viewed his drawing as simply a therapeutic maneuver.

At the time Toni left for Boston, while he had improved his outlook somewhat, he was still far from comfortable in therapy and had yet to bring under control a lifelong tendency toward intermittent depressions. Some months after moving, he phoned me to request that I recommend a new therapist in his vicinity. Knowing his past difficulty in opening up in therapy, I suggested to him that he first learn TM near where he lived, practice it for three months, and then recontact me at the end of that time.

Toni followed through on this suggestion and as soon as he learned meditation, he found it had a profound effect upon him. His meditation sessions were, from the first, deeply compelling experiences. More impressive, however, were the effects they had on his life. His troublesome depressions came under control for the first time and have remained stabilized for the past three years since he has been meditating. He became a regular and enthusiastic meditator, almost never missing his two sessions a day.

At the end of three months of meditating, Toni felt ready to re-enter therapy and at that time I referred him to a therapist in Boston. Because of the changes brought about by meditation, he had now acquired a different outlook on psychotherapy. He no longer felt that therapists were "all-powerful"; and in searching for his new therapist, he found himself sensing *his own rights* in the situation. When he started his new course of therapy he was able to talk freely and productively and use the experience to great advantage. Since the anxiety which had formerly all but paralyzed him in his treatment sessions was greatly lessened as a result of meditation, during this new course of treatment he made excellent progress.

Particularly surprising was the change in the quality of his creative work. Meditation seemed almost immediately to release a wellspring of creativity within him. Soon after learning this technique, he was completing four to five paintings a week, while at the same time holding down a full-time job as a cabinetmaker. Although he sometimes ran into fallow periods, for the most part he was astonishingly productive.

When I had the opportunity to view a showing of his paintings a year after he had stopped working with me, I was startled to see the difference in his work. His painting style had changed from an awkward, constricted, amateurish one to a powerful, artistic expression. Here was a modern artist with integrity, strength, and surprising technical mastery. His fantasy figures, somewhat reminiscent of Chagall's, were at the same time his own unique statements. Toni has, to date, exhibited his paintings and his figured pottery (which is equally original) in a number of galleries in the New York and Boston areas. He remains absorbed in his artistic work and continues to meditate with absolute regularity. In this instance, I witnessed a flowering of a vital talent which had not been evident before the artist began meditating. Obviously, meditation did not create his talent, but it seems to have released it at a strategic point in his life.

Verified anecdotes of this sort are to me more impressive than the few statistical studies presently available which deal with increased creativity as a result of practicing meditation. Means for measuring creativity on a wide scale are far from adequate at this point. We can select a few components of the creative process and identify them, but the elusive quality that makes the true artist can still only be identified by viewing his artistic work.

One or two studies measuring changes in "creativity" with meditation are worth mentioning however. A study at California State University compared a group of people who had been practicing

TM for several months with a group about to learn TM. Both were given a test for creative thinking.[9] The people who were already meditating did better on this test than those who were about to learn meditation and, as in the Hines study, the meditators showed greater ideational fluency. They also showed more flexibility and more originality in their thinking than did the non-meditators. This study, of course, has some of the flaws seen in all meditator vs. nonmeditator comparisons. We do not know whether these meditators might have scored better on creativity tests even *before* they learned to meditate.

At Harvard University, psychologist Gary Schwartz reported some different findings. When the Harvard researchers compared a group of TM teachers, with a group of nonmeditators on two standardized measures of creativity, the teachers did *no better* than the nonmeditators.[10] In fact, on some measures, they did worse. The only task on which the meditation teachers scored higher was an open-ended one where they were required to "make up a story." It looked as though being a meditator might actually *decrease* one's creativity.

The only difficulty with this conclusion is that TM teachers (Schwartz's "meditating" group) are frequently exposed to large amounts of meditation per day for extended periods of time, something which is not at all the case with the ordinary TM meditator. (Toni, described above, for example, meditates only the prescribed twenty minutes twice a day.) In addition, TM teachers as a group can be expected to have some of the same characteristics as do members of other authoritarian organizations. IMS requires them to use a completely standardized approach: they memorize their checking procedures down to the last detail of the wording and if they deviate from the prescribed wording in any respect (for example, modifying a word in the initiation ceremony) they may be required to repeat their teacher-training. I have known of some truly creative TM teachers who had to leave IMS (even though they had great respect for the TM technique) because they simply could not conform sufficiently to the strict tenets of this organization.

Using TM teachers as subjects and grading them for creativity may therefore tell us about the characteristics of TM teachers, but does it really help us understand what meditation can do for people who may be in a position to express freely the creativity that meditation can release?

Schwartz's conclusions are that meditation may enhance the free flow of associations and open up new ideas in the person, a prerequisite of creativity, but that too much meditation may interfere with the person's logical, problem-solving capacity and so dampen *that* side of creativity. He feels that while TM may enhance the first stages of creativity, if practiced to excess, "it may reduce the chance of the meditator's producing a recognizably creative product."[11] Creativity, he points out, depends on both producing novel ideas and later expressing them in a manner that makes use of rational and sequential thought. It remains to be seen, therefore, whether or not meditators typically respond well to what Schwartz calls the "necessities of creation." In the experiments at Harvard, the TM teachers did not seem able to do this.

It is instructive to recall that Toni's artistic discipline *increased* following commencement of meditation, resulting in a *more* controlled and skillful painting technique. A student to whom I taught CSM, also a painter, reported the same kind of experience after she had been meditating for several months. Her ability to exercise discipline in her creative work greatly increased. It was, in fact, the most outstanding effect that meditation had upon her and one that was most welcome. Both of these people differ from Schwartz's subjects in two important respects, however—they practiced only twenty minutes of meditation twice daily, and both were artistic *to begin with*.

What this suggests is that we need some controlled research on the effects of meditation on people who are artists as well as on ordinary meditators. We may also need to study the results of meditation on creativity in people who practice meditation *moderately* as against those who practice it more intensely.

Strengthening of Staying Power

Another link between meditation and creativity lies in a different realm. Meditation may contribute to the stamina of the artist, to his or her ability to sustain long periods of creative work. Here the results are clearly promising, although they are entirely anecdotal; I know of no formal studies in this area.

Arnold Schulman, the successful screenwriter and playwright—author (among other works) of A *Hole in the Head* (both play and movie); *Love with the Proper Stranger*; the screenplay for *Goodbye Columbus*; a recent book about an Indian spiritual leader entitled *Baba*; and twice an Academy Award nominee—is an interesting example of this since he bases his method of writing on meditation. He has practiced zazen meditation for twenty years, having studied with an outstanding Zen master, Miura Roshi, Head of the Rinzai sect in Japan.

Schulman originally learned meditation in order to cope with his problems in writing. He describes himself before beginning to practice meditation as having been disorganized, inefficient, undisciplined, and "chaotic" when writing. He followed no logical work sequence. He would often stay up all night writing and then sleep all day. He was frequently unable to get started for days and had no orderly work habits. Already a successful writer at twenty-three years of age, he realized then that he actually could not continue writing if he did not change his approach to work, which was, he says, filling him with "self-contempt." He experienced growing depression. Schulman's psychoanalysis was helping him with some other problems but could not seem to bring his writing under control.

Accordingly he cast about for auxiliary answers. First, he taught himself to concentrate thoroughly on *one thing at a time*. He found the ability to exert a gentle, firm control over his mind to be the first thing which brought about a change in his approach to work. He now seemed to have a handle on the creative process and could begin to shape it to his own ends.

He then went deeper, commencing to work with teachers of meditation and subjecting himself to the rigorous discipline of classical zazen training. Meditation has subsequently become a "way of life" for him. As he puts it, "I could no more do without meditation than I could do without air or food. It has become essential." By this he does not mean that he is "hooked" on it, but that it is so inwardly strengthening that denying it to himself is inconceivable.

Schulman regularly programs his writing efforts to take place in a meditative mood. His work is always done sitting on the floor in a half-lotus position. He works on a low table a few inches off the floor, writing either by hand or on an electric typewriter. Each night before going to bed, he sits in a semi-meditative state and reviews the story he is working on up to the point where he stopped writing, then he respectfully requests his "unconscious" to have the next sequence ready the following morning or at midnight or at four in the morning—whenever he plans to begin work again (it is, he says, important to give an *exact* time).* Having done this with complete faith that the unconscious, a "loyal servant" whom he treats with the utmost gentleness and dignity, will fulfill his request (an attitude toward work which he learned from a teacher of Raja Yoga) he then dismisses the problem from his mind and usually goes immediately to bed and to sleep. Of late he no longer has to sit in the meditative position to do this. It is so ingrained a pattern that he now can direct his next day's writing while in bed the very last thing before dropping off to sleep.

When Schulman starts working in the morning, he "unthinkingly" begins writing. He does not know what will come, but simply "lets it happen." The new sequence invariably presents itself in full as the writing unfolds and, when it does, he accepts it completely and unquestioningly. Later, in the editorial stage of his work, he will view it critically and decide how "good" or complete an answer it was.

When working on a screenplay, he sleeps at the most three or four hours a night and when awake works continuously with only brief breaks from the routine. After rising from sleep he always meditates for one full hour. Later he may do some Raja Yoga or some *asanas* (yoga postures) if he feels tired. A half hour of these postures, he claims, will substitute fully for sleep. He works sitting in a half-lotus position and maintaining to the greatest degree pos-

* This is Schulman's own system. Others might disagree with his procedures or even with this use of meditation.

sible, his meditative mood. This enables him to establish a "direct pipeline to the unconscious." His words flow forth onto the paper "mindlessly and fully." He describes this phase of work as "achieving orbit."

The problems of creativity are, Schulman feels, much like the problems of space travel. One must first get enough *thrust* to break out of the atmosphere into space. "I can only function when in orbit," he says. His means of pushing off the launching pad and breaking through is meditation. Not only does he begin his day with a long meditation, but when there is any interruption whatsoever (such as a phone call) he brings himself back into the creative mood by meditating once more, perhaps this time for fifteen or twenty minutes.

His workday thus involves a series of meditations as needed. This way he is able to sustain as much as twenty hours of highly creative work at a time. He does this without fatigue and in an almost unbroken rhythm until his writing assignment is completed. He explains that he must sweep through to the conclusion of any creative project "all in one breath."

In addition to enabling him to sustain this unusual productivity, Schulman feels meditation has assisted him in his work by eliminating the paralyzing anxiety a writer so often feels when faced with a *blank page*; the fear that can lead to endless postponement. Because meditation is not working with the conscious, logical, critical mind, he thinks this eliminates the prejudgment and fear of failure that can cause writer's block. In the meditative mood the writing flows—clearly, openly, effortlessly—and without anxiety.

We might consider this sustaining aspect of meditation an indirect contribution to creativity, but it is an important way in which meditation can assist the creative act. For some people meditation fosters the opening-up of unrealized potentials. There still remains, however, the question of which people it will do this for and under which circumstances. When is meditation effective and when not? We will now examine this problem.

14

Some Problems Arise

Meditation is not a panacea. Not everyone wants to learn it and not everyone who learns it benefits from it. Some people who do benefit from it discontinue the practice. It is also possible that other people do not need meditation because their life-style already supplies them with something equally satisfying.

Dr. Mihaly Csikszentmihalyi and his research team at the University of Chicago have a fascinating theory of pleasure based on their study of people involved in deeply gratifying activities.[1] This concept, which they call "flow," has certain things in common with the meditative mood.

According to the Chicago group, flow is present when the person is so totally involved in whatever he or she is doing that there is no time to get bored or to worry about what may or may not happen. They studied this holistic sensation that people feel when they act with total involvement—as *flow*—in structured interviews conducted with a large number of individuals involved in a wide variety of activities.

Careful analysis of these interviews revealed that games are obvious flow experiences and play is the most complete form of all. Yet playing a game is no guarantee that one is experiencing flow —it is the *ingredients* of the experience that count. If the person is totally engrossed, "lost" in the game—then he or she may enter flow.

Flow is often present in creativity. People as diverse as composers and dancers, rock climbers and chess players, surgeons involved in medical research and mathematicians working in the frontiers of their fields, all experience flow. When they do, it is often so enjoyable they are willing to forsake many other things for it, including money, fame, or comfort. In a certain sense, flow is the essential joy of living, beside which all other considerations are insignificant.

The Chicago group were the first to investigate this human experience with the methods of science and to identify what they believe to be its main elements. These they describe as follows:

—Flow is a state of *total absorption*. As an outstanding chess player describes it:

The game is a struggle, and the concentration is like breathing—you never think of it. The roof can fall in and, if it missed you, you would be unaware of it.[2]

—Flow involves centering one's attention on a *limited* stimulus field—with all else shut out. A professor of science who climbs rocks says:

When I start on a climb, it is as if my memory input has been cut off. All I can remember is the last thirty seconds, and all I can think ahead is the next five minutes.[3]

—Flow involves a kind of self-forgetfulness. This does not mean that the person in flow loses touch with his or her own physical reality or sense of existence, they may be more exquisitely aware of them than ever. What is lost is the artificial "self construct," the awareness of social roles and role-playing. The sense that "I am such and such a person, with such and such a name and status who is taking action," fades and a far more fundamental sense of self takes over. In flow there is no social "me," no *learned* awareness of "self," no ego-sense, to stand as a screen between each person and total experience. An outstanding composer says:

You yourself are in an ecstatic state to such a point that you feel as though you almost don't exist. . . . I just sit there watching . . . in a state of awe and wonderment. And it (the music) just flows out by itself.[4]

—A chess player says:

Time passes a hundred times faster. In this sense, it resembles the dream states. A whole story can unfold in seconds. . . . Your body is nonexistent—but actually your heart pumps like mad to supply the brain.[5]

—In flow the person is in *control* of his actions and his environment—he or she can cope. A dancer says:

A strong relaxation and calmness comes over me. I have no worries of failure. . . . I want to expand, hug the world. I feel enormous power to effect something of grace and beauty.[6]

—For flow to occur, the demands of the situation must be *clearcut, predictable, and not contradictory*. In flow the person must be able to know at any moment where she or he is with the activity. Rules of a game, specific training in certain skills, or rituals which are to be followed, make flow possible. They allow people participating in it to evaluate how they are proceeding without having to think about it at all, without needing to break the absorption. A basketball player says:

I play my best game almost by accident. . . . If I'm having a super game I can't tell [whether I'm playing well] until after the game. . . . Guys make fun of me because I can lose track of the score. . . .[7]

—Flow involves no goals or rewards external to itself. A young poet who is a seasoned rock climber says:

. . . You get to the top of a rock glad it's over but really wish it would go forever. . . . The justification of climbing is climbing, like the justification of poetry is writing; you don't conquer anything except things in yourself. . . . You are a *flow*. The purpose of the flow is to keep on flowing. . . .[8]

By this definition, many meditation sessions are also a form of flow. When the person is deeply into meditation, thought follows upon thought according to its own inner logic and needs no conscious intervention by the meditator; attention is strictly limited to only a few basic matters; activity is totally absorbing. The meditator is also in complete control of his or her actions and is protected from decisions by the ritual involved. During meditation there is little distinction between self and environment, between stimulus and response, between past, present, and future—attention is riveted on the intensity of the moment.

What does the concept of flow teach us about the "need" to meditate? Will a skier who regularly enters a state of flow in their downhill glides, experiencing ice and wind in perfect balance and existing in moments "outside of time," still feel like meditating later that same day, if he or she is a regular meditator? Is the need for flow ever-present, or does it wax and wane? Is there a need to balance one type of flow with another? Do people seek to alternate *active* flow experiences with those which are passive and *receptive* in nature—the age-old need to experience both aspects of life: tension and repose, the "masculine" and the "feminine," *Yin* and *Yang*?

These are crucial questions which must be answered if we are to discover whether other activities can supply the same ingredients as meditation and if they can make meditation superfluous for certain people—or perhaps for all people at certain times. It is at least plausible that some people do not need to meditate because they live with a pervasive sense of harmony in their lives. Who these people might be and why they should feel this way, however, is as yet unknown.

We do know, though, that certain people whose lives are apparently *un*fulfilling, people who are tense and driven in their behavior, are also frequently disinterested in learning meditation. Such people will not sign up to learn it when meditation is offered free as part of a curriculum, or at a guidance clinic. They remain disinterested even if their family or friends are enthusiastic about the practice. It looks as though such people are actively avoiding learning it.

Although no research has been done on tense people who avoid meditation, some clinical reports on patients who have persistently resisted suggestions that they learn to meditate, give us some clues about the reasons for such resistance.

Refusal to Learn Meditation

Meditation may run counter to some people's life-styles. This is particularly true for ambitious, driving people who hesitate to let down their pace even momentarily. Such people are usually difficult to slow down by any means. If their physician tells them they "need a good rest" for their health, they are apt to take the rest, if they agree to it at all, in their own way. They may manage to be constantly interrupted by business phone calls during a vacation: may take a dictation unit with them; or spend their holiday making business contacts. Whatever way they find to distract themselves, they are not apt to let down or become tranquil and are usually threatened by such an idea. Their self-esteem seems to rest on a vision of themselves as accomplishing something at all times: constantly measuring up to high standards, and untiringly "beating out" the next guy in line. Suspecting that meditation might slow them down, they will usually resist learning it.

Other people seem not to want to learn meditation because it means being *alone with oneself*. These are the types who tend to remain constantly occupied in order to avoid confrontation with their own selves. A patient describes this dilemma:

> When I first learned to meditate I was frightened of being alone with myself. I think that's why people set up all the things they do, all the activities in their lives, the sports, the bridge games and this and that, in order to run away from being alone with themselves. To be alone and not responsible for *doing* anything? —my first feeling about it was—"No!"

People who are overly dependent on the response of others to supply their sense of self-worth may also be afraid of sitting still with eyes closed. Without seeing others, they come face to face with a stranger in their midst, their *own self*. Such people are reluctant to "let go" of the outside world and seem automatically to shy away from the meditative disciplines. Some of them will go so far as learning meditation, but soon drop the practice.*

People needing to be in control at all times may be threatened by meditation. They often shy away from the new and unexpected in life and cannot conceive of themselves meditating because this practice is both unstructured and uncontrollable. A for-

---

* It may be useful for such people to keep their eyes open the entire time they are meditating so that they can remain in contact with the outer world upon which they depend. They may also find a form of moving meditation comforting.

mer patient was bothered by the relationship of meditation to hypnosis, for example, because he had always feared losing control under hypnosis. No amount of information about the differences between the two techniques mattered. He continued to view meditation as some sort of "mind control" that would "take over" and rob him of his right to be in the driver's seat. Needless to say, he never learned meditation although he suffered from symptoms of tension.

Added to these deep-seated reasons for not wanting to meditate are some incidental ones. I have known people who were urged so forcefully to learn meditation by overenthusiastic meditators in their family or among their friends that they resisted doing so on principle. For others it may simply be the wrong time in life for them to learn. These people may become ready to begin meditation at some point in the future.

Those Who Learn Then Quit

Perhaps more surprising than the people who do not want to learn meditation in the first place are those who learn to meditate and then quit. Their actions are often difficult to understand when taken at face value. While some people stop the practice because they are having difficulty with it, many stop just when they seem to be getting excellent results. There are a variety of reasons for dropping out, and meditating patients have provided an opportunity to explore some of them in detail.

Certain people seem to become disappointed with meditation because they have built up too many expectations around it. In their fantasy they might have seen meditation as a sort of "ideal helper," as though it were a Genie or a Fairy Godmother on whom they could depend. This is understandable because meditation is an intensely personal experience and the comfort it brings when it is working right is rather like the soothing of a kindly parent. If it does not go right for some reason, we are all somewhat disappointed. But the person who sees meditation as a "magic helper" does not just feel disappointed when it is not going right, he or she feels crushed, devastated. They may then react like a hurt child having a temper fit or one who has gone to "sulk in the corner."

A patient of mine, Rochelle, thoroughly enjoyed TM. After she commenced meditating she felt "cushioned" for the first time from the harsh accusations of some of her family members and began to interact with them more positively. She was more hopeful and experienced a sense of peace which she had not known before. She began feeling so well, in fact, that she hailed meditation as a major contribution to her life. But this picture changed when she came down with a severe case of the flu. At this time she became so weak that she was unable even to lift a glass of water to her lips. Although she tried repeatedly to meditate during her illness she found herself unable to summon up the energy to do so, even when lying down. She simply could not mentally repeat the mantra in her mind.†

As a result Rochelle felt that meditation had "deserted" her just when she needed it most. This made her bitterly angry. From then on she resented TM and refused to resume meditation after she had recovered from her illness. She could not justify this decision on logical grounds since meditation had been extremely beneficial to her, but her negative feelings were so strong she could not overcome them.

Fortunately she had an opportunity to work on this problem in psychotherapy, where we were able to explore the reasons why she had turned against meditation so strongly. Rochelle had been one of eleven children brought up in relative hardship on a country farm. When she was ill as a child, her overworked mother, finding a sick child in the family an extra burden, would remove herself emotionally from the child. She would order her to her room and rarely, if ever, visit her there. To the little girl this meant that the time when she needed parental comfort and support the most, she was abandoned.

This painful experience had shaped Rochelle's life in important

† Some physically ill patients find themselves unable to meditate although others seem to be able to do so successfully. The ability to meditate when ill seems to vary both with the person and the type of illness (see discussion in Chapter 7).

ways and now, many years later, when, as an adult, she found herself ill and entirely alone (she was at the time divorced) and tried
to meditate to comfort herself, meditation too seemed to be
"indifferent" to her. As a result she experienced a resurgence of
the despair she had felt as a child when she lay in her room ill and
alone. It was as if the meditation had changed at that moment
from an ideal "good mother" (which it had felt like up to this
point) into an indifferent "unavailable mother."

It was only as Rochelle's feelings of abandonment and personal
unworthiness began to change through therapy that she found
herself once again interested in the idea of meditating. To get her
started meditating, however, it was necessary for me to meditate
with her. She appeared to need my encouragement and support in
this experience—the presence of a sort of "mother-therapist" who
cared enough about her to stay with her. Gradually she once again
began to look upon meditation as positive and resumed the regular practice of it, with good results.

Another person who had a highly personalized reaction to meditation was a man who became enraged at his mantra because it
would not readily enter his mind when he sat down to meditate.
He was particularly angry because he felt he had spent $125 for
the mantra and it "should" come to him when he wanted it!

This man was acting toward his mantra as one might toward
another person who refused to co-operate or come when called.
He began to work on this problem in his therapy and soon
remembered that when he had been a child he had experienced a
similar fury at his mother when she paid attention to his brothers
and sisters and was not available when he needed or wanted her.
He had not been able to control his "mama" the way he wanted
to; now he could not control his mantra the way he wanted to—
both seemed to evade him. His reaction was to reject meditation
as though saying to an imaginary mother, "If you're a bad mother
and don't come to me when I want you to—then I will desert
you." The result of this personalizing of the mantra was that this
man stopped meditating until the problem of his mother could be
worked through in therapy, after which he returned to practicing
meditation with a fair degree of regularity and satisfaction.

Some people, however, stop meditating for a different reason: they have made the meditation ritual into a tyranny for themselves. Such people tend to be over-exacting about their meditation. They tell themselves that they must do it in a certain way, at a certain time, and are intolerant of the least infringement on their own part of their own rules. It is scarcely surprising that they eventually rebel and dismiss meditation as "just too much trouble."

I have found that people who react this way tend to be puritanical and harshly self-disciplining in many other respects as well. They seem to be experts at making that which is inherently pleasant into something difficult. Simple instructions of when, where, and how to meditate are interpreted by them as authoritarian commands which they deeply resent. Showing such people how to vary their meditation ritual to introduce a bit of freedom into it may do some good, but I find that in most instances insight into what they are doing is the best solution. If they can understand that they themselves are responsible for their supposed "enslavement" by meditation, and if they can begin to ease up some of their rigid demands on themselves, then they may be ready to return to meditation.

Other people may react adversely to meditation because of personal associations to the process. A friend of mine found herself becoming alarmingly depressed whenever she had to sit still with her eyes closed for TM. Because of this she soon discontinued meditating. When talking with her about this afterward, I asked her what "sitting still" brought to mind. She volunteered that as a child she was punished by being made to sit absolutely still without speaking, a condition which she had dreaded. While it is not certain that this was the reason for her depression when sitting still during meditation, it is possible that this early training may have caused her to have an antipathy to any situation which involved enforced sitting in silence. Under the circumstances, assigning her a form of meditation where she could move about and keep her eyes open might have been a solution to the problem. It is also possible that she should have been instructed to meditate for only very brief periods at a time.

It is apparent that "what is one man's meat may be another man's poison." The stillness which is such a welcome part of meditation for most people may be a frightening aspect of it for others. We have discussed tension-release during meditation. This occasionally causes someone to stop meditating entirely because deep emotions or bizarre and dreamlike thoughts during tension-release may be so intense that they cannot be tolerated. If reducing meditation time does not remedy the situation, then there seems no alternative for the person but to abandon the practice altogether and it is probably a wise idea to do so. We do not know at present what it is that prompts such occasional "allergic" responses to meditation, but it is sensible to treat them like any other allergy—by avoiding the source of the irritation.

As Maupin discovered with creative people, it may not be the *appearance* of strong emotions or bizarre thoughts that is important, but the degree of control one has over them that makes the difference. Those who feel, for whatever reason, that the process of tension-release is out of control in meditation may become alarmed and quit. On the other hand, meditation may help to make strong feelings manageable for the *first time* in a way they have never been before. One meditator describes her experience:

> I find that in meditation I am in tune with my feelings. I wouldn't listen to them before. . . . Now I find that I can experience the most devastating feelings, but meditation somehow gives me a sense that I'm in charge of them. They're not out of control, I have control of *them*.

Resistance of Self-Image to Change

The changes in outlook or behavior that result from meditation may not involve the deepest layers of personality, as we shall see, but they can be more sudden and dramatic than those which usually occur in psychotherapy. Meditation can change behavior so rapidly in some respects, in fact, that the person may be unprepared for the "new self" that develops. No matter how positive the changes, new ways which do not fit old ways can be threatening. Unless the meditator gains some understanding of what is happening, he or she may stop meditating.

A patient of mine, Margaret, had cleared up her tension-related symptoms of gastric ulcer and colitis with psychotherapy, and her depression had lifted, but her chronic tension headaches had not lessened after a year and a half of treatment. Because of this I decided that meditation might be worth trying and referred her for training in TM (I was not at this time teaching CSM). After commencing meditation, Margaret's headaches cleared up within the first few weeks and she was headache-free for the next four months—the first respite of this sort in years.

During this period she began to notice some personality changes in herself which disturbed her, however. These, she claimed, were directly due to meditation. She had formerly been self-sacrificing, playing the role of "martyr" to her husband, children, and other relatives. Now she was finding herself more aware of her own rights and compelled to stand up for herself in circumstances where formerly she would have given in.

When placed under extreme pressure at work, she used to be submissive, swallowing her resentment (and often developing a headache). Now she found herself fighting for her own point of view and certain things around the office were getting changed as a result. At home she marshaled the courage to obtain a legal separation from her long estranged, mentally disturbed husband, and stood up with strength for the first time to her teen-age sons and demanded that they stop calling her "the old lady." Apparently her manner showed that she meant what she said, because the boys treated her more gently after that, making fewer scathing comments. Clearly Margaret was becoming more self-assertive, more able to mobilize self-defensive anger when necessary, and to express it in an effective manner.

Despite the possible advantages of this new behavior, however, she began to be alarmed at the unfamiliar forcefulness of her own responses and complained that meditation was making her into "a hateful person." Her relatives, she said, especially her elderly parents, were complaining that she was no longer the "sweet" person she had been when she was more pliable.

Margaret also noticed another change in herself. She used to talk almost continuously at any social gathering, often becoming the "life of the party," but after commencing meditation she lost this compulsion to talk and would even remain silent for long periods. Because of this she now became aware for the first time of her deep sense of social uneasiness which she had hidden beneath her compulsive chatter. This too made her anxious.

Soon Margaret stopped meditating and was not able to force herself to resume the practice by any exercise of willpower, even though her tension headaches returned in full force. The personality changes brought about by meditation had been too extensive for her to assimilate. She was unprepared for them.

Before she could return to meditation it was necessary to trace, in therapy, the origin of her pervasive need to deny her own rights. As we delved into this facet of her personality, Margaret discovered that her competition with her older sister, Helen, was at the root of much of her difficulty. When they were children, Helen had been considered by their parents to be a "saint," undoubtedly headed for a religious life and certain to be a credit to the family. Margaret, on the other hand, was looked upon as a troublesome, irritating child. When she was very little, she had keenly felt this difference in attitude toward Helen but she could do nothing about it. On reaching adolescence, however, she found a "solution." At this point she developed an intense need to prove that she was more "saintly" than her exalted sister, although often this meant total sacrifice of her own wishes or needs for those of others. When Helen began to disappoint the family (she did not become a nun as expected and showed personality problems) Margaret moved into the position of being the "good" one in the family. Although she received relatively little recognition for this new role, she strove ever harder to prove how self-denying she could be.

Years later, when she learned to meditate, the "self-indulgence" of meditation threatened this vision of herself as being self-sacrificing. As meditation made her more assertive in many situations, her saintly image of herself was on the verge of being shattered. It was at this point that she stopped meditating.

After working through some of her problems in therapy, Margaret was finally ready to resume meditating. For quite a while, however, she was only able to meditate *once weekly* without building up too much anxiety. She and I would regularly meditate together for twenty minutes before her psychotherapy sessions.

This maneuver worked well because by meditating comfortably in her presence, I was demonstrating that meditation was a good and acceptable activity. Much later, looking back on this period of her treatment, she commented:

> For you to say to me "we'll meditate together"—that was granting *permission* for me to meditate—it was taking the whole problem out of my hands. I was relieved, and I could go ahead with it.

These weekly meditation sessions were deeply restful for Margaret. Her headaches once again disappeared and she began to experience personality changes typical of regular daily meditators such as a richer and more enjoyable fantasy life. In this moderate dose, she was able to handle the gradual changes in her self-concept which were occurring.

After a year at this pace, Margaret was able to return to meditating on her own once a day and has continued doing so ever since. In general she is now a more independent, self-confident, happier person who is able to accept the positive changes which have taken place in her.

Depression and Meditation

People who suffer from what is known as "chronic low-grade depression"—a lingering sense of gloom and joylessness in life—may respond well to meditation, regaining a feeling of well-being after they commence practicing it. Those with more severe depressions, however, more often than not react in a different way. Even when meditation may help them feel better, these deeply depressed persons usually stop practicing it. It may threaten their self-image or run counter to a disturbed life-style. On the basis of research on TM at the Hartford Institute of Living, for example, Dr. Bernard Glueck reports that TM has not proved useful in the treatment of patients with severe depressions when they are in what is known as a *retarded* depressed state, a state where the person is apathetic. The Hartford researchers noticed, however, that meditation will help to reduce anxiety in an *agitated* depression, a state where the patient is highly tense and restless even though depressed. Under these circumstances improvements will occur if the patient can be helped to meditate regularly. Once a patient wants to come out of any depression, they can both meditate regularly and feel the usual responses to meditation.[9]

I have noticed that severely depressed people frequently resist suggestions that they learn meditation in the first place, sometimes with flimsy excuses that can barely be convincing even to themselves. One depressed patient spontaneously told me that she did not want to learn meditation because "it might make me feel better and in a way I might not *want* to feel better."

Another patient is an example of those who quit meditation because it threatens a "depressive" life-style. Anna, a woman in her thirties who suffered from chronic (long term) depression, was obsessively indecisive about her marriage relationship. Although she found life with her husband "unbearable," she made no effort to remove herself from her painful home situation, even temporarily. She remained in her house, barely able to do housework, and otherwise tearful and inactive.

Anna talked little during her therapy sessions with me, attempting to force me to solve her problems, while at the same time resisting any constructive suggestions I might make. In the hope that meditation might replace her attitude of resignation with a more active and co-operative one, I suggested to her that she learn TM. To my surprise, she consented, took the training, and found to her own bewilderment that she began to feel decidedly positive effects from meditation. Her mood lightened, her compulsive crying spells ceased, and she began to make decisions of a meaningful sort. She also reported that she was feeling more energetic and was becoming more active. She said that meditation was making her feel "much better."

At this point, however (it being summer), both she and I left for vacation. During her month-long holiday, Anna stopped meditating entirely. Later she explained this was because she had become "angry" at meditation because it was "making me cope" and also because "it made me feel so calm that I could no longer cry or feel sorry for myself." Feeling that she must cry and must continue complaining, she had discontinued meditation and was then able to resume her despair, weeping, and self-pity. In her own words, "I had my own feelings back again."

Anna never returned to meditation, nor, in fact, did she continue long with psychotherapy, but eventually received antidepressive drugs from a physician which enabled her to get along somewhat better without essentially changing her behavior in any fundamental manner.

There seem to be several factors in Anna's wish not to continue meditation. By letting her go on vacation (and by leaving myself) I was clearly requiring her to become more independent. She may have resented this and rejected meditation to "retaliate"—I was the one who had suggested that she take it up in the first place. She was also a person who tended to make every new activity into an enslavement and meditation soon seemed to be a new "ordeal" or "duty" which she had to perform.

Probably the most important factor, however, was the fact that meditation threatened to rob her of her role as a "helpless" being whose misery was being used (unconsciously) as a club with which to control others—her husband, friends, and myself. In effect, the meditation may have been working "too well" by fostering a genuine change in attitude for which Anna was not ready. Since she did not have the personal resourcefulness, persistence, and "ego strength" of the previous patient discussed (Margaret) and her emotional illness was far more grave, the only choice compatible with her neurotic pattern was to abandon meditation.

This inability of Anna's to tolerate the pleasant aspects of meditation brings us to another curious reaction. Many people seem to abandon this practice precisely because it is making them feel too good.

Fear of Pleasure

Enjoyment constitutes a problem for many people. The idea that we should occupy our time with "useful" pursuits is widespread. A businessman may come home to rest over a weekend, only to find himself compulsively catching up on chores around the house and end up spending the entire weekend *working*. Even if he plays golf or tennis, he may make "good use of his time" by trying to improve his game or make business or social contacts. Many people work themselves into exhaustion while supposedly playing. At that point they feel harassed, cornered, and may try to escape from the whole process by "knocking themselves out."

Drinking is one escape from such tension. Attaching oneself to a TV set or newspaper is another. Our society has any number of escape devices which help us lapse into total passivity and be relieved of responsibility. They are necessary safety values for us if living is merely a mechanical duty, rather than a joyous vital process.

Meditation stands quite apart from this round of work vs. escape. It is a moment of actual presence, an aliveness which exists for its own sake and needs no justification. It goes beyond the requirements of mere survival, either material or social, and opts for joy.

The Indian spiritual leader Bhagwan Shree Rajneesh suggests that existing in the material world is but an "emergency measure" and that the true goal of man "is always to come to the flowering of the potential . . . of all that is meant by you." This flowering can only come about if you add a new dimension to your life, the dimension of the "festive":

> [Meditation] is not work; it is play . . . in business the result is important. In festivity, the *act* is important . . . any moment can be a business moment; any moment can be a meditative moment. The difference is in attitude. If it is choiceless, if you are playing with it, then it is meditative.[10] (Italics mine)

It is precisely what Rajneesh calls the "festive" attitude—a free and playful spontaneity, doing things for their own sake—which is often condemned in our society. The old dictum "Satan finds mischief for idle hands to do" may be outdated, but its spirit lives on. It is not at all unusual for meditators to report that they feel they have no right to feel as "good" as they do when they are meditating, or afterward. It may even be frightening for them to feel happy and at peace. Such people may believe they stop meditating because of practical reasons, but the underlying cause usually becomes clear if you discuss their practice with them. Their attitude about meditation is quite different from that of those who stop meditating because they find it unpleasant—typically, they have nothing but praise for meditation.

People afraid to experience the fulfillment that meditation offers, often manage to put themselves into a position where it is impossible for them to meditate properly. One woman who had learned TM and claimed to enjoy it thoroughly, consistently complained that she could never obtain a peaceful meditation at home and therefore rarely meditated. On questioning, it turned out that when she did meditate it was always in the family room of her house at a time when her husband and children were present. A peaceful meditation under these conditions was impossible and by selecting this time and place for her meditation she was depriving herself of a fulfilling experience. She could have gone to her bedroom and locked the door, or she could have meditated in the early afternoon when she first returned from work to an empty house, or even late at night, but she did none of these things. What was more, she resisted any suggestion by her meditation teacher or friends that she handle her problems constructively. She was an intensely self-denying woman—meditation promised too much happiness.

The psychotherapists I know who use meditation with their patients have all reported observing certain patients who cannot tolerate the pleasantness of this state. Dr. Bernard Glueck, for example, has noticed that some patients in the Institute of Living study seemed unable to accept the pleasurable feelings which resulted from TM and that they frequently stopped meditating rather than face the guilt that this practice brought to them.[11]

Because meditation is so inherently pleasurable, certain people may even stop meditating in order to *punish* themselves. A TM meditator describes this process when she speaks of meditation as being a form of reward:

> It's the same way you would reward yourself with candy or whatever. . . . Meditation is gentle, it's a good thing, a journey within. But if you feel you've behaved badly, you will use meditation as a weapon and say to yourself "No! You will not go to meditate! You don't deserve it! You have no right to feel that good!" . . . You don't even meditate *badly* at such a time. *You don't meditate at all.* . . .[12]

The pleasure-giving aspects of meditation may also cause special anxieties in people who have been taught to feel guilty about masturbating. It is possible unconsciously to view meditation (an experience where one is alone and gives oneself pleasure) as a "forbidden" experience, similar to masturbation. For people with masturbation guilt, something all too common in our society, meditation may be avoided because when practiced it may now create *anxiety* rather than bring about relaxation.

If allowed to continue long enough, of course, meditation itself often helps to lessen even these deep-seated guilts, because it tends to reduce self-blame. If a person allows him or herself to keep meditating for months or years, the meditation may automatically lessen their guilt about enjoying life or about sexual fulfillment.‡

These are some of the reasons we have discovered so far for people dropping out of meditation. It is instructive to look at the research evidence on this subject. The only investigator to date who has studied this problem systematically has been Dr. Leon Otis of the Stanford Research Institute. His research suggests that those who start meditating and then quit may have very different personalities from those who stick with the practice.[13]

In the first part of Otis' study, questionnaires were sent to two groups of people who had previously learned TM—one chosen at random from IMS records, the other composed of TM teachers in training. In the second part of the study, the subjects were people who had volunteered to learn TM at the Stanford Research Insti-

‡ Of course it also may not do so. In this case, professional advice on handling these problems should be sought.

tute. The questionnaire used asked about a person's history in practicing TM, any physical or behavioral changes experienced since starting it, and any changes in basic aspects of personality that the meditator had noticed since commencing to meditate. The basic personality changes were judged from the words a person chose, from a long list, to describe him or herself.

The results of these studies showed that the dropouts from TM tended to think of themselves as withdrawn, irritable, and anxiety-ridden. They checked adjectives such as moody, worried, impatient, insecure, defensive, self-conscious, perplexed or "a loner type" to describe themselves.

People who had been in TM less than six months and who were still meditating, described themselves positively, however, and thought TM had helped them. They tended to see themselves as being excitable, prompt, zestful, self-controlled, ambitious and alert people.

The meditators who had been practicing TM consistently for eighteen months or more had still a different view of themselves. They described themselves as being peaceful, alert, determined, attractive, secure, self-confident, considerate, renewed, pleasant, candid, precise, and warm—very positive attributes indeed.

Is this because TM produced all these changes in the long term meditators, or did these two groups differ from each other even before they started learning TM? Otis's results suggest the possibility that it is only those people who are strongly attracted toward the calm way of life in the first place who will tend, once they commence meditation, to stick faithfully with the practice. More insecure or troubled people may abandon meditation, perhaps because it is not helping them or perhaps because they cannot assimilate the help it does have to offer. It certainly does not take as much dedication, strength of character, or predilection for a practice to continue to do it for six months or less, as it does to remain regularly with it for a year and a half or more; many people will start things, but relatively few stay faithfully with any discipline over a long period of time. Is this perhaps the reason why the six-months-or-less group showed such different personality characteristics from the long-term meditators?

The Otis study has shown that different people respond differently to meditation, stay with it different amounts of time, and report different benefits from it. His results, taken together with our clinical observations, suggest that no blanket statement is appropriate. To assume that everyone can, needs to, or even wants to meditate seems unwarranted. At the same time, it is becoming increasingly obvious that meditation is useful for many people.

15

The Misuse of Meditation

Blocks to meditating represent one type of problem with which all of us working with meditation must deal. An entirely different difficulty arises, however, when meditation *is* embraced, but for the wrong reasons, or when it is used in an undesirable fashion.

While some people shy away from meditation, others take it up with too much intensity. If twenty minutes twice a day is beneficial, then two or three or four hours of meditating per day should be correspondingly better—or so the reasoning goes. As with any therapeutic dosage, of course, this is not the case. If one pill is prescribed, taking the whole bottle is not a good idea.

While the proper meditation time may be highly beneficial, anything over that amount may have adverse effects. As we have seen, for *some* people, even fifteen or twenty minutes of meditating at one time is too much. When we speak of overmeditation, however, we mean a much longer amount of meditation. For the average person practicing practical meditation, this might be defined as meditating more than one hour a day for the first year, and after that for more than one hour at a single sitting, or more than two hours on the same day—keeping in mind the fact that the "safe" limit may be considerably lower than this for certain individuals.

As we have seen, tension-release during ordinary meditation can produce side effects which, at times, can make for difficulty if they are not regulated. If meditation is prolonged for a matter of hours this process of tension-release is magnified many times. When a person spends this much time meditating, powerful emotions and "primary process" (bizarre) thoughts may be released too rapidly to assimilate and the meditator may be forced into sudden confrontation with previously repressed aspects of him or herself for which he is not prepared. If he has a strong enough ego, or is doing the extra meditation under the supervision of an experienced teacher, he may weather such an upsurge of unconscious material and emerge triumphant. If he has a less strong ego or has a past history of emotional disturbance, he may be overwhelmed by it, fragile defenses may break down, and an episode of mental illness occur.

This eventuality is guarded against by most responsible teachers of meditation, who strictly limit the amount of time the meditator is advised to spend at his practice. IMS, for instance, insists that the practice of TM be limited to no more than two twenty-minute sessions daily; Benson gives the same directions for his method; and we similarly limit CSM. Those who choose to meditate against these explicit instructions are usually people with deep-seated personality problems who make use of meditation in a very special way.

Overmeditating seems to be similar to other forms of addiction. Studies of drug usage have shown that those who tend to *abuse* drugs, as opposed to those who simply *use* them, show many more signs of severe personality disturbance, social withdrawal, and the like. In the same way, those who consistently overmeditate, when studied psychiatrically, most often turn out to have a previous history of addiction to drugs or to have other psychiatric problems of a serious nature.[1] Taken in heavy doses in a person with an unstable background, meditation can be dangerous.

Problems from Overmeditation

The following anecdotes illustrate some of the difficulties which may arise from overmeditation. While these examples may seem severe in terms of the psychiatric symptoms involved, they are typical of the overmeditator. To my knowledge there is no such thing as a "mild case" of true overmeditation. When a person comes to the point where he or she is meditating many hours per day, on their own and without supervision, that person usually has quite a disturbed emotional adjustment. The people concerned here already had deeply troubling personality problems. Overmeditation increased these difficulties. It appeared to push these already disturbed people over the brink, as it were, precipitating a serious psychiatric condition.

Kaye was a withdrawn young woman who consulted me when she was already in a state of incipient mental breakdown, because she had heard that I was "sympathetic to meditation." She reported that she was losing her sense of identity and was haunted by sexual terrors. Her life was chaotic. She could barely handle the simplest practical tasks and shied away almost totally from contact with people.

Kaye's experience with meditation was based on a lifelong problem. She had been an extremely shy girl with a painful sense of inferiority about her own body, which she felt to be "deformed," although this was not in reality the case. Upon graduating from high school she had found refuge from the challenges of social life by entering a Zen retreat, where she lived for two years, undergoing strict training in zazen meditation. While living there, Kaye meditated at least four hours daily. At this same time she was forbidden to speak with anyone about the strong emotions that surfaced during her meditation. She was observing a partial vow of silence which prevented her from discussing topics other than superficial household tasks.

Despite the rigor of this routine, Kaye initially benefited from being at the retreat. An ulcerative colitis which she had previously suffered from disappeared entirely. She seemed relieved at being in a quiet, protective place where she did not have to face humiliating rejections from the outside world, and her tension level reduced accordingly.

Eventually, however, an emotional "bottleneck" began to develop. Intense feelings and stressful memories were rapidly surfacing during Kaye's long hours of meditation, which she could not discuss with anyone. Because of her enforced silence she was unable to receive social support for these painful emotions and became increasingly threatened by them as time went on. Finally she found herself with a cauldron of explosive conflicts which she could no longer handle. Meditation was continually bringing up new emotionally charged material which she could not assimilate rapidly enough.

At this point, Kaye fled from the Zen center and began to travel from city to city, temporarily living with roommates who were also Zen meditators. Each time when she inevitably failed to get along with her new roommates, she became more troubled. She continued to meditate many hours a day, but without the support of the Zen center, where she had felt cared for and protected, her defenses gradually broke down and serious psychiatric symptoms emerged. At this point her meditation was no longer calming her; it was *causing* anxiety. When in desperation she finally abandoned meditation, it was too late. The rapidly developing emotional breakdown continued.

Eventually Kaye admitted herself to a psychiatric hospital. She was experiencing racing thoughts which she could not control and was suffering from intense anxiety attacks. Following a brief hospitalization, she made an appointment to see me. I saw Kaye for a few sessions before referring her for more extensive treatment than I was able to offer. During these sessions she obtained relief from outbursts of emotion which were so intense that she would tremble violently, almost convulsively, while experiencing them.

Without talking it over with me (I would have advised against it) Kaye decided to try meditation again. She had not been meditating forty-five minutes, however, when she found herself once more becoming disoriented in her thinking and experienced rising panic. On the basis of this brief attempt, we were both able to agree that she was not yet ready to return to the practice. I recommended that if she should ever resume meditating, it would be wise to do so only in a very gradual fashion, probably meditating for no more than five or ten minutes a day, until she found herself fully able to tolerate a slightly longer time than this. This advice seemed to relieve her of conflict over whether or not to recommence meditation. From that point on she was able to plan for herself and was ready to enter into a constructive treatment program.

Although traditional zazen practices such as those Kaye followed are more rigorous than the simpler centering techniques, it is unlikely that it was the zazen teaching, per se, which caused Kaye's difficulty. Many people can use this method of meditation very beneficially. Her problem seemed to have arisen from an unfortunate combination of circumstances. This emotionally disturbed, intensely withdrawn young woman had been *over*meditating in a setting which did not permit her any relief from the accumulated tensions which almost inevitably surface from such long hours of meditation. She was forbidden to talk about her feelings and could achieve no understanding of them.

A person with a healthier personality than Kaye's might have meditated constructively even under such a strict regime, arriving at a socially withdrawn but adaptive mode of life. No doubt this often occurs in monasteries, retreats, and other similar settings. Even Kaye might have withstood this excessive meditation if she had had a chance to talk over her feelings regularly so that she could assimilate them. Or, on the other hand, if she had been exposed to meditation only in *small* daily doses she might have been able to adjust to it without becoming imbalanced.

Another instance of overmeditation occurred in a TM meditator who had been carefully instructed *not* to meditate more than twenty minutes twice a day. When Dudley contacted me for advice he reported a list of symptoms sufficiently distressing to cause almost anyone to panic. While physical and neurological examinations had shown that he had no identifiable diseases, he complained of dizziness, pressure in his head, physical "rushes" that would "go to his eyes, ears, nose, and throat," and an inability to tolerate bright lights. More distressing to him, however, was his feeling that people seemed "unreal" and only a reflection of his "own consciousness." He had an intense feeling of alienation and experienced a "tremendous gulf" between himself and others. He also could experience only what was in his immediate visual field; the back of a house did not "exist" for him unless he walked around to the other side and actually saw it. If a person left the room where he was, that person ceased to "exist" until he or she reappeared. The present felt eternal. When he went to sleep he felt he was "leaving" his body; and one night when he saw a horror movie on TV he vividly imagined, in fact was convinced, that, like the figure on the screen, he was carrying ice picks in his hand. He was terrified of what he might do with them.

The more Dudley meditated, the worse these symptoms became. When he contacted me he reported that he was regularly meditating three hours a day, *plus* repeating his mantra to himself throughout the day. What was particularly significant was that Dudley claimed he had not *realized* that he should not meditate this much. Since TM teachers repeatedly stress the proper amount of time for meditation in their lectures, this young man clearly had chosen to "selectively inattend" to what they were saying. For reasons of his own, he had apparently needed to escape into an oblivion created through overmeditating.

Some of Dudley's symptoms superficially resemble some of the positive experiences reported by mystics: the disappearance of time, the eternal moment, the sense of leaving the body, the reflection of one's own consciousness in the universe. In certain circumstances these experiences are *under the control of* the person having them and are welcomed as positive occurrences, part of spiritual development. In Dudley's case, however, no amount of guidance from meditation teachers could change his chaotic experience into a conscious, positive one. He was reporting compulsive symptoms, perhaps unconsciously "borrowed" from the reports of mystically inclined people, but used for his own maladaptive purposes. They were out of his control and consistently negative.

Dudley's background emerged during the diagnostic interview. He was an "only child" still living at home with his parents at age twenty-seven and apparently closely tied to his mother. Because of this, he was unable to leave home to go to a professional school of his choice. For many years numerous personality problems had prevented him from growing up emotionally and treatment with such therapies as behavior modification and hypnosis had been to no avail. While the specific symptoms that Dudley was now experiencing were apparently *released* by overmeditation, their basic cause seems to have been the disturbed adjustment which he had had all his life. Dudley and his mother had carried on continuous psychological warfare against his father, who appeared to be the scapegoat in a triangle. The more symptoms Dudley developed, the greater his emotional stranglehold on his mother, and the greater his guilt toward his father, who was supposed to be "unsympathetic" to Dudley's many ills and to his "lack of initiative" at age twenty-seven. At night Dudley would often experience such rage against his sleeping father that he feared he might harm him.

To cope with his growing rage, frustration, and shame, Dudley had begun to "bury" himself in meditation as one might lose oneself in a drug. Obviously an intelligent man, he must have known that he should not overmeditate in that fashion, but had chosen to do this until he was literally flooded by unpleasant symptoms. When he consulted me he had recently stopped meditating entirely (a decision which I advised him to stick to) but his symptoms continued to worsen as the time to leave home and enroll in a professional school in a distant city rapidly approached. Dudley's main problem at this point appeared to be the separation anxiety which he was experiencing—he knew he would soon have to leave his mother. Coupled with this was his deep guilt at his childlike dependency on his mother and his intense hostility toward his father.

Dudley is typical of those who consistently overmeditate. His symptoms seemed to stem not so much from meditation in and of itself as from the neurotic *misuse* of meditation. When he was challenged in a single diagnostic interview to face some of the basic issues which were underlying his problem, his symptoms temporarily became much less intense. His sense of time returned and his orientation in space and sense of reality were almost entirely reinstated by the end of two hours of conversation with the therapist.

While overmeditation seems to have paved the way for Dudley's emotional disturbance, it cannot be said to have actually *caused* it, considering the ease with which, temporarily at least, his symptoms cleared up with insight. What his case teaches us is the necessity for probing deeply into the causes of excessive over-meditation. The chances are that overmeditation will be found to reflect deep emotional problems. These problems must be treated in order to effect a permanent cure for whatever symptoms arise.

This is an important point to bear in mind, because some forms of meditation presently in vogue in the West require that their followers meditate for long periods of time each day. The Divine Light Mission of "Maharaj"* J:, for example, requires a minimum of two hours of formal meditation daily from its devotees, plus the sporadic use of centering techniques throughout the rest of the day. The members of the International Society for Krishna Consciousness spend two to three hours chanting the "Hare Krishna" when awakening in the morning and follow this by additional sessions of chanting at various points throughout the day. Other groups such as the Unification Church of Sun Myung Moon also encourage similar intensive meditation-like activities in their followers. The growing influence of such "supercults" raises a number of questions about the social implications of these movements, their potential political and religious use or misuse, and the possibility of economic exploitation of followers who have been confused and rendered highly suggestible by overmeditation.

Obviously overmeditation on a wide scale can have serious consequences. In this book we are discussing the *practical* forms of meditation however, which, when properly followed, are used in moderation by regular practitioners. Teachers of some forms of practical meditation such as TM are, however, periodically required to attend residence courses where intensive regimes of meditation (up to several hours a day) are required for periods of six or more weeks at a time. Because of this, an occasional TM teacher has been known to suffer a mental breakdown requiring hospitalization either during or shortly after completion of their training. Several such cases have been called to my professional attention. In light of the heavy meditational requirement for TM

---

* The term "Maharaj" is placed in quotes for the same reason the term "Maharishi" is placed in quotes (See Note 8, Chapter 1).

teacher trainees, it would seem that a decision to become a TM *teacher* should be weighed carefully, just as a decision to undertake any other regime requiring extensive meditation must be thoughtfully investigated.

In light of the temptation to overmeditate in certain susceptible individuals and the potential risk involved for their mental health if such a person were to do so, it is essential for anyone thinking of joining a movement which includes meditation as part of its program to inquire about the amount of time he or she will be asked to spend daily in this practice. The prospective meditator may also want to look carefully at many more aspects of any purportedly "spiritual" movement they are thinking of joining to make certain their own personal liberty and freedom of thought will be preserved. Responsible training programs offering intensive meditation should supply low pressure, *noncoercive*, and supportive retreats where each participant is free to remain fully in command of their own life, to make their own decisions, and to come and go as they wish. To make certain of the noncoercive atmosphere of any large scale "spiritual" training program may take careful investigation since a number of the more notorious organizations now recruit through "front" organizations with names that are unknown and seemingly innocuous. A wise procedure for anyone who is considering attending a preliminary meeting of such an organization is first to read about the organization and their strategies from a viewpoint different from that advanced by the organization itself. A reliable source of information on this is the Ted Patrick book *Let Our Children Go!* Although it is written in a popular style, this book accurately describes the highly questionable tactics of the supercults with respect to the civil liberties and the mental and physical health of their practitioners, and it supplies valuable names and details.† A preliminary investigation of any cult's background has, it seems, become crucial if one's personal safety and mental health are to be safeguarded.

Even in the most unpressured and genuinely supportive retreat, however, as with Kaye described above, catastrophes sometimes arise, and the addition of an adequate clinical staff of trained

† Ted Patrick, *Let Our Children Go!*, New York: E. P. Dutton & Co, 1976.

mental health professionals appears essential for such programs. Because at present professionally trained assistance does not exist, however, in any of the intensive meditational programs that I know of, the decision to enter any group requiring large amounts of meditation requires careful thought. The small, decentralized meditation settings, where considerable personal guidance is afforded each trainee by a highly qualified guide or teacher, are usually preferable to the mass organizations.

These considerations do not ordinarily apply to the practical forms of meditation undertaken by the average person however. Practical meditation may add an important dimension to our lives, but it does not become a way of life. For this reason it seems to be the only type of meditation appropriate for use along with formal psychotherapy as this is used in the West. Whether, however, it can be considered a form of therapy in its *own right* is the question we will look at next.

16

A Therapist's View

"Psychotherapy," in some form or another, has been universally employed by human beings throughout the ages. Every person who tries to console a despairing friend or help a panicky child become calm is, in a sense, practicing psychotherapy—he or she is using psychological means to restore the emotional balance of another person. These common, everyday methods are based on some attempt to understand the problem, at least on an intuitive level, even though they may lack scientific sophistication. Psychotherapy, as a formal discipline, is different only in that it is systematic and practiced according to established principles which are based on our present knowledge of human nature. Psychotherapy is the formalization of the "helping hand."

There are a number of different forms of psychotherapy but in general they all have certain goals in common: to help the person become more mature, competent, effective, and be able to enjoy life more. These goals are not necessarily easy to achieve. An individual's confused views about him or herself in relation to the world or their unhealthy ways of looking at their own self are often the end product of painfully disturbed parent-child relationships, reinforced later by years of unsatisfactory life experiences. We cannot expect a psychotherapist to step in and in a short period of time undo the entire past history of the patient. Psychotherapy is, however, often effective, particularly if the patient is anxious to co-operate in a program for his or her own improvement.

The goals for psychotherapy may differ according to the person, their needs, and which forms of psychotherapy they choose. "Psychodynamic" psychotherapy seeks to resolve fundamental inner conflicts which are often unconscious and to help the patient to change on a deep level. Behavior modification therapy, as its name implies, often seeks to change only specific *behaviors* with the remainder of the personality left unaltered. Both approaches have distinct value and sometimes the two may be used in a supplementary fashion. There are other forms of psychotherapy, but the most frequently used are the "dynamic" and "behavioral" approaches just described.

To understand where and how meditation can contribute to any of these therapies we must answer two questions: How "deep" are the changes brought about by meditation, and is meditation *itself* a form of psychotherapy?

How Deep Does Meditation Go?

A study conducted at Princeton University by Christopher Ross and Hilary Brown investigated a group of TM meditators and a group of students who regularly practiced Progressive Relaxation.[1] They compared these "regular practicers" with a group of students who rarely or never practiced these same techniques. The question they sought to answer was whether regular meditation and/or relaxation leads to changes in the content of people's dreams. Dreams were chosen because they tend to be a very stable measure of personality; that is, they reflect basic conflicts and coping mechanisms which remain the same over long periods of time. In a study conducted by psychologist Calvin Hall, for example, one man's dreams collected over a fifty-year period, from early adulthood to death, were studied to see how consistent his dream content was over the years. Hall found that each dream category which he studied remained essentially unchanged for fifty years![2] In studying the dreams of other individuals, Hall also found that whenever a significant change in dream content *was* apparent, this generally represented a similarly profound change in the individual's behavior and personality. In other words, dream life does not easily change.

Ross and Brown decided that meditators' dreams might be a good way to find out if meditation can change a person's underlying personality. As we have seen, many kinds of changes have been reported in meditators over periods of only three months. These researchers set out to study changes over this same time period, but this time on a deeper level. They began by collecting a two-week daily dream diary from these subjects before they had learned their techniques of TM or progressive relaxation, and another such diary after they had been practicing their respective techniques for three months. The subjects also kept daily mood checklists during the study.

The researchers then scored the dreams for forty-eight different aspects, or "variables," which ranged from such simple characteristics as the number of characters in the dream or amount of verbal or physical aggression, to the presence of anxiety, self-reflection, bizarre imagery, or "environmental threat"—among others.

What Ross and Brown found was that the overwhelming majority of these dream scores showed no change whatever, either in the regular meditators and regular progressive relaxers or in the group that did not practice their techniques regularly at all. This occurred even though a number of the subjects reported *feeling* much better on follow-up questionnaires. The regular practicers, however, scored considerably "less anxious" on a written test which measured their level of anxiety and their daily mood checklists showed that they were "happy" much more often than they used to be before practicing meditation.

What does this mean? Did nothing happen to these subjects after they commenced to meditate or relax regularly? Does the lack of change in their dreams mean that those dramatic improvements in the lives of meditators which are so often reported to us may just be "all in the imagination"?

Decidedly not. Something *had* happened to those subjects who had practiced their techniques regularly; they were both less anxious and happier. Despite these changes, however, regular meditation and relaxation left untouched other *deeper* levels of their personalities. Their dreams and a test which reflects underlying personality dynamics by asking subjects to make up stories about pictures (the TAT) showed no changes at all over the three months. A test measuring changes in self-image—the way people tend to view themselves—also remained unchanged over the course of the study.[3]

As indicated previously, other studies *have* shown changes with meditation on tests measuring self-actualization, field independence, and other aspects of personality. None of these studies, however, employed the "projective techniques" which measure deeper layers of the personality, or dreams. The work of Ross and Brown and of Zevin (using the TAT)[4] suggests that it is these *deeper* levels of personality which often resist change through meditation.

We have noticed the same kind of limitations seen in the Princeton study, with our meditating patients. Since my husband and I have been publishing articles on meditation, patients who are long-term meditators have frequently come to us seeking therapists familiar with meditation. Some of these people have had years of intensive practice in one or another of the commonly used meditation techniques and some have even been teachers of meditation.

We have found that often these long-term meditators report they became more emotionally responsive, tranquil, insightful, and energetic after commencing meditation. Despite these gains, however, when they came to us they were still carrying disabling emotional burdens. They came for treatment because of unresolved emotional conflicts revolving around such problems as sexual adjustment, social responsibility, emotional maturity, marriage, and career, and because of various disturbing symptoms. In other words, although they had changed through intensive practice of meditation in *certain* important respects, they had not changed in others.

Some other experimental evidence bears on this question. Its results are in agreement with Ross and Brown and our clinical observations. When Dr. Leon Otis of the Stanford Research Institute administered personality tests to TM meditators and to a control group of nonmeditators who were signed up to learn the technique, he discovered that TM had no discernible effects on self-image over the year's test period for those people who continued to practice it in his experiment.[5] Otis concluded that the data "supports the notion that TM does not alter basic personality characteristics," a conclusion quite in line with that of the Princeton study.

Just as the latter found that *certain* behavior and moods did change with meditation, however, so in his study Otis also found that the TM group ranked significantly higher in enjoyment of life, restfulness of sleep, happiness, energy level, sexual adjustment, and creativity than did the control group. These changes occurred despite the fact that *deeper* personality characteristics seemed to show no difference.

Taken together, the research studies and clinical observations suggest that while the effects of meditation can be impressive, it is doubtful whether meditation can change personality in any basic sense. To effect truly deep change meditation may need to become part of a more general change in the way one lives one's life. However, practical meditation does reduce tension and improve functioning on a number of levels. This may lead to some startling changes in behavior and in the way the meditator views themself even if deep-seated emotional problems remain untouched. A patient with whom I worked at the East Brunswick Guidance Clinic illustrates this dual action of meditation. She was immensely helped by meditation, which seemed to supplement her psychotherapy, but at the same time remained unchanged in at least one basic aspect of her personality.

When Elvira came for psychotherapy she was in her mid-thirties. At that time, she was both depressed and highly anxious. She had had the sole responsibility of raising five children since her divorced husband had defaulted in child support. She was receiving welfare and three of the children were already showing severe emotional problems, her oldest son refusing outright to attend school.

Almost from the first Elvira responded to psychotherapy. Once she knew she could count on the assistance of an interested therapist she was able to use her intelligence and basic strength to begin to cope. Eventually she returned successfully to work, voluntarily removing herself from the welfare roles with a sense of pride. She was not only able to support her children and deal with them with less stress and anxiety, but her depression had lifted entirely.

One troublesome problem did remain, however. Elvira had been unable to resolve a generally destructive relationship with an emotionally disturbed lover. This unstable man was extremely possessive of her and acted more like another child in the household than an additional adult. He was intensely jealous of any attention she gave to her own children, drank heavily, and on several occasions threatened her and her family with violence. At one point he was admitted to a psychiatric hospital, where he remained for several weeks.

For some time Elvira had felt she must end this relationship for her own safety and that of the children, but she was unable to think seriously about doing this without starting to weep uncontrollably. She experienced intense guilt when she thought of "throwing him out."

As her therapy proceeded, she became much less willing to tolerate her lover's bullying behavior and experienced a growing conflict between her newfound personal dignity and her continuing dependence on his presence. At this point, she became unusually tense and on several occasions alarmed herself by drinking so heavily that she blacked out and later could not remember what had happened during the time she was drinking, something that had never occurred before. I felt it important to arrest further development of the drinking and suggested to her that she learn TM as a possible means of reducing the tension that was building up. Elvira was enthusiastic about the idea. She particularly hoped it would help her with her severe insomnia. She was now getting only three to four hours of fitful sleep per night.

Meditation was almost immediately effective. She looked peaceful, almost glowing when she came to her next therapy session after initiation, and within a few days of commencing meditation she slept restfully for a whole night. Since that time, her sleep has remained excellent even during periods when she has had to face high stress.

Her sporadic drinking stopped immediately following commencement of meditation and was never again a problem. Unexpectedly, she also lost any sense of urgency about smoking marijuana, which she had formerly used daily. She also found herself forgetting to buy regular cigarettes for herself or to smoke them when they were present in her home. In addition, she had more composure and calm at work and was experiencing a generally quieter, more understanding relationship with her children. Her most notable change, however, was her marked growth in independence. After her first three weeks of meditation, she firmly ordered her lover out of the house, despite his protests and threats, and arranged for police assistance in the event he should become violent. She then followed through with her plan to make him leave without her accustomed guilt and self-recrimination. She felt appropriate grief after he left—this had been a long-lasting and close relationship—but despite this, slept peacefully throughout the night, and attributed her ability to carry through with this decision directly to meditation.

Although some months later Elvira was reunited with this lover, this time their relationship was on a different footing. She was now more independent, having in the interim built up a number of outside activities, interests, and relationships which she would not give up and she now insisted upon her rights and those of her children. Despite this fact, however, it is clear that meditation was unable to change the underlying personality dynamics which led Elvira to select such a disturbed individual to begin with. Meditation had both "succeeded" and "failed." It had changed Elvira importantly in some respects and left her the same in others.

Is Meditation Psychotherapy?

Psychiatrist Harold Bloomfield, who is a trained teacher of TM working closely with the World Plan Organization, quotes TM's founder, "Maharishi" Mahesh Yogi, as saying that with psychi-

atric patients who regularly meditate, the role of the psychotherapist becomes one of "holding the patient's hand while TM
does the healing."[6] Dr. Bloomfield himself seems to subscribe to
this point of view although he sees dispensing drugs as an additional means for controlling more serious forms of psychiatric illness, and the occasional use of behavioral techniques and some
short-term marriage counseling (along with TM) as useful.[7]

Criticizing psychoanalysis and therapies derived from it in
which insight and the understanding of one's deeper conflicts are
fundamental, Bloomfield suggests that TM "may prove some ana-
lytically oriented techniques unnecessary"[8] and suggests that talking with a therapist about problems may even be "futile or counterproductive."[9] It is better, he feels, that a patient "move beyond
concern with previous problems to enjoy growth in the present
through the uplifting experience of *pure awareness*" (italics
mine)*[10] In support of such a concept he quotes TM's founder,
"Maharishi" Mahesh Yogi, as stating that rather than "digging
into the mud of a miserable past," one's vision should be enlarged
to "the genius and the brightness of man's inner *creative intelligence*" (italics mine).†[11] Bloomfield summarizes his position by
saying that essentially what a psychiatric patient needs from a psychotherapist is "only encouragement to meditate regularly and to
engage in dynamic activity. Once a patient becomes established in
this growth-rhythm, his need for psychiatric care may diminish
sharply."[12]

The picture Bloomfield paints for TM and its effectiveness as a
psychotherapy in its own right is a glowing one. Unfortunately,
however, it does not agree with the experience of a number of
other mental health professionals. Since my articles on the use of
meditation in psychotherapy have appeared in professional journals, psychotherapists from many different disciplines and parts of

---

* "Pure awareness" is a term for a state of objectless thought said to be obtained when a person "transcends" during the practice of TM and thereby
contacts the ultimate unchanging reality or "absolute field of pure Being."[13]
† "Creative intelligence" is a term used by TM teachers to refer to the Hindu
concept of the Absolute, or Brahman, the essential constituent of creation
which permeates all things, as this essential Being manifests itself in *prana*
(universal energy, the "motivating force of creation").[14]

the world have contacted me, volunteering information about their experiences with meditating patients. I have observed a consistency in their accounts. Almost all of these people were very encouraging about the possibilities of using meditation along with psychotherapy and have recommended it to their patients. None felt, however, that meditation was a substitute for psychotherapy; that it was effective for every patient; or that its use was invariably without problems; and none of these therapists were as impressed by its "cure-all" properties as the psychiatrists who work closely with the TM organization. With rare exceptions, they did not find that all that was necessary was to sit by and "hold the patient's hand" or dispense supplementary drugs, while meditation did the work.

Although, combined with psychotherapy, meditation can be an excellent means of helping a patient, I will not recommend it to any seriously disturbed person who is not simultaneously undergoing psychotherapy. While it *may* be effective as a sole treatment, in some instances it creates difficulties for emotionally disturbed people because of the unusually intense stress-release that such an individual may undergo. It is therefore desirable for such a person to be under the care of a trained psychotherapist while adjusting to meditation.

By this I do not mean that people who are tense or anxious or who suffer from a stress-related illness such as hypertension, may not get relief from meditation without simultaneously being in psychotherapy, or that they should not necessarily try it provided of course they remain under medical care for their physical ailment. I am speaking, rather, of people who suffer from serious psychiatric symptoms: depressions, phobias, addictions to drugs or alcohol, and other emotional disorders which require professional help. It is such people who may be a "high risk" group with respect to meditation and who should approach learning it with caution and common sense. They should be under the care of a qualified psychotherapist, should discuss their decision to learn meditation with him or her, and should *under*meditate until they and their therapist are certain the experience is benefiting them. If necessary they should also have the wisdom to stop meditating altogether if it appears that this practice is not indicated. With such precautions, they should run little risk from trying meditation and stand to gain considerable relief if it turns out to be effective for them.

My clinical observations in this respect are instructive. Over the past several years I have been consulted by a number of patients with a previous history of severe psychiatric disturbance who had happened to learn TM at a time when they were not in psychotherapy. By "severe" I mean that these people had a past history of such disturbed behavior as being a recluse for many years, living in a fantasy world where "evil forces" were feared, or had shown other evidence of serious emotional disturbance. By no means had all of them had psychiatric breakdowns requiring hospitalization, however, and many of them had never before sought psychotherapy for their problems.

These patients reported to me that disturbing psychiatric symptoms had appeared soon after they had commenced meditation, or that previous symptoms were reactivated by meditation. Three of them suffered complete mental breakdowns for which they had to be hospitalized within a matter of weeks after commencing the practice of meditation. Each attributed the breakdown to meditation, and as far as I could discern, none of them had been *over*-meditating at that time. They reported that they had not meditated more than the prescribed twenty minutes twice daily and their TM teachers later confirmed these observations. Even this moderate meditation time had apparently been too much for them. They seemed to be abnormally "sensitive" to meditation, and unable to take it even in average doses.

It is of course possible that immediate reduction in the amount of time they were asked to meditate per day, together with simultaneous psychotherapy, might have enabled these people to cope with their meditation without developing a severe psychiatric condition. On the other hand, it may be that a psychotherapist who had experience with meditation would have advised them to stop meditating entirely at this point in their lives and been correct in doing so. In any event, meditation by itself certainly did not serve as a therapy in these instances.

Our present clinical experience suggests therefore that while the changes brought about by meditation are often genuinely therapeutic, they are also incomplete, and because of the occasional undesirable side effects, meditation used *by itself* as a form of treatment for psychiatric disorders is undesirable. Conventional psychotherapy can, of course, at times be incomplete too and it may be that the combination of psychotherapy *plus* meditation will be found to be more effective in many instances than either technique used alone. A study by psychologists Leah Dell Dick and Robert Ragland at the University of Oklahoma showed that people who obtained counseling from a student mental health center responded better to a *combination* of meditation and psychological counseling, than they did either to meditation *alone* or to counseling alone.‡[15]

The Meditating Therapist

Quite apart from any effects that meditation may have on patients, several of my meditating psychotherapist colleagues and myself have noticed changes in our work *with* patients after we commenced meditation.

We have experienced personal benefits from practicing meditation which have no doubt contributed indirectly to our professional skills, but our methods of *dealing* with patients have changed too. Several of us, my husband and myself included, have noticed that our ability to sense patients' moods has sharpened since we commenced meditating. We are also more effortlessly aware of their deeper struggles and unconscious conflicts. My husband, Dr. Ephron, has had the experience of watching his meditation sessions actually assist him directly in his work. On a number of occasions when he had been particularly puzzled about a certain patient's problem, he found that during his next meditative session after seeing the patient, he experienced vivid mental imagery. When studied later on, these imagined scenes turned out to contain new and accurate insights into the patient's difficulties.

‡ Psychotherapists interested in using meditation with patients will find further information in Appendix.

Often they contained an answer to a problem which had been baffling.

One young woman was unable to work out a deep-seated problem relating to her fiancé. She left my husband's office on a particular day frustrated because she could not understand her compulsion to attack her lover, whom in many ways she loved and whom she felt she genuinely wanted to marry. During his own meditation session later that afternoon, although not consciously thinking about this patient and her problem, Dr. Ephron visualized King Lear surrounded by two of his daughters; the daughters in the scene were being destructive and exploitive toward their father. As in the play by Shakespeare, they had reduced him to rags and to madness. While still meditating, the name of this patient flashed into his mind and the scene seemed to be a symbolic statement of her problem. Perhaps, he thought, this young woman, together with her divorcée mother, had deliberately tried to exploit the girl's wealthy father and use his riches for their own needs. Could the fact that she had never faced her own guilt at her destructive exploitation of her father be one of the causes of this young woman's present discomfort in the presence of men, and of her defensive need to attack *them* as though *they* were the "monsters?"

During her next psychotherapy session, he explored this by asking her whether she and her mother had ever treated her father as though he were, in effect, like King Lear. The patient was startled at the wording of the question, replying that her father had often complained to her mother and to herself by saying: "*I feel like King Lear* in this house." This information led to a productive session in which the patient could, for the first time, examine the validity of her father's complaints that he was being treated badly in his own home. By doing this, she was able to explore the manner in which she had developed her own exploitive patterns and how they were still contaminating her relationships—both toward her father and toward other men in her life, including her fiancé, a young man of great wealth.

On the occasions when meditation brings about this kind of insight into a patient's problems, the free-floating attention of the meditative state makes it possible for the therapist to combine his or her previous observations of the patient in such a way that a creative insight emerges. This is much like other creative syntheses in the meditative state which lead to artistic achievement or scientific discovery.

Several of us in psychotherapeutic work have also noticed that our ability to understand the symbols in a patient's dreams and to help the patient deal constructively with these symbols has increased since we have been meditating. It is as though we ourselves were now more comfortable with this "primary process" material since it is often the type of material that the meditative state brings about. Another difference is our increased "staying power." When patients' appointments follow one another in a long succession over the course of the day, we now have less of a tendency to become fatigued or drowsy from work stress, an occupational hazard in the "sitting professions."

Psychotherapists are also at times called upon to face severe bursts of hostility from patients. Expression of such hostility can be a useful, even necessary part of the treatment for the patient, but may be stressful for the therapist, particularly if the patient's angry outburst is unexpected. My husband and I have found that since we have been meditating, our ability to cope with such negative reactions on the part of patients has improved. I, for example, will no longer feel as threatened by a patient's sudden outburst; it is as though I were now "cushioned" from it. I therefore have a more balanced and constructive attitude toward what the patient is doing. This seems to be an extension of my generally greater tolerance for irritating or potentially upsetting situations which has developed since commencing meditation.

Meditation may also foster the kind of "evenly suspended attention" when listening to patients in psychotherapy that Freud considered essential to psychotherapists. Freud pointed out that deliberate attention to what the patient is saying during treatment may actually prevent a deeper understanding of the real meaning of his or her comments.[16] Instead of actively listening, he therefore advised the psychotherapist to "turn his own unconscious like a receptive organ toward the transmitting unconscious of the patient." As we have seen, the nondirected goalless state achieved during meditation brings about a greater than usual openness to inner and outer impressions and an increased awareness of emotional reactions. Perhaps meditation might be considered an exercise designed to strengthen the very "psychic muscles" necessary to achieve Freud's ideal state of evenly suspended attention.

This aspect of meditation seems to be related to what psychologist Terry Lesh discovered when she studied the effects of meditation on clinical psychology students studying to be psychological counselors. Empathy (that is, the ability to "feel with" another person as though his or her feelings were your own) cannot really be taught, yet it is essential for good psychotherapy. Lesh wondered whether meditation might improve the capacity of future psychologists to empathize with their patients.

She chose to study the effects of zazen meditation on the development of empathy. What she found was that empathetic ability significantly improved in those counselors who reguarly practiced meditation during the course of the study, and either did not improve or got worse in the two groups of psychological counselor trainees who did *not* practice meditation.[17] Lesh's study and our own observations have led us to think that learning meditation might be a valuable addition to their standard training for students entering the mental health professions.[18]

With respect to the relationship between meditation and psychotherapy, I would suggest that meditation can be a most useful partner to psychotherapy, but that this alliance seems to work best when it is a partnership in the true sense of the word—each discipline supplementing the other.

IV

Explaining Meditation

A Governing Apparatus

Evidence with respect to meditation's effectiveness is impressive; it seems to be a powerful method for changing certain aspects of personality. We now need to ask where this power comes from. What is meditation's "secret?"

In trying to understand why meditation has the pervasive effects it does, we seem to be watching many different streams flow into a river whose potential force can be explained only by the totality of its waters. Many factors converge in meditation, lending to it their combined power, something that is above and beyond the effects of any single component.

To understand why meditation works we are in somewhat the position of the three blind men in the familiar folk tale, who tried to find out what an elephant "was" by using their sense of touch alone. The first man came back to report that he knew what an elephant was, it was a *great pillar* (he had felt its leg). The second reported that he was certain he knew what it was, it was a *rough carpet flapping in the breeze* (he had felt its ear). The third reported that he had cleared up the matter—an elephant was a new piece of weaponry—a *curved lance* (he had felt its tusk). All of the men were partially right. All were wrong. The elephant "was" neither his leg, his ear, nor his tusk, although these were all legitimately parts of him.

It is the same with meditation. While we may consider various explanations for its effectiveness we need to remember that meditation is something quite different from any one of these and that our limited understanding will give us only part answers. We will start with the theory that meditation acts as a governing apparatus which maintains a natural balance in terms of the amount of stimulation we respond to at any given time.*

Meditation as Sensory Deprivation

All forms of meditation shut out the external world to a greater or lesser extent. When meditating we withdraw from distracting sights, sounds, and other sense impressions which ordinarily bombard us. This is done by focusing our attention somewhere else—usually upon a single unchanging or reptitive stimulus. Meditation might even be described in part as a form of self-imposed "sensory deprivation," as if, every time we meditated, we entered an "isolation chamber" of our own making.

While this comparison may seen obvious, it raises some questions. Sensory deprivation, at least in its extreme forms, is by no means considered desirable in all instances. There is a good deal of evidence which indicates that being seriously deprived of external input or stimulation can be painfully disorganizing, and sometimes even dangerous to survival. Long before our modern experiments on perceptual deprivation, people learned that sensory isolation imposes severe stress. Solitary confinement has been a major punishment throughout history and the accounts of people changing under these circumstances, "losing their minds," or suddenly becoming "willing to talk" are familiar. People placed alone in a monotonous environment without human contact for long periods of time may go insane, and animals will show similar kinds of withdrawal, regression, and possibly eventual death under these circumstances.

While these undesirable effects had long been known, it was not until the 1950s that experimental evidence began to accumulate about the need for living beings to have sensory input. The

* The expression "governing apparatus" is used as Webster's describes a "governor"—a contrivance giving automatic control (as of pressure or temperature)," except that in this case a *psychobiological* balancing process is referred to.

first important research in this area began at McGill University in Canada.[1] There researchers set about constructing an artificial environment called an "isolation chamber," which reduced sensory stimulation to a minimum, and then studied people's reactions to being placed in it for varying lengths of time. Later on, a number of other researchers also constructed such chambers. Each experimental setup differed slightly, but they all had in common a "soundproofed" room (no room is completely soundproof but these approximated it) and some way of shutting out patterned vision.

In the McGill experiments the chamber was dimly lit but the subjects wore translucent goggles which prevented them from seeing forms or shapes of any kind. In some of the other laboratories the room was completely dark. In almost all of the experiments the sense of touch was reduced to a bare minimum; subjects wore gloves, kept their arms and legs in cardboard cylinders to eliminate touch sensations, and were told to move as little as possible. In one series of experiments conducted by neurophysiologist John Lilly, subjects were kept immersed in a tank of water to reduce sensation even further.[2]

What effect does such a radical cutting off of the ordinary varieties of sensory input have on people? It seems that several things can happen, but just what depends on the particular person and the circumstances of isolation.

In the McGill experiments, the first thing most subjects did was go to sleep. After awakening, they often sang to themselves or clapped the cardboard cylinders together or played mental word games. This "trying to keep occupied" phase was described as being increasingly unpleasant and following it the subjects tended to enter a different kind of mental state. Then thinking often became disorganized and rambling, and vivid images appeared. These were usually similar to presleep "hypnagogic" images. Sometimes, however, they were "as real as life" and could be considered hallucinations. Many of the subjects reported this phase of their experience as being "like a dream while awake." The subjects might "see" rows of little men marching or people skiing down slopes, or they might "hear" things such as a music box tinkling or a voice speaking to them. Some subjects had sensations of bodily strangeness such as a feeling that their mind "seemed to be a ball of cotton wool floating above my body."[3]

The McGill experimenters found that the subjects became more and more unstable as the experiment proceeded. They were either ecstatically pleased over insignificant things or unusually upset by them. When they finally emerged from the isolation chamber they seemed dazed and objects often appeared two-dimensional. Colors were apt to appear far deeper and more intense than normal, and a number of subjects said that their thinking was confused, and reported headaches, mild nausea, and fatigue. These symptoms often lasted up to twenty-four hours. Directly after the experiment the subjects generally showed a sharp drop in their scores on tests of reasoning, indicating a temporary fall-off in intellectual capacity.

On the basis of a long series of such experiments, the McGill investigators concluded that their research provided direct evidence for a kind of dependence of man on his environment that had not been previously recognized. It seems that people cannot function in a logical, directed, integrated manner without a constant stream of sensory input. Since our nervous system is a receiver as well as a sender, if it has nothing to *receive*, then it may be thrown out of gear.

Just how it will be affected, however, depends on the amount of stimulation still remaining. No experimental laboratory has as yet succeeded in depriving a human being *entirely* of stimulation. Some sense impressions are always perceived by the person, even if these are minimal impressions of touch, taste, or smell. The studies done so far have only been able to *reduce* the intensity of stimulation, and to monotonize the environment. Usually they give some form of repetitive, unvarying stimulation to the person so that he or she experiences a constant sameness of input. In the McGill experiments, this monotony or sameness consisted of low illumination and constant noise from the ventilating system and there were no effective precautions against sudden large body movements which occasionally provided some stimulation. In some of the experiments after McGill, such as Lilly's water immersion tank, there was a greater reduction of sensory input—total darkness and floating in body temperature water—which reduced almost all touch sensations, but there was still some sensations from occasional movements of the water, leakage of sound into the tank and other uncontrollable factors. Nevertheless, some of these later experiments differed from the McGill ones in being *relatively* free of stimulation and there are apparently some differences between these two types of experiment in terms of their effects.

The most excessive symptoms, such as severe disorganization of thought and hallucinations, are interestingly enough produced by *monotonous stimulation* rather than by the near elimination of all stimulation. When stimulation is all but totally eliminated, thought distortion and hallucinations tend to taper off and finally stop and the person enters an almost stuporous condition where he or she is largely nonreactive. It is as if the sending and receiving apparatus had temporarily gone out of commission under these conditions. As soon as enough light is reintroduced, however, so that it can be seen through diffusing goggles, or if a steady monotonous sound is reintroduced, then the hallucinations are likely to return.[4]

This finding may shed some light on how the meditative state works. Meditation, like the McGill experiments, reduces stimulation well below ordinary daytime levels but it does not reduce it *totally*; some monotonous form of stimulation still continues. In meditation this may be the repetition of the mantra over and over again; staring at one unchanging object; ritual gestures; attending to one's breathing; and so forth. The sensory deprivation experiments suggest that the most effective way to change our pattern of thinking is to create a monotonous stimulation which does not have much "meaning" to it. This is exactly what meditation appears to do.

While the practical forms of meditation, and the McGill type of isolation where some unpatterned sensory input is still allowed, are quite similar, the withdrawn state of samadhi is a different matter. Samadhi appears similar to the near total elimination of sensory input obtained in some of the more radical sensory deprivation experiments. If, as has been suggested by psychologist Charles Brownfield,[5] eliminating sensory input almost entirely simply puts the sending and receiving apparatus out of commission, this might explain why the mental state of samadhi is reported to be so different from that of ordinary meditation. The bodily distortions, visions, unusual sensations, or fragmented thoughts which arise during the less strenuous kinds of meditation are said to be left behind in samadhi and the experience is that of a "great void." The mental apparatus, as we know it, appears to be in a condition of suspended animation during this state.

The *effects* of the monotonous, unpatterned stimulation of the McGill type of sensory isolation chamber are also similar to the *effects* of meditation. Meditators frequently report vivid dreamlike imagery (although this rarely achieves the vividness of hallucinations unless they have been meditating for very long periods of time at one sitting). Meditators also frequently report distortions of body image; that their thinking has become much looser in its organization (almost uncontrolled); and that they are experiencing intense emotions during meditation. But if meditation and sensory isolation can produce similar effects, why then is meditation so often described as pleasant and highly desirable, while sensory isolation is often felt to be unpleasant, disturbing, undesirable?

If we examine the experimental reports carefully we will notice something that may not be apparent at first. Not *all* of the subjects who have undergone even the most severe sensory deprivation have had unpleasant experiences or shown disorganization of thinking, hallucinations, or any unusual behavior at all. *Some* have gone through several days of such isolation quite comfortably.

Perhaps even more interesting is the fact that for some people sensory isolation is reported to be a positive experience. Accounts by solitary sailors, polar explorers, lifeboat survivors, and other people forcibly isolated for long periods of time and exposed to highly monotonous environments show that it is not unusual for such people to report that once they became accustomed to the isolation experience and found a way to cope with it, they then underwent a "transformation." At some point the isolation seemed to become an important growth experience for them and many of these people reported being able to achieve a new integration of personality as a result.

It was these and similar reports which led a group of researchers in the 1950s to think that sensory isolation might have some *healing* properties. What would happen, they wondered, if one were to expose a group of emotionally disturbed people, say psychotic patients in a hospital, to such conditions? Might the isolation possibly be of help to them?

In 1956 such an experiment was conducted by researchers Azima and Cramer in Montreal.[6] These experimenters placed psychiatric patients in an isolation chamber quite similar to the one used in the McGill experiments, for periods lasting from two to six days, depending on the patients' own responses to the situation. As in all other sensory isolation experiments, the subjects could terminate the experience whenever they wished to. While some of these patients' symptoms got worse with sensory deprivation, the symptoms of some other patients, especially those suffering from depressions, were very much improved. This improvement lasted after they came out of the isolation chamber and did not disappear. These patients now showed greater motivation, more socialization with other patients, and greater self-assertiveness. Some of them responded so well to sensory isolation, in fact, that they improved to the point of being discharged from the hospital. This was particularly interesting in light of the fact that some of those who could be discharged in this manner had been long-standing chronic "incurable" hospitalized patients.

What had their experiences during isolation been like? At first these patients reported a typical disorganization of thinking—but for them disorganization seemed to be followed by "reorganization." Self-assertiveness and "constructive aggression" seemed to become available to them and psychological testing after the experience showed that they had suffered no loss of concentration or efficiency as a result of isolation. A number of these patients became more receptive to psychotherapy afterward, too. In general, patients whose major illness was depression seemed to benefit the most while others, who were diagnosed as being "hysterical personalities," tended to become *more* anxious and disturbed when placed in isolation.

These results led another investigator, A. Harris, to try placing schizophrenic patients in sensory isolation.[7] When he did this he found that they tolerated the experience much better than normal persons and that for many of them, the intensity of their hallucinations was reduced or eliminated as a result of the sensory isolation. Other researchers then followed this same line of investigation with practically unanimous agreement as to the value of sensory isolation for certain types of psychiatric patients.†

Why do certain patients respond well to sensory isolation while others do not? Psychologist Charles Brownfield attempted to discover the reason by testing subjects to find out whether they were predominantly "sensation seeking" or "sensation avoiding."[8] Most people lean a bit toward one or the other of these two extremes. Sensation-seeking people are those who tend to reach out for new and exciting experiences, new tastes, adventures, novel environments, travel, and other forms of stimulation. Sensation-avoiding people are those who tend to withdraw from anything new, tending to stick to the tried and true and to plan out everything in advance in order to avoid the unknown.

Brownfield reasoned that sensation-avoiding people might find sensory isolation both pleasant and possibly therapeutic because it would help them achieve the reduction of stimulation they need. On the other hand, sensation-*seeking* people might find it extremely painful to be shut away from the stimulation which *they* require. In order to test these assumptions, he assembled a group of "normal" people and a group of psychiatric patients and gave them tests to determine whether they were sensation-seeking or sensation-avoiding. He then asked those who wished to volunteer for sensory isolation, to remain in isolation for twenty-four hours if possible.

Though Brownfield had only a few patients in his final pilot

† The sensory isolation chamber is still unknown, however, as a form of treatment in any psychiatric hospital, despite the fact that electroshock therapy, a treatment much more radical than sensory isolation, is still being used.

study in the isolation chamber due to technical difficulties, the results were in the direction he predicted. Sensation-seeking subjects, when placed in the chamber, all reported discomfort, anxiety, or boredom. Sensation-avoiding subjects, on the other hand, frequently reported that they felt *better* after they had been in the isolation chamber than they had before—they described themselves as now feeling comfortable, relaxed, and calm. When questioned afterward, the sensation seekers said they would never want to go through the procedure again, whereas those who were sensation avoiders seemed eager to revolunteer at the earliest possible opportunity.

Perhaps this line of research applies to meditation, too. Can it be that sensation seekers find the partial sensory isolation of meditation uncomfortable, or even anxiety-provoking; while sensation avoiders find it comforting and even healing? Furthermore, we might wonder whether in the overstimulating environment of our modern world, we may not all require *some* sensory deprivation at times, to right the balance.

A Governing Apparatus

Since meditation changes our stimulation level, can it act as a governing apparatus, helping us maintain the proper balance between too much and too little stimulation? Each of us seems to have our own "best" level of stimulation—a level which is neither too high nor too low for our proper functioning. In addition, we are able to tolerate more stimulation at certain times than at others. We probably all function better if the range of stimulation that we have to deal with is kept within our own best level, but keeping it within these limits requires effort.

Most of us when in a dull, unstimulating environment for too long become restless. We then get up, walk around, stretch our muscles, talk to someone or do something "interesting"—we are eager for "input." On the other hand, if we hear children shouting, the TV blaring, the lawn mower next door roaring, and a dog barking, we will usually try to get away to some quieter place. We continually act to adjust the level of stimulation to make it as pleasant and comfortable for ourselves as possible. If we are unable to do this satisfactorily, then our functioning may take a sharp drop.

Perhaps meditation helps us with this balancing of sensory input because it brings about a *mild* form of sensory deprivation which still contains some sensory input, usually repetitive and monotonous, such as the thought of a mantra or awareness of breathing. As we have seen, when sensory deprivation is too extreme or prolonged, people may react to it with loss of efficiency or even anxiety and distress, just as they often react adversely to overmeditating. An adjustment process is not helped along by overdoing, and this may be why the practical forms of meditation achieve the excellent results they do. They shut out *some*, but not *all*, sensory input and they do this only for a relatively short period of time.

Sensory Overload

There have been many studies of sensory deprivation, but surprisingly little attention has been given to the opposite—what happens when human beings or lower animals are bombarded with stimuli. Too much stimulation can be annoying and, carried to an *extreme*, overstimulation can seriously break down the adequacy of our mental or physical functioning. The strategies of the "third degree" and of "brainwashing" are based on this principle. If a prisoner or someone else whose behavior is being manipulated is kept overstimulated by constant bombardment with intense sights, sounds, or sense impressions for hours on end, day after day, the clarity of his or her thinking processes eventually breaks down. At this point people often become susceptible to suggestions or willing to comply with demands which, in a more rational state, they would reject.

Primitive tribes or other groups may purposely create a sensory overload by means of rituals, singing, dancing, or whirling in order to bring about ecstatic trance states, but under conditions where there is no escape, sensory overload can have a different effect. If animals are subjected to intense stimuli such as loud noises, bright flashing lights, or impressions of rapid motion over long periods of time, a wide variety of serious symptoms occur. The heart rate and blood pressure of a group of rats subjected to these conditions, for example, changed in a manner indicating that the animals were undergoing severe stress—their adrenal hormone levels shot up, all manner of symptoms of anxiety were shown, and in a number of instances, death occurred.[9]

When animals are packed together in cages where they are subjected to constant inescapable stimulation from other animals, the consequences are serious. What happens has been described as the "behavioral sink." By this is meant that the behavior of these animals deteriorates until there is an extreme breakdown in social behavior; normally co-operative animals become hostile and destructive to each other. There is also a sharp increase in the death rate of the animals with many early deaths which would not normally have been expected. The effects of overcrowding on animals has been studied because of the possible implications this may have for man. If overcrowding breaks down the inner controls of animals to such a radical degree, what happens to human beings confined to the constant overstimulation of ghettos in large cities?

These are important questions for us to ask in an age where sensory overload seems to be the order of the day. Without realizing it, the average person faces an ever increasing amount of sensory bombardment in his or her daily life. An obvious example of this is the so-called "electric circus," where intense lights, sounds, and colors are flashed in rapid succession so that the mind cannot adapt to it and an altered state of consciousness is created. Ordinary rock music played over any amplifier which is turned up very loud is also a sensory overload. The music may stimulate the nervous system to eventual exhaustion, at which point perceptions and thoughts become altered and the listener may feel temporarily "high." What such overstimulation, taken in large doses, may be doing to one's nervous system or other bodily systems in the long run, is unknown, however; although we do know that sounds greater than 75 decibels (typical acid rock over an amplifier is at least 108 decibels) increase the pulse and respiration and that very loud noises leave us shaky. Increasing numbers of people, particularly young people, are exposed to such noise, and recent tests have shown that by the time they have reached college age, 61 per cent of young people in today's population (a generation exposed to unusual amounts of high noise) show some loss of hearing acuity.

Such activities as listening to very loud hi-fi or going to rock concerts or to electric circuses are intentionally sought. Hopefully not *all* of us are exposed to conditions of sensory overload unless we want to be—or are we? The unfortunate fact is that we may no longer realize when we are faced with sensory overload because this condition has become so much a part of our life-style. High-pressure advertising messages and dramatically presented newscasts are flashed to us constantly over the mass media. Billboards and supermarket shelves demand our attention with brightly colored competing displays. The noise of cars, motorcycles, and planes intrudes into even the quietest country resort. And these are but some of the ways that high levels of stimulation invade our lives.

What makes matters even more difficult is that with over-stimulation, our normal tendency to withdraw from intense stimuli seems to be dulled. At this point, instead of withdrawing from excitement, we may actually reach for more. A familiar example is young children staying up for a special occasion who become overstimulated, and then refuse to go to bed although what they now need most is quiet. If left to their own resources, such children may drive themselves to an even higher pitch of excitement until they "go to pieces." Perhaps this tendency to drive ourselves to more and more exhausting levels of stimulation is one reason why meditation is beginning to be looked upon favorably by so many people in the modern world. We may sense that we are being caught in a trend which, unless we stop it, may continue until we drop in our tracks.

Human beings, interestingly enough, are the only animals who observe a 17-hour period of continuous wakefulness. Lower animals periodically nap throughout the day. Awakening for an hour or so and then going back to sleep, they take catnaps throughout their active hours. Only humans force themselves to remain almost constantly awake, a feat for which we must be trained. Infants and young children, who are not yet trained in this manner, still require naps, while older people who can no longer conform as easily to this training again require naps during the day.

Because humans do not have periodic sleep we may need other ways of reducing the input we are receiving. As suggested earlier, under natural conditions we all tend to lapse into a "meditative mood" at certain times during the day. Perhaps these moods perform the same function for us as catnaps do for animals. The research on ultradian rhythms which shows that reverie states occur at roughly one-and-a-half-hour intervals throughout the day in people, suggests that a tendency to retreat periodically from the stimuli which are pounding at us is still built into our nervous systems, even though we may refuse to allow ourselves to indulge in this to any degree. Nature does not seem so ready to let us off the hook, however. We periodically take coffee breaks, eat, smoke cigarettes, or daydream even while we are on the job. Perhaps we are not so different from the lower animals after all.

One of the most effective ways for us to re-establish a balance between too little and too great an amount of stimulation may be to meditate. It is interesting that people in boring, *low*-stimulation conditions such as some forms of imprisonment, frequently report comfort and refreshment from meditation. For them, the mental activity supplied by meditation seems to give them the *stimulation* they need—again suggesting that meditation acts as a governing apparatus. If meditation restores us to a state of inner balance with respect to the adjustment of our stimulation level, its effects upon our health, both physical and mental, may be considerable.

Rediscovering Our Natural Rhythms

Retreating from the sensory input of waking life into the stillness of meditation is only one way of describing this state however. When we meditate we do not retreat into a mere absence of external stimulation, but into the *presence* of something else. When one level of stimulation is removed—that of the world which often acts on us in ways convenient to *it* rather than to us

—we are released to sense more subtle forms of stimulation. In the quiet of the meditative state, we may become attuned to the voices of the body which are ordinarily obscured by waking activity.

Meditation seems to be the only natural state which is sufficiently still, and at the same time sufficiently *alert*, so that when we are in it we can clearly perceive our own inner rhythms. People often report that during meditation they hear the beating of their own hearts or sense their breathing as an important occurrence. They sometimes report that they can hear the rushing of blood through their head or sense other minute and delicate bodily processes usually obscured by activity.

We might compare our insensitivity to bodily processes when active to our inability in the daytime to perceive stars in the sky. Although they are present twenty-four hours a day, we cannot see them when the sun is up because its brilliant light obscures them. When the sun sets, however, the far more subtle lights of the celestial bodies are readily seen and it is as though a host of stars had "appeared" in the sky. So it is with meditation, which removes us from the bright light of activity to the softer light of inner awareness—away from one level of perception toward an entirely different one. When we cease to perceive ourselves in active interaction with the world, we seem to be free to see ourselves in our rhythmic livingness.

It does not seem to be coincidence therefore that established meditative systems often make use of components which reflect natural bodily rhythms. Our positive response and sense of peacefulness with respect to the rhythms of heartbeat, breathing, and other bodily processes may go back as far as human memory extends. Regularly repeated sounds or rhythmic movements are widely recognized as soothing. Parents from all cultures and eras have rocked agitated infants to quiet them, or have repeated affectionate sounds in a lilting manner or have bounced their babies on their laps with an intuitive awareness of the soothing effects that these rhythmic activities have on them.

Dr. Reginald Lourie, of the George Washington University School of Medicine, has studied the role of such rhythmic patterns in the development of children.[10] He reports that as they grow, a certain number of healthy children supply their own rhythmic patterns. At two to three months of age, a few of them are rocking or moving their heads, the only part of their bodies over which they have some control. At six to ten months of age, even more are rocking their heads, while others have now taken up increasingly dramatic forms of rhythmic activities such as banging their heads against the crib or getting up on hands and knees to rock vigorously back and forth.

In some of these children, these rhythmic movements are transitory, lasting only until about age two or three. But in others such movements remain much longer. Tracing these rhythmic activities through various stages of development, Lourie has found that while at first rhythmic activities seem to be done predominantly for pleasure—a number of children will rock when they have had a particularly satisfying meal or are praised, or are successful or admired, or are having pleasant thoughts—by the end of the first year these rhythmic patterns seem to have changed in purpose. Now they have become a means of relieving *tension* and are used when the child is angry, frustrated, tired, bored, or hungry. This tension-relieving aspect of rhythm continues throughout life and is useful for all of us, the basis, it seems, of many habits which serve to release tension.

Sooner or later, of course, these rhythmic activities meet with interference from adults who are annoyed or even alarmed by the disturbance they make, and pressure is put on children to stop them. No matter what ingenious devices are employed, however, they do not stop these activities. The children may seem to conform to the wishes of the adults around them but they do not actually give up the rhythmic patterns—they simply substitute others. Tooth grinding, ear pulling, finger tapping, nose rubbing, and other newer, more disguised forms of repetitive activity now evolve and may continue for a long time. The reach toward the comforts that rhythm brings seems too deeply entrenched to be easily abandoned.

Recently a group of scientists studied this profound effect of rhythm on the human being, in the laboratory. To find out whether the sound of the human adult heartbeat, similar to the sound of the mother's heartbeat which the child has become accustomed to before birth, might have a particularly soothing effect on newborn infants, psychologist Lee Salk of the Rockefeller Institute in New York City studied a large group of newborns in a hospital nursery, observing them from immediately following their birth until the time they were four days old.[11] All of these infants were treated according to the ordinary routine of the nursery except for one thing—they were continuously played a tape recording of a normal adult heartbeat sound (seventy-two beats per minute) over an intercom, without interruption day and night, for the first four days of their lives.

Salk had originally intended to have another group of infants hear the heartbeat speeded up to an abnormally fast sound (128 beats per minute) but he quickly discontinued this part of the experiment. This speeded-up heart rate turned out to be so upsetting to the infants that their crying increased dramatically and they showed other agitated behavior. The fast heartbeat sound had to be discontinued for the well-being of the children. For the sake of comparison, therefore, Salk selected a group of newborns for whom no tapes were played at all during the first four days in the nursery. These infants were just treated according to regular hospital routine.

The results of the experiment were striking. Seventy per cent of the infants who heard the heartbeat rhythm increased in body weight over the first four days as against only 33 per cent of the infants who did not hear the heartbeat rhythm—a highly significant difference. Crying was heard in the nursery only 38 per cent of the time among those children who were listening to the heartbeat rhythm as against 60 per cent of the time among those children who did not hear the heartbeat played. Since there was no difference at all between the two groups in the amount of food they consumed, why did the experimental group gain more weight? Salk suggests that since the more contented group had less exercise from crying, this may account for their weight gain. He has expressed the theory that the mother's heartbeat is one of the major sounds heard by the fetus before birth and that the unborn infant may have learned to associate these rhythmical heartbeat sounds with the relatively tension-free state in the womb. After birth, the mother's heartbeat (or other similar rhythms) may be soothing because of this early conditioning.

Perhaps nowhere do we get so profound a statement about the deep rhythms of the intrauterine state as in the writings of Dr. Frederick Leboyer, the French obstetrician whose pioneer work in obstetrical methods is changing delivery room procedures in many parts of the world. Leboyer indicates that before birth the infant is in "perpetual motion." Even when his mother is asleep, there is always the great rhythm of her breathing, of her diaphragm, and of course there is the steady sound of her pulse beat. Then, about a month before delivery, uterine contractions (far less intense than those of labor) begin, lasting a whole month—the ninth. Leboyer emphasizes the infinitely slow rhythm of these contractions and advises the hands holding the newborn infant to "remember the slowness, the continuous movement of the uterine contraction, the 'peristaltic wave' the child grew to know so well during the final month before its birth. . . ."[12]

Leboyer feels that lovers rediscover this visceral slowness instinctively:

> . . . to make love . . . is to plunge again into the world before birth, before the great separation. It is to find again the primordial slowness, the blind and all-powerful rhythm of the internal world, of the great ocean. . . .[13]

Psychoanalyst Joost Meerloo, reasoning along somewhat the same lines, has also suggested that the unborn child's early experiences with heartbeat rhythms may be the basis for the profoundly soothing effects of poetry, music, and dance. Perhaps, he says, these rhythmic experiences are all grounded in "various reminiscent feelings of a lost long ago and far away happiness."[14]

Aside from the fact that we may have *learned* to connect natural rhythms with soothing experiences before birth, it is also possible that we may instinctively find those regular rhythms that approximate the normal rhythms of our own bodies to be deeply comforting because, physiologically, they signify that "all is well" and nature is running smoothly. A study at Princeton set out to investigate this possibility by looking at the way in which undergraduate college students responded to various types of syncopated (two-beat) rhythms sounded on a drum.[15] These drumbeats were first carefully regulated as to speed and then recorded on tape so that we were able to obtain five different speeds.

We wanted to find out what effect various rhythms might have on the mood of the listener—whether people responded differently to rhythms that were closer to the speed of the normal heartbeat than they did to those which were farther from it. Our results strongly supported the notion that adults are more comfortable with rhythms within the normal adult heartbeat range. The subjects rated rhythms in this range (the recorded speeds of sixty and seventy-two beats per minute) as making them feel "relaxed," whereas they rated rhythms which were either much faster or much slower than the normal heartbeat range as making them feel "tense" and "anxious."

These soothing effects of bodily rhythms may help explain some of the deeply calming effects of meditation. Repetition of the mantra is a profoundly rhythmic activity, as is one's own breathing. Even as the meditator is paying attention to his or her particular meditational focus, other rhythms such as heartbeat and respiration often come sharply into awareness during meditation. We may be more profoundly aware of these natural rhythms then than at any other time. In the previously mentioned questionnaire distributed to TM and CSM meditators, 74 per cent of those who responded reported being *more* aware of bodily processes such as breathing and heartbeat during meditation than they were ordinarily, and 43 per cent said they were *far* more aware of such processes during that time. By contrast, only 26 per cent reported that they were *less* aware of bodily processes during meditation or that they saw no change.

Not surprisingly, a number of meditational techniques have made these natural bodily rhythms their object of focus. As we have seen, zazen meditation demands careful attention to one's breathing and the techniques of Hatha Yoga (the Yoga of "postures" or physical exercises) is based on a subtle co-ordination between physical activity and breathing—a co-ordination that we tend to lose during our waking life. When we harmonize our actions and our breath, breathing becomes a central regulating rhythm which gives many people a feeling of centeredness and calm.

Even when attention is not consciously directed to these bodily rhythms, there seems to be a natural tendency to focus upon them. During regular mantra meditation, although the subjects we questioned had never been instructed to link their mantra to their breathing rhythm (in fact, they were told *not* to make any effort to do this), 76 per cent of the meditators who filled out the questionnaire reported that their mantra spontaneously linked itself up with the rhythm of their breathing, either sometimes or often, and 6 per cent said it was *always* linked to breathing. Only 18 per cent said the mantra was *never* linked to it.

The regularly repeating mantra, or other repetitive meditational devices, or attention given to the rise and fall of the breath, can create a deep sense of calm. An entry in my own meditation journal describes this:

> . . . The waves of the mantra washed over me repeatedly. I felt them physically, slowly pulsing through me. . . . At various times the mantra was a soft spread of light; a cushion caressing my face; a cloud of mist rhythmically dispersing; the echoing toll of a distant bell; a faint sensation over and around my eyes; or just quiet beats. Sometimes I had no imagery. At such times, it was as though the mantra were some deep biological presence existing amidst profound silence.

By inducing natural rhythms during meditation, rhythms only as rapid or as slow as the person wishes them to be at the moment, we may be extending an ancient, intuitive knowledge of the calming effects of rhythm to an activity appropriate for adults as well as children. Meditation may be one of the most comforting of the rhythmical activities available to us after childhood ends, restoring through its lulling repetitions, a natural balance between tension and repose.

Shifting Gears

Shifts occur during meditation—radical changes in perspective, more subtle changes in energy utilization. These can be looked upon as directed and purposeful adjustments, shifting our entire tuning apparatus to a different wavelength than we are accustomed to.

Meditation and Shift in Cognitive Mode

One of the most important aspects of meditation is a change in cognitive (thinking) *mode*. During meditation the verbal, logical "self" that reasons in orderly sequences and is highly aware of time, seems to dim out. It is replaced by a different "self"—one that we usually encounter only under special circumstances such as sleep onset, when our mind drifts among images and impressions whose content and meaning we feel or know only intuitively. The self we know during meditation operates in a dim but intimate world, removed from considerations of time and involvement with past and future. Our "interior speech," that ever present running stream of words that occupies our thinking during regular activity, is either stilled or relegated to a background role. In the meditative sphere of our being, images and an awareness of space are often the most real aspects of our experience.

It now appears that these two modes of experiencing—the logical, linear, verbal one and the alogical, simultaneous, spacial one—

may have their basis in the organization of the brain itself. The brain of all higher animals, including humans, consists of two distinct hemispheres which in their own ways are like two separate continents.* These hemispheres are connected by tracts of nerve tissue which form the great cerebral commissures; the larger and most familiar of these tracts of nerve fibers is known as the *corpus callosum*. This communication-bridge between the hemispheres enables information to be transferred from one side of the brain to the other.

Some years ago two researchers, Ronald Meyers and R. W. Sperry, made a surprising discovery. When the connections between the two halves of the brain were cut, each hemisphere was able to function independently as though it were, in itself, *a complete brain*. This was first found to be true with laboratory animals and later proved to be equally the case in human beings who for medical reasons had had to undergo operations in which their corpus callosum was surgically severed.[1] Ordinarily, when we learn to do a simple task with one hand, we can perform the same task (although often we do it awkwardly) with the other hand—as the old saying goes, our left hand "knows" what our right hand is doing, and vice versa. This is not so with those who have had their corpus callosum cut, however. Meyers and Sperry discovered that such people had no transfer of learning from one hand to the other, even on a very simple manual task. The other hand had to start its learning process from scratch, as it were, each time, as though it were the hand of a completely separate person. The most intriguing thing about this research and its follow-up studies in the California Institute of Technology, however, was the discovery that the operated subjects' two different hands (or their two different sides of the visual field) were able to learn different *kinds* of things. Both competent in its own way, their fields of specialization were quite different.

* The right hemisphere controls the *left* side of our body and in right-handed people, the left hemisphere is said to be "dominant." Left-handed people show a somewhat less consistent pattern: in some the left hemisphere is dominant; in some the right hemisphere is dominant; and a few have mixed dominance.

The left side of the brain could remember language and handle mathematical problems; the right side could not; or what it could learn about this was extremely rudimentary compared to the virtuosity of the left side of the brain. While the right side of the brain was able to *recognize* written and spoken words, it could not reproduce them; it was in effect, mute. On the other hand, the right side of the brain excelled in the recognition of faces, in estimations of space, in the ability to assemble blocks in order to duplicate a printed design, and in the ability to draw a cube in three dimensions. The *left* hemisphere-directed hand, however, could not seem to visualize or reproduce anything three-dimensional in a picture. The researchers concluded that these studies "demonstrate conclusively that in a split-brain situation, we are really dealing with two brains, each separately capable of mental functions of a high order."[2]

Laboratory findings are not our only evidence concerning two separate modes of consciousness which may be linked to the actual structure of the brain. The laboratory experiments are supported by a large number of clinical studies. Neurosurgeons over the years have collected a great deal of information on patients who have had brain disease or been injured in one hemisphere only. This medical evidence has shown that injury to certain portions of the *left* hemisphere will cause loss of speech (aphasia), but that the right hemisphere appears so unessential for this function that it is even possible for a person to have had his or her entire right hemisphere destroyed, and still be able to use language normally and with no loss of vocabulary, *provided the left hemisphere remains intact*. The person to whom this happens will, however, probably lose *other* capacities such as the ability to recognize faces, form visual images mentally, estimate space accurately, or perform musically.

Musical sensitivity seems to depend heavily on a well-functioning right hemisphere. There is a famous neurological case of a composer who suffered a massive stroke in the left hemisphere of his brain. This left him totally unable to speak, but amazingly his ability to compose music was not only unimpaired by the stroke, it actually improved! This man's best work, in fact, was done *after* his stroke.[3] Can it be that his "logical" left hemisphere had been hampering his ability to create music? When his left hemisphere was "knocked out of commission" by the stroke, did this "free" him to realize his right hemispheric potential for musical composition?

In another instance, a prominent painter suffered a sudden and severe loss of the capacity for speech—evidence that his left hemisphere had been damaged. His *artistic* activity remained undisturbed, however. In fact, after his speech loss, the intensity and sharpness of his artistic work was even accentuated. It was as though the person unable to speak and the artist lived together in him on "two distinct planes."[4]

Such observations suggest some interesting possibilities. Can *normal* people suffer from a conflict between the two halves of their brain? Is it possible that one of the hemispheres sometimes interferes in the smooth and complete functioning of the other? Does one side of the brain perhaps struggle to "right a balance" if the other side has been usurping too much control? Could such a conflict perhaps contribute to the disbalances and splitting of functions and of awareness that sometimes lead to what we call mental illness? And could a technique which reduced the dissonance between the hemispheres, bringing them into a more harmonious working relationship with each other, perhaps aid emotional adjustment and the integration of the total personality?

An intriguing speculation which relates to this problem has recently been suggested by psychologist Paul Bakan, who has proposed that there may be a cyclical alternation of hemispheric dominance during the twenty-four-hour day.[5] Since brain wave recordings show evidence of a relatively greater activation of the right hemisphere during REM sleep (as might be expected on logical grounds since dreams are predominantly made up of visual and spacial imagery rather than representing abstract logical reasoning), perhaps then the REM cycle represents a periodic reassertion of right hemispheric activity throughout the night. This might, Bakan suggests, be paralleled in the daytime by the ultradian rhythm of daydreaming—those reverie states which, as we have seen, tend to recur at regular intervals throughout the day. Perhaps the ultradian daydream rhythm is related to shifts in the relative dominance of the right and left hemispheres? If this is so, then a need to restore some kind of natural balance or "equality" between the hemispheres might be served by both REM sleep at night and by reverie states during the day. Because of our predominantly left hemisphere-oriented culture, is it possible that our somewhat neglected right hemisphere may in this manner force its influence upon us—"insist" on having times when it holds sway?

While the relationship between meditation and hemispheric dominance is not yet clear, the possibility of a harmonizing of the two hemispheres during meditation is suggested by research in several different laboratories.

On the basis of their EEG studies on TM meditators at the Hartford Institute of Living, Drs. Bernard Glueck and Charles Stroebel feel that meditation may have its greatest impact on the individual precisely because of a harmonizing of brain waves from all parts of the head (including *both* hemispheres) which may be induced by this technique. These researchers, studying the brain waves of experienced TM meditators, found that as these people began to meditate, the density of alpha waves recorded from the machine's leads on their scalps increased rapidly. What was particularly interesting, was the extent of the brain that appeared to be caught up in this alpha rhythm. The alpha waves "swept forward" until they involved the entire dominant hemisphere of the brain, the frontal areas as well. Then, within a relatively short period of time (frequently no more than one or two minutes) the *opposite* hemisphere showed the same prominent alpha rhythm— the brain waves of both hemispheres were now in synchrony.

Other researchers have confirmed these findings. Neurologist J. P. Banquet observed the same marked uniformity of electrical activity from all areas of the brain in his laboratory. Like the Hartford researchers, he reported that during meditation alpha waves rapidly spread synchronously (in phase with one another) from the back to the front of the brain and that after about five minutes of meditating, recordings indicated that the dominant and the "silent" hemispheres of the brain were now in phase with one another. This kind of "hypersynchrony," as he called it, is usually seen only with different, slower varieties of brain waves and in states of drowsiness or sleep. It is unusual for a person in the alerted awake state to have brain waves synchronized in this fashion and the implication is that during meditation the two hemispheres of the brain may be able to "work together" in a fashion not possible under other circumstances. By encouraging this synchrony between the two halves of the brain, meditation may foster the integration of our two basic modes of thinking—the analytical (left hemispheric) mode and the synthesizing and intuitive (right hemispheric) mode.

Man's highest achievements obviously require the complimentary workings of thought processes from both sides of the brain. Intuition and hunches must be shaped through logical, disciplined thinking to form a work of art. The most rigorous scientific and philosophical reasoning requires the enrichening leaven of hunch and inspiration to make it fruitful. Man thus needs a harmony, a coming together of his two "selves" into one mind, one being. Perhaps such an integration is one reason for the sense of wholeness experienced by meditators who find the technique working for them. In a literal sense, meditation may be making us more "together."

Deposing the Ego

Another way of looking at the shift in our mode of thinking during meditation is to see this change as a move away from control by the ego. Our ego—that part of our thinking-acting self which we interpose between ourselves and our environment—is something we construct carefully, slowly, painstakingly from infancy on. Forming the ego is somewhat like building a house by hand—lifting each brick, weighing it in our hands, trying it out in a particular place, fitting it in, and then cementing it. The structure develops gradually.

The ego is not static as a building is, however. It is a decision-making apparatus which enables us to weigh each thing we do, monitoring our acts to insure that we behave both consistently and in a manner appropriate to the situation. The ego performs many roles. It is our bookkeeper, calculating the psychological and physical cost to us of each act we contemplate. It is our consultant, predicting future trends on the basis of past experience. And it is our executive, organizing our days, hours, and minutes. As an executive, it is empowered to establish priorities, grant exceptions, mete out rewards and punishments, offer incentives for hard work, and plan for future expansion.

The ego is so effective in its organization that it can make large numbers of decisions all at once because these are based on pre-established rules and principles. It can also count on one of the most efficient computers in the world—the human brain. Without the ego's organization we would not do well in a complex world where decisions must constantly be made. We need it—at least up to a point.

The question is one of balance. Up to a certain point the ego seems to serve us—beyond that we may start to serve *it*. If the ego is in the driver's seat *all* the time, then direct experience fades away because a welter of "corporate" decisions begin to interpose themselves between even the simplest sense experiences and ourself. The superstructure weighs each incoming impression, decides to file it under a particular category, and acts according to the "organization's" rules when processing it. The machinery is so smooth that we need never contaminate ourselves with the uncertainty of the new; everything falls into place and is processed efficiently. We are not allowed to contact the world directly any more, that would be inefficient. Life "out there" becomes mechanized, our taste buds dull, our vision flattens, our thoughts lose vitality, and some intangible scent is gone from the air. All contingencies are taken care of—but are we truly alive?

Young children know nothing of this potential superstructure since their ego is rudimentary, just enough to get by. When they pick up a box to examine it—they look at it. They are not involved in decision making, labeling, or predicting. They are unconcerned with alternatives or the repercussions of their actions. They look at the box. They touch it, turn it slowly, bite it, throw it, pick it up again, shake it, stare at it. There is total absorption in their face and body. They are incredibly still, eyes are wide, fastened on the box in unwavering gaze, their face is flushed, lips parted—they are examining the box. That is *all* they are doing. Lost in the complex web of ego concerns, we all too often allow to slip from us this simple capacity for total experiencing. The revival of this lost capacity would seem to be one of the most valuable of the gifts that meditation offers us.

The freeing of the grip of the ego in meditation is related to "deautomatization," a process which psychiatrist Arthur Deikman considers an essential aspect of meditation.[6] "Deautomatization" is the opposite of "automatization"—the natural process of making our activities, both physical and mental, automatic so that we can perform them without having to think about them. Most of our activities are automatized. Our vision, for example, automatically skips a great many intermediate steps which we once had to practice when we were infants. When an adult "sees," this is actually the end result of a complicated process which is no longer conscious. People who have been blind all their lives from cataracts, but who as adults have had surgery so that their vision is cleared, actually have to be painstakingly taught to "see." What they experience when the bandages are first removed is a confusion of impressions. These newly operated patients cannot organize and analyze the visual field into *forms*. All they can clearly discern are colors. It will take many months before they can learn to identify as simple a form as a square or a circle— something which has become automatic for the sighted person.[7]

Automatization is obviously useful, but *over*automatization can lead to difficulty. When too large a portion of our experience is automatized, we become "a walking bundle of habits." The price we pay for efficiency is the loss of what the Zen philosophers call the "mind of a beginner." It seems therefore that we need both a necessary amount of automatization and a healthy degree of *non*automatization to allow us to experience life fully. Can meditation help us restore this balance by "deautomatizing" some of our ways of thinking and perceiving? Deikman feels it can do so and that deautomatization may be one of the most significant effects of meditation.

In order to investigate this notion he taught subjects to meditate using a blue vase as an object to focus attention on. The instructions were to concentrate on seeing the vase "as it exists in itself without any connection with other things." The subjects were to exclude all other thoughts or sensations and let the perception of the vase "fill their entire mind."[8]

The people who participated in Deikman's experiment reported that in the course of a series of meditation sessions, their perception of the vase changed markedly. Often its color became deeper, more vivid or "luminous." Sometimes it changed form, becoming larger or smaller, or distorted in shape. At times it seemed to become two-dimensional, its boundaries blurred, or it melted into the background. In some cases it seemed to move. One subject reported that she had "merged with the vase," losing her sense of individual identity. Following the meditation session another subject looked out of the window at a park below and reported seeing things in a most unusual fashion. The objects on the landscape looked ". . . scattered all over the lot, not hung together in any way." Later he explained that "the view didn't organize itself in any way . . . there were no planes, one behind the other . . . everything was working at the same intensity . . . like a bad painting which I didn't know about until I got used to it so I could begin to pick out what was going on in the painting. I didn't see the order to it or the pattern to it or anything and I couldn't impose it, it resisted my imposition of pattern."[9]

Deikman concluded that in the above instance this man's experience resulted from a "deautomatization of the brain's structures," that is, of the learned patterns which ordinarily provide visual organization of a landscape. Apparently his ability to focus attention selectively was also deautomatized, for each thing in the landscape *equally* claimed his attention, none of them standing out while others receded. Normal figure-ground (depth) perception also seemed to be deautomatized—the planes did not recede as they normally would.

While the deautomatization of these subjects did not carry over into their ordinary waking life for more than a short period following meditation, what remained were pleasant feelings of newness, aliveness, closeness to the subjects' own feelings and to the world. The deautomatization of meditation does not therefore appear to be an end in itself but a means to an end; that of allowing a kind of reorganization to take place within the personality.

There is an interesting parallel between the responses of Deikman's subjects after meditation and the way in which the operated cataract patients saw the world with naïve untutored vision —both groups could not organize the visual field according to our habitual ways. The deautomatization of the subjects meditating upon the vase is also similar to experiences which may take place under the influence of drugs such as LSD, mescaline, and the like.

Deikman stresses the fact that the breakdown of automatization which took place in his subjects did not occur at random, nor was it a destructive force. It seemed directed toward a specific purpose—to permit the adult to gain a new, fresh perception of the world by freeing him temporarily from ingrained habitual ways of experiencing which had him trapped. In this way the constructive, creative forces within the person, the forces which seek to build, grow, and put together experiences in new and richer ways, may be given access to "fresh materials." These materials come from both the imagination and the senses, they are new ways of looking at experience. Deautomatization is not to be looked upon as a way of "going back" or "losing ground" or "regressing," but rather as the undoing of a pattern "in order to permit a new and perhaps more advanced experience."[10]

Deikman points out that while drugs and extreme forms of sensory deprivation may produce similar types of deautomatization, the effects achieved through these external means appear not to be nearly as long-lasting and are not as deeply inspiring or meaningful as those produced by the individual himself, through his own efforts, as he meditates over long periods of time. It seems to be when it is taken in *small doses*, worked at conscientiously, and kept under voluntary control, that the deautomatization process can be used most constructively, enabling the person to gain freedom to rebuild his or her approach to life in a new and meaningful manner.

Energy Shifts During Meditation

Any discussion of the changes which take place in meditation is incomplete without considering some of the reasons for these changes advanced by the great meditative traditions. These so-called "esoteric" explanations for the effects of meditation are of course not presented by meditation teachers as possibilities; they are advanced as though they were proven facts. In actuality, they are belief systems based on revelations obtained during states of radically altered consciousness. Because they are usually presented as dogma, not as hypotheses, it is customary for scientists to dismiss them out of hand. This is unfortunate because it automatically removes these influential beliefs from the realm of experiences which invite systematic study, leaving them in a mystical area which is labeled "unscientific."

The Yoga concept of prana, for example, is central to the Indian view of meditation and its effects, but is such a broad, all-inclusive concept that it is exceedingly hard for the Western mind to grasp. Prana refers at once to a number of seemingly different things. It is said to be the vital energy or breath drawn into the body through the lungs, the vital energy absorbed through meditation, and ultimately a universal breath or energy of which the individual's energy field is "but one manifestation."

Prana is said to be present in all forms of matter from inert minerals to man himself. While it permeates matter, however, it is *not* matter, but rather an energy or force that animates it. This universal energy is thought to be manifested as gravitation and electricity, as muscular energy, as the energy that radiates through nerve impulses, and as the energy back of thought processes. Both the driving force which animates pure thought and the driving force behind the simplest mechanical movement are but different manifestations of prana; and air, food, water, light are in turn media through which prana is carried. Thus we are said to absorb prana through the food we eat, the liquids we drink, and the air we breathe. Prana can also penetrate totally and directly without recourse to these mediating factors. The whole body, in fact, is said to be controlled by prana, which in turn regulates every cell. Describing the overwhelming all-inclusiveness of this concept, Swami Vishnudevananda says:

> If we look at the vast ocean, we see big or small waves arise and dissolve with innumerable small bubbles. But, the background of all these waves and bubbles is the same vast ocean. Everything from the smallest bubble to the biggest waves is connected with the ocean though in appearance they differ. Similarly every human being or animal or plant is connected with the infinite ocean of energy or *prana*. In reality, wherever there is motion and life, behind (this) there is the storehouse of pranic energy.[11]

In the Yoga tradition, various forms of meditation are designed to open up blocks which are said to prevent the free flow of prana through the living being. While this view of meditation applies to the more advanced techniques used for spiritual development, a modified view relating to the practical Westernized forms of meditation is possible to envision. Such a view, it seems, is what the proponents of TM propose as an explanation for the effectiveness of their technique. Their leader, "Maharishi" Mahesh Yogi, refers to an entity he calls "creative intelligence," which is said to be a universal source of energy upon which each person draws during meditation. "Creative intelligence" is clearly a Westernized name for prana as an expression of the manifesting Being or Brahman.†[12]

While the notion of tapping into a universal energy source during meditation is as yet only theory and not scientific fact, it is not inconceivable that some as yet unidentified energy exchange may take place on some level during meditation. Theories of energy transfer are becoming more sophisticated. The effects of cosmic energy fields operating over vast distances are, for example, being systematically studied in such disciplines as biometeorology. If there is such an energy transfer in meditation, however, it must

† Brahman is the all-pervading transcendental reality of Hindu religion which is considered the source of all things and the bearer of all possibilities that are susceptible of actualization.

follow laws very different from those of the limited, readily observable energy forms that we know such as electricity. A fundamental energy source, if it exists, could probably be studied only through extremely subtle means by techniques not yet available to science. Perhaps a type of energy transformation such as is implied in the concept of prana is not so far removed from the concepts of mass–energy transformations which underlie the notions of modern theoretical physics. Certainly the presence of unknown forms of energy is not an unfamiliar concept to scientists working on discovering the properties of invisible and immaterial force fields. For this reason we should maintain an open-mindedness toward those explanations of meditation which conceive of the practice in terms of either the transfer or stabilizing of energy systems, or as a merging of individual energy systems with much broader energy fields. Were such concepts to prove correct, in whole or in part, they would certainly represent an important, indeed a fundamental, aspect of meditation.

In a similar way, the Zen concept of the Individual Mind or Little Mind (the ego) merging during meditation into what is described as Big Mind, draws upon similar reasoning and is derived from the same source—the intuitively conceived views of persons in states of altered consciousness, often during meditation. These views suggest a certain parallelism with some concepts in modern physics which conceive of the universe as looking, in the words of Sir James Jeans, "more like a great thought than like a great machine."[13] At present, however, we still have to consider this concept as belonging to the realm of metaphysics rather than to the spheres of physics or biology, its relationship to scientific inquiry remaining, as yet, no more than a speculative one.

Meditation, then, is a time when the organism shifts gears from the active to the receptive mode; from a state of ego dominance to a state where the ego is subordinate and can be partially dispensed with; from a state of automatization to one of deautomatization. It may also be a time when the organism experiences a shift from the dominance of one cerebral hemisphere to a state of concordance or harmony between both hemispheres of the brain; and perhaps a time when it experiences a shift from limited contact with some as yet unidentified energy source toward a more deep fundamental contact, or "flowing with," that source.

Whatever the status of some of these conjectures turns out to be, one thing is certain. A change from our ordinary way of experiencing goes on during meditation which in many respects is fundamental. Can it be, therefore, that entering this state regularly, day in and day out, brings about an equally profound change in our lives because we consistently *learn* from these shifts during meditation? We will now look at this possibility.

Natural Lessons

It could be argued that to confine meditation to a few minutes twice a day is to contradict its basic nature. Meditation is not only a formal practice, but a way of being in the world, an approach to life. Ultimately, we can probably benefit most from it if we allow its spirit to permeate our behavior.

That this often occurs spontaneously with regular meditators is indicated by the fact that many people report a change in their outlook on life as a result of meditating. Meditation seems to extend beyond the meditation session proper and affect the tenor of their lives. The question is why this should be so. Perhaps the answer will become clear if we consider the difference between meditation and dreaming.

Like meditation, dreams occur on a mental plane separate from that of daily life. It is often difficult to remember them, and when we do, they may seem alien to our waking perspectives. Meditation, on the other hand, while it too differs from everyday life, is nevertheless an alert, *wakeful* experience. We often evaluate on an intuitive level while meditating, and much of what goes on may be recalled later. Because it partakes of waking existence in this manner, meditation is in a unique position to affect the way we react to ourselves when we are *not* meditating. The wakeful "lessons" of meditation can carry over to other areas of our waking lives.

When we speak of the effects of repeated daily or twice-daily meditations, we are talking about lessons to which we are *regularly exposed*, making the potential influence of meditation on our lives considerable. A person who engages in a practical form of meditation for two twenty-minute sessions daily, is spending forty minutes each day meditating. Following each twenty-minute session, many meditators are also taught to remain for two to three minutes with eyes closed as they slowly "come out of" meditation. In this way, a total of about forty-six minutes each day is spent in a state of inner communion, an amount interestingly close to the time per day spent in the fifty-minute psychoanalytic hour. Unlike the psychoanalytic patient, however, the regular meditator spends this time with him or herself not three or five times a week, but every day—seven days a week. Viewed this way we can see why meditation often brings about personality change. It is useful to consider some of these lessons of meditation.

Meditation as Desensitization

We have mentioned systematic desensitization, the technique used in behavior therapy to treat phobias and other conditions which produce anxiety but we will examine it a bit more closely now because it seems to parallel the meditative state in certain important respects. Basically, systematic desensitization works in steps, the first being relaxation. After a person learns to put him or herself into a state of relaxation at will, they work with a therapist to construct what is called a "hierarchy" of the items that disturb them. If, for example, the person is afraid of spiders, with the therapist's help they will work out a graded list of imagined spider-threats. At the top of the list will be the least threatening contact the person can think of with respect to spiders—perhaps the word "spider" mentioned casually in a conversation—at the bottom, the most threatening spider-contact they can possibly imagine.

Systematic desensitization proper commences with the client relaxing deeply* and imagining his or her least threatening spider-

---

* He or she may make use of progressive relaxation or be asked to visualize a calm scene, or use some other technique to achieve this relaxation.

contact for a few seconds. As soon as they feel the slightest anxiety, they must return to relaxing deeply. This process continues over a number of sessions until bit by bit, against a background of calm, the person learns to tolerate each item on the list and can finally cope with the last, most threatening item. This method works because if a frightening response is produced in the presence of deep relaxation it seems to lose its "charge." Eventually the person may be ready to continue the desensitization process by working with real spiders instead of imagined ones. This is the final stage of retraining.

It is obvious that the situation in which a person undergoing systematic desensitization finds him or herself is similar in certain respects to that of the meditating person. In meditation the object chosen as the focus of meditation—a mantra or one's own breathing, for example—becomes a powerful "signal" to turn attention inward. Eventually this meditational focus can bring about deep relaxation when the person has been contemplating it only for a few seconds. Against the background of this "signal" for relaxation, many different kinds of thoughts, images, and sensations are experienced.† As these impressions and sensations float through the mind, the meditator is at the same time paying attention to his soothing focus. In this way, a deeply relaxed and quiet state becomes coupled with a rapid review of a great variety of experiences, both verbal and nonverbal. What is particularly important is that this massive drift of imagery and sensations during meditation is entirely *self*-initiated—that is, the person's own nervous system releases these impressions. This is an important aspect of the meditative process.

The relationship to systematic desensitization becomes clear as we watch what happens when this stream of consciousness continues during meditation. As thoughts, images, and sensations float through the mind, the meditative state appears to neutralize them. No matter how unfruitful a meditative session may *seem* to

† These thoughts occur during all forms of meditation and are particularly prominent during periods of tension-release. Although they may not receive much *deliberate* attention from the meditator, who is paying attention to his or her object of focus, their presence alone, against a background of relaxation, is sufficient for desensitization to take place.

the person when it is occurring (occasional sessions may, as we have seen, even be stressful) the most frequent comment of meditators afterward is that they find themselves emerging from meditation with the "charge" taken off their current concerns or problems. In both meditation and systematic desensitization, disturbing material has been reviewed in the presence of a predominant mood of quiet and relaxation and as a result the disturbing material has lost some of its "charge."

Does this mean then that meditation is just another form of behavior modification? It seems obvious that meditation is not just this and it is important to notice the difference between the two techniques. In systematic desensitization a therapist identifies the areas of anxiety in consultation with the patient. Together they define one specific problem (say, the fear of spiders) and then develop an organized plan for dealing with it. Patient and therapist then construct the list of feared situations, and the two cooperate in handling a *single isolated problem* in a step-by-step fashion.

In meditation, however, only the meditator is involved in the desensitization process. No one else's opinions are sought; no collaboration is required. The nervous system of the meditator releases the material to be "desensitized" when and if "it" feels the time is correct to do so. Although this is an entirely automatic process, the meditator himself can be said, in a sense, to "choose" the material to be neutralized on any particular day. In other words, the person who benefits from this experience is the one who has control over it. Also, during meditation a single problem is not isolated to be dealt with in a step-by-step organized fashion, but rather a host of problems seem to surface simultaneously to be dealt with *all at once*; a procedure of striking efficiency.

The brain of the meditator during meditation seems to behave, in fact, much like a computer programmed to run material through demagnetizing circuits to take off the charge. A computer can be set up to handle large amounts of data at one time and in the same way we might imagine subsystems within the brain scanning memory banks at lightning speed to select those contents of the mind which fit certain criteria. It seems likely that the material receiving priority for desensitization would be those items which are "judged" to be most urgent—provided that, at the moment, the brain-computer has determined that they can consciously be tolerated without too much anxiety. We seem to have a self-protective mechanism operating to determine if it is "safe" to surface certain thoughts or feelings during meditation—an automatic safety brake, as it were.‡ Such judgments and decisions are in no way outside of the capacity of the higher brain centers. As a matter of fact, the ability to make such subtle computations almost instantaneously is what makes the human brain infinitely more complex, sensitive, and effective than any electronic computer yet devised.

Meditation might be visualized then as a time when the brain, simultaneously weighing the considerations just mentioned and many others, makes a decision to surface certain mental contents rather than others for "demagnetizing" during the particular meditation session. A process such as this would give meditation a clear advantage over systematic desensitization when it comes to the scope of material that could be processed at one time. While systematic desensitization may be the most efficient treatment if we want to get at a limited problem such as a phobia, for handling a wide range of interrelated problems, meditation seems more efficient. As psychologist Daniel Goleman suggested, it may be a "global" (all-inclusive) form of desensitization.[1]

Meditation would seem to be ideal for desensitizing purposes. It is portable, we can "carry" it with us; it gives us an opportunity to handle emerging problems before they have had a chance to cause trouble; and because it is a process entirely under our own control, we are not ordinarily forced when meditating to deal with material that is too emotionally distressing. Such a process may affect the tenor of our lives outside of meditation as well. We are learning that we can process tensions as they arise, rather than

‡ Safety brakes may not operate when a machine is used improperly. Similarly, if meditation is used improperly (for example through overmeditation), or if a person is "allergic" to small amounts of meditation, this braking function seems to be thrown out of gear. Thoughts and feelings which are *not* easily tolerated may then surface.

allow them to fester. This may give us a new sense of being in control of our own moods and of the impact which life has upon us.

Self as "Being"

If translated into words, another fundamental lesson of meditation might go something like this:

> As I sit here quietly in my meditation, I *exist* even though I am separate from others. . . . I am now a being unto myself. . . . I am separate from lover, friend, mother, father, therapist, whomever . . . but in my meditation I do not sense this separateness as loneliness, I know it as closeness to myself and to life. . . .

Meditation is surprisingly complete in itself. When in this state, the outer world may threaten us, sights and sounds may pound at us for attention, but we recognize that none of this fundamentally changes "who" we are. Through it all, the quiet intake and outflow of breath goes on, the gentle rhythms of our pulse coordinate with the soundless beat of our mantra or with the motion of our breathing, and we know that whatever else may or may not happen, *life goes on.* This sense of sureness about our existence tends to linger with us after meditation and changes our perspective in many ways. Matters which formerly distressed us may shrink to relative unimportance alongside of this immediate experience of livingness. This lesson may lay the base for a new sense of identity, a new awareness of strengths and resources, increased feelings of personal rights—developments which, as we have seen, are often reported by meditators.

During meditation we are also learning not to force our minds or bodies to do what we "want" them to do or what we believe they "should" do, but rather to follow gently where they lead. This experience of trusting the wisdom of our own inner selves makes meditation an unusual experience for the average Westerner. Our society encourages us to manage ourselves as though we were objects, to force ourselves to do things (or not to do them). This is the by-product of a culture that measures work efficiency in terms of speed of production—the more we force, the greater the profits. Many of our personal problems, in fact, may be the products of our pathological time-oriented culture. In an agricultural society people learn to have infinite patience with the slow and compelling rhythms of nature and so may develop a somewhat different attitude—a greater appreciation for the value of waiting and watching, of flowing with the stream rather than fighting it. Meditation may lead us to such a receptive attitude as well, for we cannot meditate if we *try* to meditate, only if we *permit* meditation to occur.

The lesson of accomplishing through simply letting something happen can carry over into our ordinary lives. It is particularly important in terms of our ability to experience pleasure, because most pleasurable activities depend on our being able to *allow* them to happen.

In the new sex therapies, for example, increasing emphasis is placed on teaching people to forget about trying to achieve orgasm (or to achieve at all).[2] Instead, they are instructed to view the various sensations they experience during sexual activity as justification for the experience. A leisurely, nonstriving play experience, free of all demands and judgments about performing "correctly" or "incorrectly"—an experience without goals, with every step its own reward—seems to lead to the ultimate in pleasure and intimacy between partners. Essentially this is an expression of what we have called the "meditative mood" in the sexual experience.* When a person finally stops trying to be a lover, and experiences the luxury of having fun, when he or she "lets" everything happen and "makes" nothing happen, then the natural wisdom of the self takes over and a fulfilling sexual experience is achieved.

Learning Self-Permissiveness

Self-blame may be reduced through another of meditation's lessons. Children are often effectively shamed by looks and gestures

* A recent EEG study conducted at the New Jersey College of Medicine and Dentistry has shown a marked shift to right hemispheric dominance during orgasm—an indication of the involvement of the right hemisphere of the brain (the intuitive, holistic side) in sexual experience.[3]

of others around them even before they can understand language, but they are usually *scolded* through words. In this manner they come to blame themselves elaborately in verbal terms, mentally repeating: "I am a bad child"; "I am sloppy"; "dirty"; "dumb"; "selfish"; or whatever other disapproving terms they have learned to apply to themselves. Unfortunately they do this long after parents, teachers, and friends may have ceased to criticize them in this manner. The phrase "a still small voice" to refer to the conscience was therefore well chosen; our conscience is in many respects a "voice." If we tune down the language centers during meditation and allow the wordless aspects of experience to come into the forefront of our consciousness, we tend to "take the teeth out of" much of our self-blame.

In meditation, self-criticism seems to recede, along with other abstract verbal concepts, until it remains only a distant whisper. Simultaneously there seems to be desensitization during meditation of the wordless experiences of shame from very early childhood. This two-pronged attack on self-blame—the reduction of our self-criticizing statements about ourselves and the removing of the "charge" from early nonverbal shame experiences—is a powerful one. As a result, when meditating, we are often able to experience even the least desirable aspects of ourselves without anxiety. We readmit them to awareness, "make friends" with them, as it were, and in this way can exert constructive control over them.

These and other aspects of meditation constitute a profound self-education. Repeated daily over a period of time, these lessons form a conglomerate of experiences and attitudes which can affect our outlook in fundamental ways. One of the most profound lessons of meditation comes from temporarily experiencing the totality of ourselves, a totality which is unknowable through the limited concepts of our rational mind alone. In this sense, meditation opens up fresh vistas, unexplored territories. Where this new "meditative" awareness is likely to lead us, as a society, is the final question we will consider.

V

Conclusion

The Promise of the Future

It is evident that meditation has its limitations. It is not useful in all instances where tension-reduction may be sought, nor does it appeal to everyone. Despite this, it has advantages that set it apart from other familiar methods for relieving stress.

The practical forms of meditation are so easy to teach that almost anyone can learn them in one or two properly conducted instruction sessions. Even more important, these practical forms of meditation are "self-reinforcing," that is, they constitute their own reward. People *look forward* to meditating. Because of this, they are more apt to remain meditating over a period of time than they are to continue other daily regimes for relieving stress. These advantages make meditation probably the most effective of all known relaxation techniques for assisting large groups of people to counteract stress. This is a high qualification for usefulness in our society.

For those who are accustomed to think of "scientific" advances as man-made inventions or machines, this may be difficult to accept however. Can the carefully studied and controlled use of a natural practice be more effective in bringing about relaxation than manufactured devices such as pharmaceuticals or biofeedback machinery?

As we progress in scientific knowledge, it is increasingly clear that answers crucial to our survival are often found by working closely with the processes of nature and respecting their wisdom.

In the long run this may be far more productive than fighting against natural principles or trying to "subdue" them. Meditation fits into a general trend to uncover the potential of natural processes. It is simple. It relies on no gadgetry. It is available to all. In tune with the present social and research emphases, it is therefore likely to play an increasingly important role in contemporary life. Although this role may not always be constructive—misuse of meditation by the supercults for purposes of political or religious control, or the promotion of sensationalized versions of meditation taught without proper safeguards for consumers, are negative possibilities—on balance, it seems to have an exciting potential.

In Medicine

In the future, the meditative techniques may be used extensively along with conventional medical treatments for many of the stress-related illnesses. If the medical world can overcome initial doubts about its scientific validity, the way will be open, for example, for using meditation in hospital settings. Taught to preoperative patients, it might be an excellent preparation for surgery. Since a less stressed patient is known to be a better surgical risk, a therapist trained in teaching a variety of meditational and other relaxation techniques could be scheduled to meet with the patient on the day or evening before surgery. Not only would the meditation itself be calming, but the rapport established between meditation teacher and pupil—often a close and meaningful one—might additionally ease the distress of this period.

What could be useful for the surgical patient could also benefit other hospitalized patients as well. Not all seriously ill people can be expected to learn to meditate, but some could certainly do so, and others might find that some other relaxation technique worked well for them. A relaxation specialist on the hospital staff could have a wide repertoire of meditation and relaxation techniques at his or her command and be trained in selecting the appropriate one for a particular personality.

An additional medical use of meditation might be as an analgesic or pain reducer. The technique of meditating upon one's pain in order to reduce it can be very effective.* Related to the area of pain control is the possible use of meditation in *thanatology*, the new science dealing with ways of aiding the dying patient to come to terms with his or her experience in a more peaceful manner. At the Maryland Psychiatric Research Center, a group of psychiatrists headed by Dr. Stanislav Grof have achieved some remarkable results with terminal cancer patients using meditative states induced through the administration of LSD under carefully standardized conditions. After taking this medication, the patients are gently guided into that depth of consciousness which they personally can best tolerate. The resulting transformation in their view of themselves often brings about a difference in their entire medical and psychological condition. Though it may not prolong their lives, it can radically change the quality of their final days and months. In a controlled study with this procedure, these researchers found a marked lessening of depression, anxiety, and pain in most of the patients who had received this treatment. These people also tended to be less afraid of dying, to feel less isolated, and to cause fewer "problems" for the hospital staff.[1]

While it might be argued that these results were due to the use of a chemical agent (LSD) and had nothing to do with the induction of a meditative mood, this seems extremely unlikely. LSD is known to be dependent for its effects upon the atmosphere or "setting" in which it is taken. A sensitive guided experience by expert therapists was an essential part of the Maryland study, and the therapists actively helped the patients to achieve states of consciousness which can be identified as similar to some of the profound meditative states.

It is also possible that meditation will be found to speed up the healing process. A number of informal clinical reports suggest that this might be so† and a pilot study at the University of Pennsylvania Hospital suggests that gum infections may heal more rapidly in patients practicing meditation.[2] A special form of medita-

* See description in Chapter 6.
† See the account of the post-surgical meditator in section "Meditating when Ill" in Chapter 7.

333

tion is also being used clinically to assist healing in cancer patients. Dr. O. Carl Simonton, former chief of radiation therapy at the Travis Air Force Base in California, has successfully used a form of meditation which involves some guided imagery (together with cobalt radiation and psychotherapy) to treat cancer. While Simonton's technique is not identical with "meditation" as we have described it in this book—that is, it is not merely a simple centering exercise—he is making use of a strong meditative mood for healing purposes. His patients are asked to enter a state of deep relaxation for fifteen minutes three times daily, during which time they are mentally to picture their own cancer and vividly imagine their white blood cells, like a small "army" of helpers, clearing away the debris left by the radiation treatments and effectively promoting healing. They end up by visualizing themselves as completely well and healthy. Simonton's promising results suggest that research which involves the meditative mood in special formats should be explored further. Out of 50 patients in one research study who were treated by his method, 37 (or 74 per cent) had either "good" or "excellent" responses and only 4 of these 50 patients had a "poor" response, despite the fact that a number of them had very extensive disease. Of the "excellent" respondents (12 in number), 8 had been given less than a 50 per cent chance for cure.[3]

Medicine may also prescribe the use of practical forms of meditation more or less continuously throughout the day for special purposes. A hypertensive or "Type A"‡ behavior person who is advised by his physician to "slow down," "enjoy" himself more, or "stop worrying" is being asked to change his whole way of life, his *attitude* toward living, and even his conception of what life is all about, rather than simply alter a few habits. To accomplish this, variations of meditation may even need to be introduced into the *activities* of such a person in addition to its regular scheduled daily use. Forms of walking meditation practiced with eyes open, engaged in at intervals throughout the day, may serve, for example, to deepen and reinforce the effects of regular meditation.

‡ "Type A behavior" is a form of compulsive overactivity which has been shown to be prevalent in heart-attack-prone individuals.[4]

Meditative exercises accompanying simple activities such as cooking, tennis, or swimming, may be assigned, and could serve to lessen the stress of life in an effective manner. Interweaving of the meditative mood with everyday living is regularly practiced by many who are trained in spiritual disciplines and may be the reason why their lives seem to be pervaded with a natural calm that seems foreign to an action-oriented Westerner.

Although such changes in routine may be out of step with the standards of a technological society which measures efficiency in terms of work output and goods produced rather than in terms of human resources conserved, such a program may be the therapy of choice for those people who have become casualties of our society —people who suffer physical and emotional damage because they are overinvolved in our rapid pace of life and cannot "get off the merry-go-round." Special techniques designed to facilitate the generalization of the meditative mood to many aspects of their lives, could in effect give such people a retraining in living.

In Psychiatry

We have already discussed some of the potential uses of meditation in psychiatry. It may be widely used for the relief of anxiety and should be of considerable help to patients suffering from chronic fatigue or sleep disturbances. It will no doubt be explored for treating the addictions and for prison psychiatry, and may also be used along with psychotherapy to treat the milder forms of depression.

Besides these specific applications, psychotherapists may use meditation extensively as a general "facilitator" of adjustment. Maladaptive behaviors such as irritability, low frustration tolerance, an uncontrollable temper, and others may regularly be treated by using some form of meditation along with psychotherapy. Strong submissive trends or a poor sense of identity in a patient could automatically suggest to the psychotherapist the use of meditation. Combined with psychotherapy it may also be used to help patients become more emotionally "alive" and better able to sense their deeper problems. Meditation will almost certainly be tried with systematic desensitization and other behavior modification techniques, since present research suggests that it can be as effective for inducing deep relaxation as the muscle-relaxing strategies, and often far simpler to learn.

It seems likely that psychotherapists will increasingly teach their own patients to meditate rather than relying on outside meditation teachers or organizations. This will insure their supervising their patients' meditation in a clinically appropriate manner and perhaps assigning an appropriate mantra for each patient's condition based on research on the effects of sound on personality. Some psychotherapists may meditate together with their patients on occasion; and in group therapy, group meditations may be found useful for increasing rapport between participating group members.

In Education

Use of meditation in the school system is likely to increase when it is realized that nonreligious forms of meditation can be taught by regular school personnel without any additional expense or inconvenience to the school system. However there may be some initial difficulties in the way of adoption of meditation in the schools. The devotional aspects of TM, along with the Hindu religious philosophy underlying it, have been the cause for a growing legal battle over whether or not TM should be taught in the American public school system.* This is a battle that does not concern the nonreligious, scientifically devised forms of practical meditation, but which may cause some confusion in the mind of the public with regard to meditation in general.

There is always the danger that *all* techniques of meditation may be rejected by certain groups because of the mistaken conclusion that there are no forms of meditation which are truly secular. As Benson, Woolfolk, myself, and other researchers have shown, however, scientifically devised forms of meditation are an effective

* To obtain a detailed summary of these issues and information on the religious background of the TM movement, the reader can write to the Coalition for Religious Integrity, Box 75, Maplewood, N.J. 07040.

alternative to religious forms of meditation for practical and clinical purposes. It would be my supposition that the result of the present legal controversy with respect to TM may be that large institutions such as schools, hospitals, and the like will increasingly turn to standardized forms of meditation that are entirely free of any religious connotations—if indeed they turn to meditation at all.†

If the schools do take it up, their use of meditation will probably involve regular "meditation breaks" to ease tensions in the classroom and help the students concentrate. To be effective such breaks will need to be more than mere token silences such as the one-minute "meditation" pause recently instituted in Connecticut schools, where children were told to sit still, remain quiet, and "meditate," without any explanation of what this meant. When children sit still doing nothing they are likely merely to squirm or giggle. At any rate, they are not meditating in the sense that we have been describing this process. Like people of any age, children must be taught *how* to meditate.

If meditation becomes widespread in the school system, its instruction may be carried out by classroom teachers who are experienced in one of the meditative techniques. An alternative plan may be to have special relaxation instructors on the school staff who will go from classroom to classroom imparting skills in the various meditation and relaxation techniques. Meditation can also be taught as part of physical education programs, possibly together with some Yoga training in physical postures and breathing exercises (Hatha Yoga).

Group meditation may be found useful directly before examinations to help reduce test anxiety, and students may be taught how to "break up" their homework into short study-blocks, interspersing these with mini-meditations in order to increase staying power during long hours of study. Teachers may discover that the atmosphere in the classroom is improved when the class meditates together. Where I have seen this done, class discussion afterward

† The U. S. Navy has, for example, recently endorsed the use of Benson's meditation technique (taught by one of its own staff members) in a program of Leadership and Management Training for Navy recruits at San Diego.

was more spontaneous; the students were less defensive and more co-operative with one another.

Meditation may also be found useful in programs teaching creative skills. Meditating before commencing the day's work on a creative project could become a recognized means of diminishing self-criticism and permitting an easy flow of ideas. Used intermittently during long hours of work, it might also be widely adopted as a way of "recharging the battery," and increasing energy and enthusiasm. Many creative people will also no doubt become aware of its usefulness in handling blocks to creativity.

In Business and Industry

Corporations may take to using meditation but probably only if it proves effective for increasing productivity. Whether workers on a production line will produce more rapidly if they meditate is unproven, but relaxed people usually handle jobs more easily, efficiently, and accurately than tense ones, which should make meditation an asset. The health of meditating workers will also tend to be better (fewer stress-related illnesses) and this could lead to a reduction in absenteeism. Possibly certain forms of addiction will be helped by meditation as well—a fact which should appeal to business. Meditation breaks during the day may also improve job satisfaction and make for greater alertness and fewer mistakes, thus cutting down on work accidents. Because of its potential benefits in these areas, meditation is likely to be adopted by those businesses and industries with the foresight to see that such improvements in the quality of the work, health, and job satisfaction of employees could turn out to be extremely profitable in the long run, even though a meditation program might involve sacrificing a few moments a day in production time for meditation breaks.

On the executive level meditation may be accepted sooner. Meditation fosters initiative, imagination, and independence, and these traits are, at least theoretically, highly desirable in executives. Since executives are also prone to be "Type A behavior" people, executive meditation breaks are not difficult to envision becoming company policy. In the same way, the use of group meditation before "brainstorming" sessions might create a greater flow of ideas; meditation before board meetings might lead to more harmonious teamwork among participants; and periodic meditation breaks during day-long conferences could be extremely relieving to people forced to concentrate for many hours on the presentation of detailed information.

Institutions such as hospitals, schools, or businesses using large-scale programs of meditation will probably use a number of *different* forms of meditation rather than any one form. Presumably these will be taught by a relaxation expert on the staff who will be on hand at all times to deal with problems which might arise. Not having allegiance to any particular form of meditation or relaxation, such specialists will be in a position to select whichever technique might be most suitable for each person; switch it when necessary for another; introduce promising new techniques when these become available; and conduct suitable comparison studies among techniques.

Meditation Western Style

The West's first approach to any new technique is usually analytic—the technique is broken down into its components and studied. As we begin to take meditation seriously, this will undoubtedly be one of the first things that will happen. Different kinds of meditative techniques will be dissected (sometimes beyond recognition), experimented with, and then either reassembled in something like their original form, or combined with other techniques such as biofeedback, physical exercise, muscle relaxation, or others. They will then be used for practical purposes and may bring about some interesting innovations in our popular life-style, the most prominent of which will be the meditation break and the meditation room.

If meditation is introduced into the programs of large organizations, a meditation room will be a necessity. Since it need only be a simple place, partially soundproofed and with a few comfortable straight-back chairs, low lighting, a carpet, and perhaps a green plant or so, the modest cost of establishing such a room may be a good investment in terms of the relief it can bring to people who need it during a pressured day at the office. When for one semester we set up such a meditation room in the Psychology building at Princeton, students expressed a strong sense of loss when it had to be dismantled.

Religious institutions, of course, have traditionally supplied sanctuaries in churches or temples where people could be alone and turn inward in a tranquil atmosphere. With the decline of participation in the organized religions in recent years, this manner of evoking the meditative mood is no longer available for many; an additional reason why modern men and women may be in need of a socially sanctioned retreat—a meditation break or a meditation room—which is respected by others.

Not only may institutions find it to their advantage to schedule meditation breaks in a systematic manner, but this practice may become accepted in social gatherings as well. My husband and I have found that when we have guests who are meditators, they are usually delighted with the suggestion that we all meditate together before dinner. After we have done so, we feel closer to one another, and the usual social role-playing is gratefully set aside.

It seems likely that the West will first use meditation as an emergency measure, putting it to work to patch up imbalances, counteract some of our society's excesses, and perhaps make "the system" work better. Companies may use it so that workers will complain less; the military so that soldiers can tolerate battle stress better; and school systems to insure that children are less trouble to their teachers. But will meditation remain only a palliative—tame and under our control?

While some of the larger institutions may initially view it as strictly utilitarian and manageable, it is doubtful if meditation, however fragmented or disguised, is likely to become simply a means of smoothing the machinery of any society. Meditation, even in the practical forms we have been considering, has an im-

340

pact on values, and value changes brought about by its wide-scale use could conceivably alter some of our basic emphases as a society.

Toward a New Perspective

With large groups of people practicing meditation, we may find a number of unexpected shifts occurring in our outlook. One such shift may be a new view of our life-pace. Meditation widely practiced could lead to a collective easing of life-pace and a new use of whatever time becomes available in a society facing economic hardships and other forms of continuing stress. Not only would the meditation be an anti-stress measure, but it could be of considerable help to people who have been unwittingly brought up to be compulsive "workhorses." Often Westerners are nonplussed when they have to slow their hectic pace momentarily to spend time with themselves. We may plunge into escapist activities to obliterate the necessity of doing so. It is possible that meditation can make a major contribution toward effective use of time since it teaches us to spend a greater portion of it simply "living," less in compulsive accomplishing. Widely practiced, meditation may result in a gradual lessening of our present overemphasis on *extrinsic* rewards (those rewards derived from advantages outside of the experience itself, such as money, power, or prestige) and an increased emphasis on *intrinsic* rewards (the rewarding aspects of experience valued for *its own sake*).

A society influenced by the meditative point of view will also be likely to develop an interest in and respect for the human body different from that which Westerners have known in the past. One of the fundamental lessons of meditation is that we exist as *living beings*. This realization may lead to renewed interest in that which is healthy and an aversion to that which is unhealthy, for ourselves and our environment. A society with a meditative perspective may well avoid foodstuffs, environments, or activities which run counter to natural rhythms, just as individual meditators now tend to shy away from the abuse of addictive substances.

If this happens, a new kind of ecological awareness may flow from a deep inward conviction of our own interrelatedness with all that surrounds us—our fellow human beings, animals, plants, and the resources of the earth.

If society absorbs the lessons of meditation we will be less apt to view science as an inevitable battle between man and natural forces, less eager to define scientific achievement as the winning of yet another round in our fight to "conquer the earth." Instead, we may begin to heed the gentle voices of order and balance that come to us from the natural world. This should result in our supporting a science and technology that work hand in hand with nature, instead of fighting against it.

The widespread use of meditation could also bring about a greater sensitivity to what are often called spiritual values. This does not necessarily mean that participation in organized religion will increase, although conceivably it might, but rather that we will come to accept some intangible aspects of life more readily. This change of attitude will stem from the meditative experience itself, an experience that reflects the flow of life with all its inevitability and unknowable essense. Because of this contact with that which is natural and essential, a population of meditators might come to feel, at last, a unity with the universe. This in turn could conceivably help change our basic way of viewing human destiny and ultimately our own role on this planet.

Notes

Introduction

The meditation instructions at the commencement of this section (in some cases paraphrased) are drawn from the first eleven books below:

1. A. Watts, "The Art of Meditation," in *What Is Meditation?*, ed. John White (Garden City: Anchor Press/Doubleday, 1974), p. 34.
2. TM Instructors, as quoted in P. D. Hemingway, *The Transcendental Meditation Primer* (New York: McKay, 1975), p. 29.
3. J. H. Schultz and W. Luthe, *Autogenic Methods*, 6 vols. (New York: Grune, 1969), Vol I, p. 7.
4. TM Instructors, op. cit., pp. 17 and 29.
5. H. Johari, *Dhanwantari* (San Francisco: Rams Head, 1974), p. 76.
6. M. Sadhu, *Meditation* (London: George Allen, 1967), p. 72.
7. TM Instructors, giving International Meditation Society standard lectures on Transcendental Meditation, Edison, N.J., January 15, 1973.
8. H. H. Bloomfield, M. Cain, D. T. Jaffe, and A. Rubottom, "What is Transcendental Meditation?," in *What Is Meditation?*, ed. John White (New York: Anchor Press/Doubleday, 1974), p. 88.
9. S. N. C. Yati, "Entering the World of Meditation," in *What Is Meditation?*, ed. John White (New York: Anchor Press/Doubleday, 1974), p. 42.
10. B. R. Dass, *The Only Dance There Is* (Garden City: Anchor Press/Doubleday, 1974), p. 50.
11. TM Instructors, as quoted in Hemingway, op. cit., p. 17.

12. M. Ullman, S. Krippner, and A. Vaughan, *Dream Telepathy* (New York: Macmillan, 1973).
13. L. LeShan, *The Medium, the Mystic and the Physicist* (New York: Viking, 1974).
14. S. Grof, *Realms of the Human Unconscious* (New York: Viking, 1975).
15. C. T. Tart, *States of Consciousness* (New York: Dutton, 1975); *Transpersonal Psychologies*, ed. C. T. Tart (New York: Harper, 1975).

CHAPTER 1: *The Ageless Practice*

1. A. J. Maslow, *Toward a Psychology of Being*, (rev. ed., 1968) (Princeton, N.J.: Van Nostrand, 1962).
2. Meditation Journal of George Edington (personal communication).
3. For a comprehensive review of the various forms of meditation, see J. Naranjo, "Meditation: Its Spirit and Technique," in *On the Psychology of Meditation*, ed. J. Naranjo and R. Ornstein (New York: Viking, 1971).
4. E. Conze, *Buddhist Meditation* (New York: Harper, 1969), p. 83.
5. B. S. Rajneesh, *Dynamics of Meditation* (Bombay: A Life Awakening Publication Movement Publication, 1972), p. 130.
6. M. Mahesh Yogi, *Transcendental Meditation* (New York: New Am. Lib. [Signet], 1963).
7. D. Denniston and P. McWilliams, *The TM Book* (Allen Park, Mich.: Versemonger Press, 1975).
8. The name Mahesh Yogi (or Yogi Mahesh) is the appropriate designation for one trained as a Yogi with the first name of Mahesh (renunciants are not concerned with their last name because they traditionally do not reveal their past). The Sanskrit term "Maharishi" placed before Mahesh Yogi's name, designates a rare "high" state of consciousness traditionally said to have been attained only by seers or prophets of the Vedas who received revealed knowledge from the "sound within" rather than from the scriptures. To refer to the modern exponent of the TM movement by such a term may be quite appropriate for TM teachers, if this is the way they view their own guru, but not being an objective description, it does not seem to have a place in a scientific consideration of meditation. In this book, therefore, without implying any disrespect to the leader of the TM movement, the term "Maharishi" is placed in quotes.
9. Researchers interested in obtaining information about teaching

this technique can write to Dr. P. Carrington, Department of Psychology, Princeton University, Princeton, N.J. 08540.

10. R. K. Wallace and H. Benson, "The Physiology of Meditation," *Scientific American* (February 1972), pp. 84–90; R. K. Wallace, H. Benson, and A. F. Wilson, "A Wakeful Hypometabolic Physiologic State," *American Journal of Physiology* 221 (1971), pp. 795–99; R. K. Wallace, H. Benson, A. F. Wilson, and M. D. Garrett, "Decreased Blood Lactate During Transcendental Meditation," *Federation Proceedings* 30 (1971), p. 376.

11. H. Benson, *The Relaxation Response* (New York: Morrow, 1975).

12. Ibid., p. 114.

13. D. Tolliver, "Personality as a Factor Determining Response to Two Different Meditative Techniques" (Senior Thesis, Princeton University, 1976).

14. L. Fehmi, "Open Focus Training" (Paper presented at the Annual Meeting of the Biofeedback Research Society, Monterey, Calif., February 5, 1975). Researchers interested in obtaining information about this technique can write to Dr. Fehmi at 905 Herrontown Rd., Princeton, N.J. 08540.

15. R. L. Woolfolk, L. Carr-Kaffashan, P. M. Lehrer, and T. F. McNulty, "Meditation Training as a Treatment for Insomnia," *Behavior Therapy*, in press.

CHAPTER 2: *Is Meditation Unique?*

1. E. W. Maupin, "Meditation," in *Ways of Growth*, ed. H. A. Otto and J. Mann (New York: Viking, 1968), pp. 189–98.

2. R. E. Shor, "Hypnosis and the Concept of the Generalized Reality-Orientation," in *Altered States of Consciousness*, ed. C. T. Tart (New York: Wiley, 1969), pp. 233–50.

3. Ibid., p. 241.

4. R. White, "A Preface to a Theory of Hypnotism," *Journal of Abnormal and Social Psychology* 36 (1941), pp. 477–506.

5. N. Kleitman, *Sleep and Wakefulness* (Chicago: Univ. of Chicago Press, 1963), pp. 329–38.

6. L. Chertok and P. Kramarz, "Hypnosis, Sleep and Electroencephalography," *Journal of Nervous and Mental Disease* 128 (1959), pp. 227–38; A. L. Loomis, E. N. Harvey, and G. A. Hobart, "Electrical Potentials of the Human Brain," *Journal of Experimental Physiology* 19 (1936), pp. 249–79; J. B. Dynes, "Objective Method for Distinguishing Sleep from the Hypnotic Trance," *Archives of Neurology and Psychiatry* 57 (1947), pp. 84–93; A. Kasamatsu and T. Hirai, "An Electroencephalographic

Study on the Zen Meditation (Zazen)," in *Altered States of Consciousness*, ed. C. T. Tart (New York: Wiley, 1969), pp. 489–501.

7. Kasamatsu and Hirai, op. cit.
8. A. Maslow, as quoted in Shor, op. cit., p. 249.
9. J. H. Schultz and W. Luthe, *Autogenic Therapy*, 6 vols. (New York: Grune, 1969).
10. J. Breuer and S. Freud (1893), "Studies on Hysteria," in *Standard Edition of the Complete Psychological Works of Sigmund Freud*, ed. J. Strachey, Vol. II (London: Hogarth, 1955).
11. S. Freud (1895), "The Psychotherapy of Hysteria" in J. Breuer and S. Freud, "Studies on Hysteria," in *Standard Edition of the Complete Psychological Works of Sigmund Freud*, ed. J. Strachey, Vol. II pp. 255–305. (London: Hogarth, 1955).
12. E. Jacobson, *You Must Relax* (New York: McGraw, 1934).
13. E. Jacobson, *Progressive Relaxation* (Chicago: Univ. of Chicago Press, 1938); *Modern Treatment of Tense Patients* (Springfield, Ill.: C. C. Thomas, 1970); *Biology of Emotions* (Springfield, Ill.: C. C. Thomas, 1967); *Tension in Medicine* (Springfield, Ill.: C. C. Thomas, 1967).
14. J. Wolpe, *Psychotherapy by Reciprocal Inhibition* (Stanford: Stanford Univ. Press, 1958).
15. D. A. Bernstein and T. D. Borkovec, Excerpt from *Progressive Relaxation Training Record* (Champaign, Ill.: Res. Press, 1973).
16. B. B. Brown, *New Mind, New Body* (New York: Harper, 1974).
17. E. E. Green, A. M. Green, and E. D. Walters, "Voluntary Control of Internal States," *Journal of Transpersonal Psychology* 2 (1970), pp. 1–25.
18. Kasamatsu and Hirai, op. cit.
19. G. Schwartz, "Biofeedback, Self-Regulation and the Patterning of Physiological Processes," *American Scientist* 63 (1975), pp. 314–24.

CHAPTER 3: *The Scientist Takes Note*

1. E. Green and A. Green, "The Ins and Outs of Mind-Body Energy," *Science Year*, 1974, Field Enterprises, Chicago, Ill.
2. For a description of current experimentation with psychedelic drugs see R. Ashley, "The Other Side of LSD," *New York Times Magazine*, October 19, 1975.
3. For a description of biofeedback research see B. B. Brown, *New Mind, New Body* (New York: Harper, 1974).
4. P. K. Bagchi and M. A. Wenger, "Simultaneous EEG and Other

Recordings During Some Yogic Practices," *Journal of Electroencephalography and Clinical Neurophysiology* 10 (1958), p. 193.

5. B. K. Anand, G. S. Chhina, and B. Singh, "Studies on Sri Ramanand Yogi During His Stay in an Air-Tight Box," *Indian Journal of Medical Research* 49 (1961), pp. 82–89.

6. P. K. Bagchi and M. A. Wenger, "Electrophysiological Correlates of Some Yogi Exercises," *Journal of Electroencephalography and Clinical Neurophysiology* 7 (1957), pp. 132–49.

7. B. K. Anand, G. S. Chhina, and B. Singh, "Some Aspects of Electroencephalographic Studies of Yogis," *Journal of Electroencephalography and Clinical Neurophysiology* 13 (1961), pp. 452–56.

8. A. Kasamatsu and T. Hirai, "An Electroencephalographic Study on the Zen Meditation (Zazen)," in *Altered States of Consciousness* ed. C. T. Tart (New York: Wiley, 1969), pp. 489–501.

9. H. Bloomfield, M. Cain, and D. Jaffe, *TM: Discovering Inner Energy and Overcoming Stress* (New York: Delacorte Press, 1975); D. Denniston and P. McWilliams, *The TM Book* (Allen Park, Mich.: Versemonger Press, 1975).

10. R. K. Wallace, "Physiological Effects of Transcendental Meditation," *Science* (March 27, 1970), pp. 1751–54; R. K. Wallace, H. Benson, and A. F. Wilson, "A Wakeful Hypometabolic Physiologic State," *American Journal of Physiology* 221 (1971), pp. 795–99.

11. P. B. C. Fenwick, "Metabolic and EEG Changes during Transcendental Meditation" (Paper read at conference on "TM: Research and Application," Institute of Science and Technology, University of Wales, Cardiff, 1974).

12. Wallace, 1970, op. cit.

13. J. Allison, "Respiratory Changes During the Practice of the Technique of Transcendental Meditation," *Lancet* (April 18, 1970), pp. 833–34.

14. Ibid.

15. N. N. Das and H. Gastaut, "Variations de l'Activité Électrique du Cerveau, du Coeur, et des Muscles Séquelletiques au Cours de la Méditation et de l'Extase Yogique," *Journal of Electroencephalography and Clinical Neurophysiology*, Supp. 6 (1957), pp. 211–19; Wallace, 1970, op. cit.; Wallace, et. al., 1971, op. cit.; J. P. Banquet, "EEG and Meditation," *Journal of Electroencephalography and Clinical Neurophysiology* 33 (1972), pp. 449–58.

16. Banquet, op. cit.

17. L. S. Otis, "TM and Sleep" (Paper presented before the An-

nual Meeting of the American Psychological Association, New Orleans, 1974); J. Younger, W. Adriane, and R. Berger, "Sleep during Transcendental Meditation," *Perceptual and Motor Skills* 40 (1975), pp. 953–54; R. R. Pagano, et al., "Sleep During Transcendental Meditation," *Science* (January 23, 1976), pp. 308–10.

18. Otis, op. cit.
19. Banquet, op. cit.
20. B. C. Glueck and C. F. Stroebel, "Biofeedback and Meditation in the Treatment of Psychiatric Illness," *Comprehensive Psychiatry* 16 (1975), pp. 303–21.
21. L. Goldstein, personal communication to the author, March 1976, New Jersey College of Medicine and Dentistry, Piscataway, N.J.
22. Wallace, 1970, op. cit.
23. G. E. Schwartz, "Pros and Cons of Meditation: Current Findings on Physiology and Anxiety, Self-Control, Drug Abuse and Creativity" (Paper delivered before the 81st Annual Convention of the American Psychological Association, Montreal, 1973); Glueck and Stroebel, op. cit.
24. D. Orme-Johnson, "Autonomic Stability and Transcendental Meditation," *Psychosomatic Medicine*, 35 (1973), pp. 341–49.
25. Ibid.
26. D. J. Goleman and G. E. Schwartz, "Meditation as an Intervention in Stress Reactivity," *Journal of Consulting and Clinical Psychology*, 44 (1976), 456–66.
27. Wallace, et al., 1971, op. cit.
28. M. Jones and V. Mellersh, "Comparison of Exercise Response in Anxiety States and Normal Controls," *Psychosomatic Medicine*, 8 (1946), pp. 180–87; F. Pitts, "The Biochemistry of Anxiety," *Scientific American* (February 1969), pp. 69–75.
29. H. Ritterstaedt and H. Schenkluhn, "Measuring Changes of the Skin Temperature During the Practice of Transcendental Meditation" (Unpublished paper, Max Planck Institute, Germany, 1972); R. K. Wallace and H. Benson, "The Physiology of Meditation," *Scientific American* (February 1972), pp. 84–90.
30. H. Benson, B. R. Marzetta, and B. A. Rosner, "Decreased Systolic Blood Pressure in Hypertensive Subjects Who Practiced Meditation," *Journal of Clinical Investigation* 52 (1973), p. 8a.
31. H. Benson, *The Relaxation Response* (New York: Morrow, 1975).
32. K. S. Blasdell, "The Effects of Transcendental Meditation Technique upon a Complex Perceptual-Motor Task," in *Scientific Research on the Transcendental Meditation Program: Collected*

Papers, ed. D. W. Orme-Johnson and J. T. Farrow, Vol. I (New York: Maharishi International University [MIU] Press, in press); A. G. P. Rimol, "Transcendental Meditation and Its Effects on Sensory and Motor Perception" (Senior Thesis, Princeton University, 1974).

33. M. Pirot, "The Effects of Transcendental Meditation Upon Auditory Discrimination," in *Scientific Research on the Transcendental Meditation Program: Collected Papers,* ed. D. W. Orme-Johnson and J. T. Farrow, Vol. I (New York, MIU Press, in press).

34. F. M. Brown, W. S. Stewart, and J. I. Blodgett, "EEG Kappa Rhythms During Transcendental Meditation and Possible Perceptual Threshold Changes Following" (Paper delivered to the Kentucky Academy of Sciences, November 13, 1971).

35. E. Braütigam, "The Effect of Transcendental Meditation on Drug Abusers" (Research report, City Hospital at Malmö, Sweden, December 1971); S. Nidich, W. Seeman, and T. Dreskin, "Influence of Transcendental Meditation: A Replication," *Journal of Counseling Psychology* 20 (1973), pp. 565–66; P. D. Ferguson and J. Gowan, "The Influence of Transcendental Meditation on Anxiety, Depression, Aggression, Neuroticism and Self-Actualization," *Journal of Humanistic Psychology,* in press; L. A. Hjelle, "Transcendental Meditation and Psychological Health," *Perceptual and Motor Skills* 39 (1974), pp. 623–28; S. Shackman, "The Effect of Two Relaxation Techniques on Anxiety, Self-Concept and Personality Growth" (Senior Thesis, Princeton University, 1974); D. Ballou, "The Transcendental Meditation Program at Stillwater Prison," in *Scientific Research on the Transcendental Meditation Program: Collected Papers,* ed. D. W. Orme-Johnson and J. T. Farrow, Vol. I (New York: MIU Press, in press).

36. Shackman, op. cit.; Glueck and Stroebel, op. cit.

37. A. I. Abrams, "Paired-Associate Learning and Recall: A Pilot Study of the Transcendental Meditation Technique," in *Scientific Research on the Transcendental Meditation Program: Collected Papers,* ed. D. W. Orme-Johnson and J. T. Farrow, Vol. I (New York: MIU Press, in press).

38. D. E. Miskiman, "The Effect of Transcendental Meditation on the Organization of Thinking and Recall (Secondary Organization)," in *Scientific Research on the Transcendental Meditation Program: Collected Papers,* ed. D. W. Orme-Johnson and J. T. Farrow, Vol. I (New York: MIU Press, in press).

39. M. J. MacCullum, "Transcendental Meditation and Creativity," in *Scientific Research on the Transcendental Meditation Program:*

Collected Papers, ed. D. W. Orme-Johnson and J. T. Farrow, Vol. I (New York: MIU Press, in press).

40. R. W. Collier, "The Effect of Transcendental Meditation upon University Academic Attainment," in *Scientific Research on the Transcendental Meditation Program: Collected Papers*, ed. D. W. Orme-Johnson and J. T. Farrow, Vol. I (New York: MIU Press, in press).

41. D. R. Frew, "Transcendental Meditation and Productivity," *Academy of Management Journal* 17, no. 2 (1974), pp. 362–68.

42. Hjelle, op. cit.

43. W. Seeman, S. Nidich, and T. Banta, "Influence of Transcendental Meditation on a Measure of Self-Actualization," *Journal of Counseling Psychology* 19 (1972), pp. 184–87; Ferguson and Gowan, op. cit.

44. Ballou, op. cit.; M. Cunningham and W. Koch, "The Transcendental Meditation Program and Rehabilitation: A Pilot Project at the Federal Correctional Institute at Lompoc, California," in *Scientific Research on the Transcendental Meditation Program: Collected Papers*, ed. D. W. Orme-Johnson and J. T. Farrow, Vol. I (New York: MIU Press, in press).

45. M. Shafii, R. Lavely, and R. Jaffe, "Meditation and the Prevention of Drug Abuse," *American Journal of Psychiatry* 132 (1975), pp. 942–45.

46. R. Honsberger and A. F. Wilson, "Transcendental Meditation in Treating Asthma," *Respiratory Therapy: The Journal of Inhalation Technology* 3 (1973), pp. 48–81.

47. Benson, op. cit.

48. C. Allen, "Possible Psychological and Physiological Effects of Transcendental Meditation on Aphasic Patients" (Unpublished paper, University of Michigan, 1973).

49. C. Simonton, "The Role of the Mind in Cancer Therapy," in *Psychiatry and Mysticism*, ed. S. R. Dean (Chicago: Nelson-Hall, 1975), pp. 293–308.

50. C. Allen, "Possible Effects of Transcendental Meditation on Stuttering" (Unpublished paper, University of Michigan, 1973).

51. Glueck and Stroebel, op. cit.; P. Carrington and H. S. Ephron, "Meditation as an Adjunct to Psychotherapy," in *New Dimensions in Psychiatry: A World View*, ed. S. Arieti and G. Chrzanowski (New York: Wiley, 1975), pp. 262–91.

CHAPTER 4: *The Other Side of Research*

1. P. B. C. Fenwick, "Metabolic and EEG Changes during Transcendental Meditation" (Paper read at conference on "TM:

Research and Application," Institute of Science and Technology, University of Wales, Cardiff, 1974).

2. R. K. Wallace, "Physiological Effects of Transcendental Meditation," *Science* (March 27, 1970), pp. 1751–54.

3. M. West, "The Effect of a 20 Minute Period of TM on the Performance of a Short Term Memory Task" (Paper presented at conference on "TM: Research and Application," Institute of Science and Technology, University of Wales, Cardiff, 1974).

4. A. I. Abrams, "Paired-Associate Learning and Recall: A Pilot Study of the Transcendental Meditation Technique," in *Scientific Research on the Transcendental Meditation Program: Collected Papers*, ed. D. W. Orme-Johnson and J. T. Farrow, Vol. I (New York: MIU Press, in press).

5. R. Shaw and D. Kolb, "Improved Reaction Time Following Transcendental Meditation," in *Scientific Research on the Transcendental Meditation Program: Collected Papers*, ed. D. W. Orme-Johnson and J. T. Farrow, Vol. I (New York: MIU Press, in press).

6. M. Shook, "The Effects of TM on Simple and Complex Reaction Time" (Senior Thesis, Princeton University, 1976).

7. D. Daniels, personal communication to the author, April 1976.

8. D. Denniston and P. McWilliams, *The TM Book* (Allen Park, Mich.: Versemonger Press, 1975).

9. M. Shafii, R. Lavely, and R. Jaffe, "Meditation and Marijuana," *American Journal of Psychiatry* 131 (1974), pp. 60–63.

10. S. Shackman, "The Effect of Two Relaxation Techniques on Anxiety, Self-Concept and Personality Growth" (Senior Thesis, Princeton University, 1974).

11. J. C. Smith, "The Psychotherapeutic Effects of Transcendental Meditation with Controls for Expectation of Relief and Daily Sitting," *Journal of Consulting and Clinical Psychology*, in press.

12. Ibid; M. Shelly, personal communication to the author, Kansas University, Lawrence, Kans., February 1976; P. Davies, personal communication to the author, Kansas University, Lawrence, Kans., February 1976; L. S. Otis, "TM and Sleep" (Paper presented before the Annual Meeting of the American Psychological Association, New Orleans, 1974).

CHAPTER 5: *Learning How to Meditate*

1. J. C. Smith, "Transcendental Meditation and Anxiety" (Dissertation proposal, Michigan State University, 1973), p. 29.

Notes

CHAPTER 6: *The Challenge of Tension-Release*

1. J. H. Schultz and W. Luthe, *Autogenic Therapy*, 6 vols. (New York: Grune, 1969), Vol. I.
2. Ibid., Vol. I, p. 29.
3. Ibid., Vol. II, p. 12.
4. Ibid., Vol. V, pp. 180–81.
5. Ibid., Vol. IV, pp. 119–23.
6. Ibid., Vol. V.
7. Ibid., Vol. VI.
8. L. S. Otis, "The Psychobiology of Meditation: Some Psychological Changes," paper presented before the Annual Meeting of the American Psychological Association, Montreal, 1973.
9. A. A. Lazarus, "Psychiatric Problems Precipitated by Transcendental Meditation (TM)," *Psychological Reports*, in press.
10. R. Woolfolk, quoted in Lazarus, op. cit.

CHAPTER 7: *How to Use Meditation Under Stress*

1. J. H. Schultz and W. Luthe, *Autogenic Therapy*, 6 vols. (New York: Grune, 1969), Vol. III, p. 154.
2. Ibid., Vol. III, p. 158.
3. Ibid., Vol. III, p. 172.
4. L. Boudreau, "Transcendental Meditation and Yoga as Reciprocal Inhibitors," *Journal of Behavior Theraphy and Experimental Psychiatry* 3 (1972), pp. 97–98.
5. K. S. Blasdell, "The Effects of Transcendental Meditation Technique upon a Complex Perceptual-Motor Task" in *Scientific Research on the Transcendental Meditation Program: Collected Papers*, ed. D. W. Orme-Johnson and J. T. Farrow, Vol. I (New York: MIU Press, in press).
6. A. G. P. Rimol, "Transcendental Meditation and Its Effects on Sensory and Motor Perception" (Senior Thesis, Princeton University, 1974).
7. D. Goleman and G. E. Schwartz, "Meditation as an Intervention in Stress Reactivity," *Journal of Consulting and Clinical Psychology* 44 (1976), pp. 456–66.
8. Schultz and Luthe, op. cit., p. 183.
9. Ibid., p. 184.

CHAPTER 8: *Some Intriguing Rhythms*

1. N. Kleitman, *Sleep and Wakefulness* (Chicago: Univ. of Chicago Press, 1963), pp. 145–47.
2. G. G. Luce, *Body Time* (New York: Bantan Bks., 1973), p. 45.

Notes

3. H. Johari, *Dhanwantari* (San Francisco: Rams Head, 1974).
4. N. Kleitman, pp. 363–370.
5. H. S. Ephron and P. Carrington, "Rapid Eye Movement Sleep and Cortical Homeostasis," *Psychological Review* 73 (1966), pp. 500–26.
6. T. Wada, "Experimental Study of Hunger in its Relation to Activity," *Archives of Psychology* 8 (1922), pp. 1–65.
7. S. Friedman and C. Fisher, "On the Presence of a Rhythmic Diurnal, Oral Instinctual Drive Cycle in Man: a Preliminary Report," *Journal of the American Psychoanalytic Association* 15 (1967), pp. 317–43.
8. M. B. Sterman and D. McGinty, as quoted in G. G. Luce, *Biological Rhythms in Psychiatry and Medicine*, (Chevy Chase, Md.: National Institute of Mental Health, 1970), p. 26.
9. D. F. Kripke, F. Halberg, T. Crowley, and G. V. Pegram, in Luce, op. cit., p. 26.
10. D. F. Kripke and D. Sonnenschein, "A 90 Minute Daydream Cycle," *Sleep Research* 2 (1973) p. 187.
11. M. Gauquelin, *The Cosmic Clocks* (Chicago: Regnery, 1967).
12. G. G. Luce, *Biological Rhythms in Psychiatry and Medicine* (Chevy Chase, Md.: National Institute of Mental Health, 1970).
13. M. Takata, "Blood Serum and the Sunrise," *Symposium Internationale sur les Relations Phénoménales Solaire et Terrestriale* (Brussels: Presses Académiques Européennes, 1960), p. 172.
14. C. F. Stroebel as quoted in Luce, op. cit., pp. 104–7.
15. E. D. Weitzman, H. Schaumberg and W. Fishbein, "Plasma 17-Hydroxycorticosteroid Levels During Sleep in Man," *Journal of Clinical Endocrinology and Metabolism* 26 (1966), pp. 121–27.
16. Johari, op. cit., p. 76.
17. R. Hittelman, *Guide to Yoga Meditation* (New York: Bantam Bks., 1969), p. 180.

CHAPTER 9: *The "Mystery" of the Mantra*

1. R. E. Ornstein, *The Psychology of Consciousness* (New York: Viking, 1972), p. 122.
2. D. Retallack, *The Sound of Music and Plants* (Santa Monica, Calif.: De Vorss, 1973); P. Weinberger and M. Measures, as quoted in P. Tomkins and C. Bird, *The Secret Life of Plants* (New York: Avon, 1974) p. 167.
3. H. Roffwarg, J. Herman, and S. Lamstein, "The Middle Ear Muscles: Predictability of Their Phasic Activity in REM Sleep from Dream Materials" (Paper presented before the Association for the Psychophysiological Study of Sleep, Edinburgh, 1975).

4. D. Moltz, "Effects of Internally Generated Sounds on Mood," (Senior Thesis, Princeton University, 1976).
5. A. Daniélou, *Hindu Polytheism*, Bolligen Series (New York: Pantheon Bks., 1964), p. 335.
6. S. Bhatnagar, personal communication to the author, September 1975.
7. Daniélou, op. cit., p. 334.
8. Ibid., pp. 334–35.
9. K. W. Morgan, ed., *The Religion of the Hindus* (New York: Ronald, 1953), p. 168.
10. Ibid., p. 169.
11. Ornstein, op. cit., p. 167.

CHAPTER 10: A *Few Nagging Questions*

1. P. Wienphal, *The Matter of Zen* (New York: New York University Press, 1946), p. 22.
2. M. Sadhu, *Meditation* (Hollywood: Wilshire Bk., 1973), p. 97.
3. B. R. Dass, *Be Here Now* (New York: Crown, 1971), p. 83.

CHAPTER 11: A *New Partnership*

1. B. C. Glueck and C. F. Stroebel, "Biofeedback and Meditation in the Treatment of Psychiatric Illness," *Comprehensive Psychiatry* 16 (1975), pp. 303–21.
2. J. Donnelly as quoted in D. Rhinelander, "Disagreement at Institute Ends TM Use as Treatment," Hartford *Courant*, October 3, 1973, p. 1.
3. H. S. Ephron, personal communication to the author, April 1976.
4. H. Benson and R. K. Wallace, "Decreased Drug Abuse with Transcendental Meditation: a Study of 1862 Subjects," *Congressional Record*, 92nd Cong., 1st sess. June 1971, Serial №92-1.
5. M. Shafii, R. Lavely, and R. Jaffe, "Meditation and Marijuana," *American Journal of Psychiatry* 131 (1974), pp. 60–63.
6. M. Shafii, "Smoking Following Meditation" (Unpublished paper, University of Michigan Medical Center, Ann Arbor, Mich., 1973).
7. M. Shafii, R. Lavely, and R. Jaffe, "Meditation and the Prevention of Drug Abuse," *American Journal of Psychiatry* 132 (1975), pp. 942–45.
8. P. D. Hemingway, *The Transcendental Meditation Primer* (New York: McKay, 1975), p. 151.
9. L. S. Otis, "The Psychobiology of Meditation: Some Psychological Changes" (Paper presented at the Annual Meeting of the American Psychological Association, Montreal, 1973).

10. A. Weil, *The Natural Mind* (Boston: Houghton, 1972).
11. Ibid., p. 68.
12. H. Benson, *The Relaxation Response* (New York: Morrow, 1975).
13. R. Honsberger and A. F. Wilson, "Transcendental Meditation in Treating Asthma," *Respiratory Therapy: The Journal of Inhalation Technology*, 3 (1973), pp. 79–81.
14. Benson, op. cit., p. 109.
15. Glueck and Stroebel, op. cit.
16. M. H. Silverman and E. L. Hartmann, "Transcendental Meditation and Sleep" (Paper presented before the Association for the Psychophysiological Study of Sleep, Edinburgh, 1975).
17. D. E. Miskiman, "The Treatment of Insomnia by the Technique of Transcendental Meditation," in *Scientific Research on the Transcendental Meditation Program: Collected Papers*, ed. D. W. Orme-Johnson and J. T. Farrow, Vol. I (New York: MIU Press, in press).
18. R. L. Woolfolk, L. Carr-Kaffashan, P. M. Lehrer, and T. F. McNulty, "Meditation Training as a Treatment for Insomnia," *Behavior Therapy*, in press.

CHAPTER 12: *More Open to Life*

1. Meditation Journal of Harmon S. Ephron (personal communication).
2. B. C. Glueck and C. F. Stroebel, "Biofeedback and Meditation in the Treatment of Psychiatric Illness," *Comprehensive Psychiatry* 16 (1975), pp. 303–21.
3. Meditation Journal of George Edington (personal communication).
4. M. Hines, "Meditation and Creativity: A Pilot Study" (Senior Thesis, Princeton University, 1970).
5. W. Linden, "Practicing of Meditation by School Children and Their Levels of Field Dependence-Independence, Test Anxiety, and Reading Achievement," *Journal of Consulting and Clinical Psychology* 41 (1973), pp. 139–43.
6. K. R. Pelletier, "Increased Perceptual Acuity Following Transcendental Meditation," in *Scientific Research on the Transcendental Meditation Program: Collected Papers*, ed. D. W. Orme-Johnson and J. T. Farrow, Vol. I (New York: MIU Press, in press).
7. D. James, "The Short-Term Effects of Transcendental Meditation on Field Independence: A Pilot Study" (Unpublished paper, Princeton University, 1976).

8. E. Fromm, *Man for Himself* (New York: Rinehart, 1947).
9. *Ibid.*; K. Horney, *The Neurotic Personality of Our Time*, (New York: Norton, 1937; H. S. Sullivan, *The Interpersonal Theory of Psychiatry* (New York: Norton, 1953); C. R. Rogers, *On Becoming a Person* (Boston: Houghton, 1961).
10. H. Shecter, "The Transcendental Meditation Program in the Classroom: A Psychological Evaluation of the Science of Creative Intelligence," in *Scientific Research on the Transcendental Meditation Program: Collected Papers*, ed. D. W. Orme-Johnson and J. T. Farrow, Vol. I (New York: MIU Press, in press).
11. D. Ballou, "The Transcendental Meditation Program at Stillwater Prison," in *Scientific Research on the Transcendental Meditation Program: Collected Papers*, ed. D. W. Orme-Johnson and J. T. Farrow, Vol. I (New York: MIU Press, in press).
12. M. Cunningham and W. Koch, "The Transcendental Meditation Program and Rehabilitation: A Pilot Project at the Federal Correction Institute at Lompoc, California," in *Scientific Research on the Transcendental Meditation Program: Collected Papers*, ed. D. W. Orme-Johnson and J. T. Farrow, Vol. I (New York: MIU Press, in press).

CHAPTER 13: *The Creative Meditator*

1. M. Dellas and E. L. Gaier, "Identification of Creativity: The Individual," *Psychological Bulletin* 73 (1970), pp. 55–73.
2. T. V. Lesh, "Zen Meditation and the Development of Empathy in Counselors," *Journal of Humanistic Psychology* 10 (1970), pp. 39–74.
3. E. W. Maupin, "Individual Differences in Response to a Zen Meditation Exercise," *Journal of Consulting Psychology* 29 (1965), pp. 139–45.
4. M. Hines, "Meditation and Creativity: A Pilot Study" (Senior Thesis, Princeton University, 1970), p. 11.
5. S. Suzuki, *Zen Mind, Beginner's Mind* (New York: Walker/Weatherhill, 1970).
6. A. Kostler *The Action of Creation* (New York: Macmillan, 1964).
7. R. May, *The Courage to Create* (New York: Norton, 1975), p. 67.
8. Hines, op. cit.
9. M. J. MacCullum, "Transcendental Meditation and Creativity" in *Research on the Transcendental Meditation Program: Collected Papers*, ed. D. W. Orme-Johnson and J. T. Farrow, Vol. I (New York: MIU Press, in press).
10. G. E. Schwartz, "Pros and Cons of Meditation: Current Findings

on Physiology and Anxiety, Self-Control, Drug Abuse and Creativity" (Paper delivered before the 81st Annual Convention of
the American Psychological Association, Montreal, 1973).
11. G. Schwartz, "TM Relaxes Some People and Makes Them Feel
Better," *Psychology Today*, April 1974, p. 43.

1. M. Csikszentmihalyi, *Beyond Boredom and Anxiety*, (San Francisco: Jossey-Bass, 1975).
2. Ibid., p. 39.
3. Ibid., p. 40
4. Ibid., p. 44
5. Ibid.
6. Ibid.
7. Ibid., p. 47
8. Ibid.
9. B. C. Glueck, personal communication to the author, July, 1976.
10. B. S. Rajneesh, *Dynamics of Meditation* (Bombay: A Life
Awakening Movement Publication, 1972), p. 60–62.
11. B. C. Glueck, "Current Research on Transcendental Meditation"
(Paper delivered at Rensselaer Polytechnic Institute, Hartford
Graduate Center, Hartford, Connecticut, March 1973).
12. Meditation Journal of Sally B. Eaton (personal communication).
13. L. S. Otis, "The Psychobiology of Meditation: Some Psychological Changes" (Paper presented before the Annual Meeting of
the American Psychological Association, Montreal, 1973).

1. B. C. Glueck, "Current Research on Transcendental Meditation"
(Paper delivered at Rensselaer Polytechnic Institute, Hartford
Graduate Center, Hartford, Connecticut, March 1973).

1. C. A. Ross, "The Effect of Two Relaxation Techniques on Mood,
Sleep and Dreams" (Senior Thesis, Princeton University, 1974).
2. C. Hall, "Frequencies in Certain Categories of Manifest Content
and Their Stability in a Long Dream Series," *American Psychologist* 3, 1948, p. 274.
3. S. Shackman, "The Effect of Two Relaxation Techniques on
Anxiety, Self-Concept and Personality Growth" (Senior Thesis,
Princeton University, 1974).
4. W. A. Zevin, "Effects of Transcendental Meditation on Loneli-

ness Anxiety as Measured by the TAT" (Unpublished paper, Department of Psychology, Princeton University, 1974).

5. L. S. Otis, "The Psychobiology of Meditation: Some Psychological Changes" (Paper presented before the Annual Meeting of the American Psychological Association, Montreal, 1973).

6. H. H. Bloomfield, M. Cain, and D. Jaffe, *TM: Discovering Inner Energy and Overcoming Stress* (New York: Delacorte Press, 1975), p. 127.

7. H. H. Bloomfield and R. B. Kory, *Happiness: The TM Program, Psychiatry, and Enlightenment* (New York: Simon & Schuster, 1976).

8. H. H. Bloomfield, M. Cain, and D. Jaffe, op. cit., p. 141.

9. Ibid., p. 137

10. Ibid.

11. Ibid.

12. Ibid., p. 143.

13. M. Mahesh Yogi, *Transcendental Meditation* (New York: New Am. Lib. [Signet], 1963), p. 23.

14. Ibid., p. 36.

15. L. D. Dick and R. E. Ragland, "A Study of Meditation in the Service of Counseling," *Journal of Humanistic Psychology*, in press.

16. S. Freud (1912), "Recommendations to Physicians Practicing Psychoanalysis," in *Standard Edition of the Complete Psychological Works of Sigmund Freud*, ed. J. Strachey (London: Hogarth, 1958), Vol. XII, p. 112.

17. T. V. Lesh, "Zen Meditation and the Development of Empathy in Counselors," *Journal of Humanistic Psychology* 10 (1970), pp. 39–74.

18. P. Carrington and H. S. Ephron, "Meditation and Psychoanalysis," *Journal of the American Academy of Psychoanalysis* 3 (1975), pp. 43–57.

CHAPTER 17: *A Governing Apparatus*

1. W. H. Bexton, W. Heron, and T. H. Scott, "Effects of Decreased Variation in the Sensory Environment," *Canadian Journal of Psychology* 8 (1954), pp. 70–76; B. K. Doane et. al, "Changes in Perceptual Function After Isolation," *Canadian Journal of Psychology* 13 (1959), pp. 210–19; W. Heron, B. K. Doane, and T. H. Scott, "Visual Disturbances After Prolonged Perceptual Isolation," *Canadian Journal of Psychology* 10 (1956), pp. 13–18; T. H. Scott et. al., "Cognitive Effects of Per-

ceptual Isolation," *Canadian Journal of Psychology* 13 (1959), pp. 200–9.

2. J. C. Lilly and J. T. Shurley, "Experiments in Solitude in Maximum Achievable Physical Isolation with Water Suspension of Intact, Healthy Person" (Paper read, in part, at Symposium on Sensory Deprivation, Harvard University Medical School, Boston, 1958).

3. Bexton et. al., op. cit.

4. Doane et. al., op. cit.

5. C. A. Brownfield, *The Brain Benders* (Jericho, N.Y.: Exposition, 1972).

6. H. Azima and F. J. Cramer, "Effects of Decrease in Sensory Variability on Body Scheme," *Canadian Journal of Psychiatry* 1 (1956), pp. 59–72.

7. A. Harris, "Sensory Deprivation and Schizophrenia," *Journal of Mental Science* 105 (1959), pp. 235–37.

8. Brownfield, op. cit.

9. A. M. Ludwig, "Sensory Overload and Psychopathology," *Diseases of the Nervous System* 36 (1975), pp. 357–60.

10. R. S. Lourie, "The Role of Rhythmic Patterns," *The Five-Minute Hour* (Ardsley, N.Y.: Geigy Pharmaceuticals, January 1976).

11. L. Salk, "The Role of the Heartbeat in the Relations Between Mother and Infant," *Scientific American* March 1973, pp. 24–29.

12. F. Leboyer, *Birth Without Violence* (New York: Knopf, 1975), p. 60.

13. Ibid., p. 62

14. J. A. Meerloo, "The Universal Language of Rhythm," in *Poetry Therapy*, ed. J. J. Leedy (Philadelphia: Lippincott, 1969), pp. 52–66.

15. J. Markowitz, "The Effects of an Externally Generated Rhythm on Mood" (Senior Thesis, Princeton University, 1974).

CHAPTER 18: *Shifting Gears*

1. R. W. Sperry, "The Great Cerebral Commissure," *Scientific American*, January 1964, pp. 42–52; M. S. Gazzaniga, "The Splint Brain in Man," in *The Nature of Human Consciousness*, ed. R. E. Ornstein, (San Francisco: Freeman, 1973), pp. 87–100.

2. Gazzaniga, op. cit., p. 98.

3. A. R. Luria, L. S. Tsvetkova, and D. S. Futer, "Aphasia in a

Conductor," *Journal of Neurological Sciences* 2 (1965), pp. 288–92.

4. T. Alajouanine, "Aphasia and Artistic Realization," *Brain* 71 (1948), pp. 229–41, as quoted in J. E. Bogen, "The Other Side of the Brain: An Appositional Mind," in *The Nature of Human Consciousness*, ed. R. Ornstein (San Francisco: Freeman, 1973), pp. 101–25 (quoted on p. 106).

5. P. Bakan, "Dreaming, REM Sleep, and the Right Hemisphere," (Paper presented before the Association for the Psychophysiological Study of Sleep, Edinburgh, 1975).

6. A. J. Deikman, "Experimental Meditation," in *Altered States of Consciousness* ed. C. T. Tart (New York: Wiley, 1969), pp. 199–218.

7. M. Von Senden, *Space and Sight* (Glencoe, Ill.: Free Press, 1960).

8. Deikman, op. cit., p. 201.

9. Ibid., pp. 207–8.

10. Ibid., p. 217.

11. S. Vishnudevananda, *The Complete Illustrated Book of Yoga* (New York: Julian Press, 1960), p. 226.

12. M. Mahesh Yogi, *Transcendental Meditation* (New York: New Am. Lib. [Signet], 1963), p. 35.

13. Sir James Jeans, *The Mysterious Universe* (Cambridge, England: Cambridge, 1937), p. 122.

CHAPTER 19: *Natural Lessons*

1. D. Goleman, "Meditation as Meta-Theraphy: Hypothesis Toward a Proposed Fifth State of Consciousness," *Journal of Transpersonal Psychology* 3 (1971) pp. 1–25.

2. H. S. Kaplan, *The New Sex Therapy* (New York: Brunner/Mazel, 1974).

3. H. D. Cohen, R. C. Rosen, and L. Goldstein, "Human EEG Laterality Changes During Sexual Orgasm," *Archives of Human Sexuality*, in press.

CHAPTER 20: *The Promise of the Future*

1. S. Grof, *Realms of the Human Unconscious* (New York: Viking, 1975).

2. I. M. Klemons, "Changes in Inflammation Which Occur in Persons Practicing Transcendental Meditation" (Unpublished paper, Pennsylvania State University, 1972).

Notes

3. C. Simonton, "The Role of the Mind in Cancer Therapy," in *Psychiatry and Mysticism* ed. S. R. Dean (Chicago: Nelson-Hall, 1975), pp. 293–308.
4. M. Friedman and R. H. Rosenman, *Type A Behavior and Your Heart* (New York: Knopf, 1974).

Appendix

FOR CHAPTER 4

Even under the most favorable conditions, researchers regularly report a 20 per cent dropout rate from the average TM group during studies lasting only several months. If they last longer, the dropout rate may go higher (Smith, for example, reports a 59 per cent dropout rate among the TM meditators in his study, over a six month period).* The above rates occur under experimental conditions in subjects who have a high incentive to remain with the experiment. Meditators in the general community who are not in a research study constitute a different population.

The most encouraging figures on the TM attrition rate for the community at large have been reported by Dr. Mohammad Shafii. Contacting 187 people who had taken TM training in the past, he determined through a series of telephone inquiries that only approximately 30 per cent of these people had discontinued meditation. Other studies, however, have reported a higher dropout rate which seems to vary with age. When Dr. Maynard Shelly of Kansas University studied 263 high school students who had learned TM, 71 per cent said they had either completely stopped or rarely meditated any more.† In a pilot study on a group composed mostly of *college* students, Dr. Penelope Davies obtained a 53 per cent dropout rate from TM for those who had been meditating for three to six months and a 60 per cent dropout rate for those who had been meditating more than three years.‡ These figures roughly correspond with our estimate on the

* J. C. Smith, "The Psychotherapeutic Effects of Transcendental Meditation with Controls for Expectation of Relief and Daily Sitting," *Journal of Consulting and Clinical Psychology*, in press.
† M. Shelly, personal communication to the author, Kansas University, Lawrence, Kans., February 1976.
‡ P. Davies, personal communication to the author, Kansas University, Lawrence, Kans., February 1976.

TM dropout rate on the Princeton University campus, which appears to be about 50 per cent. Similarly, Dr. Leon Otis found that after eighteen months of practicing TM, a group of adult meditators showed an approximate 50 per cent dropout rate from the practice.* His figures also showed a clear-cut variation with age. His report suggests that older subjects tend to stay with TM whereas younger subjects tend to drop out.

* L. S. Otis, "TM and Sleep" (Paper presented before the Annual Meeting of the American Psychological Association, New Orleans, 1974).

Appendix

Case of Bette J: About six months after commencing TM, Bette J., a young woman in her mid-twenties, began to notice an unusual pattern of tension-release occurring during all of her meditation sessions. Originally it took the form of pressure in and around her eyes and was sufficiently unpleasant to make her spontaneously reduce her meditation time to three sessions per week. After three months, the eye pressure switched to a series of fast, rhythmic blinks during meditation, with mental repetition of the mantra disappearing as these muscle contractions now began to constitute her entire meditation.

As the months passed, the muscle contractions progressed downward over her face, changing to a wrinkling of her nose, then to rhythmic contortion of her entire lower face, and finally to a series of extremely rapid sucking movements. At this point she found that she wanted to increase her meditation to six sessions per week, and did so. Several months later, her left arm began to jab up and down from the shoulder in co-ordination with the mouth and jaw muscles and following this, both arms began automatically to flail about during meditation, sometimes knocking pillows off the couch where she sat while meditating. Although these meditations were understandably described as "somewhat tiring," she usually felt quite relaxed *afterward*.

Bette reported no particular associations to the eye or nose contractions, but when the side effects began to involve her mouth (about a year later) she spontaneously reported that the feeling reminded her of the "sucking of a nursing baby." She then recalled the fact that her mother had been extremely depressed and remote from her when she was an infant and that she had been deprived of fulfilling nurturing early in life.

When her meditation began to involve movements of her jaw,

364

Bette commented that as a child she had rarely talked, because when she had done so, no one around her had paid attention. From a child who rarely spoke, she had become an adult who chattered compulsively but still in a manner to which people paid little attention.

It is interesting that Bette's tension-release symptoms proceeded, as it were, on a schedule of their own and that it was only as they progressed downward, reaching a lower part of her face, that she began to have insight into their meaning. Similar to the reports of the autogenic therapy trainees, Bette seems to have experienced a very specific and personally meaningful sort of tension-release during her meditation which has led to some important changes in her life. At the present time a previously rather wooden facial expression has been replaced by a bright animated one; she has recently developed graceful, vivacious hand gestures which give her a much more alive and attractive appearance; and she has taken up a number of athletic activities which involve movements of the whole body, particularly the arms.

Case of Adriane M.: This patient's reaction to meditation reflects her deep-seated sexual problems, for which she had sought psychiatric treatment. At the time she learned CSM, she was undergoing psychoanalytic psychotherapy and her first entry in her meditation journal expresses a positive outlook on the meditation:

> In tonight's meditation it was quite easy to move into a pleasurable state allowing myself to give up some control. . . . I began feeling sexually aroused; my body began to go into an orgasmic state. I never allowed myself to feel this way before with men, but kept telling myself, "It's a good feeling"—

This sexual opening up was followed by strong counter reactions, both in her actual life and during her meditation session the following morning:

> This morning it was difficult for me to relax during meditation. . . . I had a fight with my boyfriend on the phone last night. I was still angry with him in the morning and would not let my body relax. *I think I was actually warding off the sexual feelings I had in my last meditation.*

Despite conflict over her newly awakened sexual feelings, pleasurable body sensations asserted themselves again during Adriane's next meditation session:

> I quickly calmed down and my body started feeling great. . . . Then I went into another semi-orgasmic state. I felt pleasurable feelings throughout my body but I felt like I wanted to have an

orgasm. I had intense vaginal sensations—I've never had vaginal feelings before. . . . I kept blocking these sexual feelings . . . then I tried talking to myself about how it's okay to have these feelings and look at how great my body was feeling. I gradually enjoyed all this sexual feeling. . . . It was hard coming out of meditation.

Soon after this, tension-release during meditation became overly intense. Over the next several days Adriane's meditation journal details a number of distressing incidents resulting from a *too rapid release* of sexual feelings during meditation:

I had intense sexual feelings as soon as I started meditating and felt myself trying to fight them because I could not go to work wanting to have an orgasm all day. I was so aroused that I wanted to have sex with anybody but of course, I wouldn't. . . .

And later that day:

I couldn't wait to get home from work to meditate. I had to get rid of this sexual feeling or I felt I would go crazy. I had intense feelings all day about wanting to see my analyst—not sexual feelings—just very warm feelings. I usually have to hide my warm feelings. . . .

The release of her rigid controls over her sexual responses was occurring too rapidly and the flooding of sexual material was becoming anti-therapeutic. Recognizing this, Adriane's analyst recommended to her that she reduce her meditation sessions to ten minutes, and meditate only *once* a day:

My analyst told me I can only meditate for 10 minutes once a day, rather than the usual amount of time until I feel more comfortable. I felt much better hearing that because then I felt that I could control my own feelings completely. That was to be the only rule of meditation [the timing] and if I could control that, then I could control myself completely. . . .

Despite her difficulty in adjusting to the tension-release symptoms, meditation *was* affording Adriane some benefits:

I can't believe how great I've been feeling, despite the sexual tension. I feel like I'm functioning on another level. I feel so happy all the time and overlook a lot of things that used to bother me.

As long as she continued to hold meditation time down to ten minutes, she reported a more satisfying experience:

I feel I'm not as "crazy" during meditation now. My feelings are not as intense. I feel more comfortable now that things are less dramatic.

Unfortunately Adriane did not systematically keep her meditation to the prescribed ten minutes a day, but started to increase it to twenty minutes twice daily despite her analyst's admonition to the contrary. Whenever she meditated for longer periods of time, too rapid release of sexual feelings again occurred and repressed wishes and fantasies of an anxiety-provoking nature began to surface. At this point, disturbing material concerning sexual feelings toward her own father began to emerge during her meditation sessions:

I am becoming more emotional [between meditation sessions]. I cry all the time over TV programs. I laugh a lot too when I'm watching TV. I wish I could just calm down during meditation without feeling so sexually aroused. . . .

I had a hard night with my dreams. I was afraid to meditate this morning because I didn't want to see my father dead again as he had been in the dream. It was strange—he was alive this morning and wanted to have sex with me. I was real young and he was gentle with me. I really didn't know what was happening. I felt aroused but I tried to make those feelings go away. I think I actually let him have sex with me. . . .

Tonight I only meditated for 10 minutes 'cause I was hungry. I felt like I was 4 or 5 years old and was swinging on my swing at home. My dog and ducks and cat were with me. I was sexually aroused when swinging. . . .

One time, after she had meditated the prescribed ten minutes in the morning, her evening meditation went well:

Tonight I had a great time meditating. This is how it should be. I felt so calm. I blocked out all the noise from outside. I had just pleasant feelings—nothing frightening or intense like at other times. Just relaxed. I couldn't make myself uncomfortable if I tried. It was hard for me to stop—I felt like I could sit here forever.

Adriane's sexual problems were a reflection of the personality difficulties for which she had sought psychiatric treatment. What is important from the standpoint of understanding the meditative process is the manner in which her tension-release symptoms reflected these underlying problems.

Appendix

Notes for psychotherapists considering using meditation with patients:

1. When dealing with patients with strong guilt about meditating, we have found it useful to ask them not to meditate except just before, or during, their psychotherapy sessions. This way guilt reactions to the enjoyment of meditation may be immediately worked on in therapy, and the therapist can give support to the patient.
2. If a psychotherapy session is unproductive, interrupting it to meditate with a patient may be a useful strategy. More often than not, meditation is followed by insights on the patient's part into his or her current problems. Strategic meditation of this sort may also be useful to calm agitated patients so that they can constructively deal with their problems. *Overuse* of meditating with a patient is undesirable, however. It is not only time-consuming but may allow meditation to become associated in the patient's mind with the presence of the therapist. This is obviously counterproductive since one of meditation's chief values is that it is an independent, *self-directed* therapeutic endeavor.
3. It is wise to limit the interpretation of the *contents* of a patient's meditative session to times when the patient has spontaneously reported the contents of the meditation session without being asked to do so, and is clearly distressed about it. This indicates that he or she both needs and wants to work through some special anxiety with regard to a particular meditation session. Primary process material which surfaces during meditation is often highly symbolic and reflective of the patient's problems, but should not ordinarily be interpreted, just as the contents of a creative product, equally

368

revealing in its own way, is best left "unanalyzed." Meditation's chief value is that it is an *intra*personal experience, where no self-evaluation or self-criticism takes place. Bringing a therapist into the meditation via his or her interpretations of meditative contents, may eventually destroy the patient's freedom to meditate.

Index

Index

375

Index

preparatory, 115–24; presurgical, 117; and productivity, 231–40; and prolonged emotional stress, 126–28; psychological effects of, 51–54, 189–204ff.; and psychosomatic illness, 108, 204–10; and radical changes in perspective and energy utilization, 211ff., 306ff., 320–27, 331–42; "readiness," 135ff.; reducing time for, 99–102, 109; as a regular practice, 86–88; research, xvii, xix, xx–xxii, 3–20, 37ff., 55–72, 190–210, 211ff. (*see also* specific aspects, developments, kinds, problems, studies); resistance to, 244–46, 250–60; and self as "being," 325–26; side effects (discomforts and problems), 86–87, 92–95ff., 261–70, 281, 346ff. (*see also* specific kinds, problems); spacing, 152–53; and stamina and creativity, 237–40; as a state of inner solitude, 230, 245, 250; for stress, 111–32 (*see also* Stress); suiting to the person, 182–83; techniques, 5–36, 75–91 (*see also* specific meditation techniques); tension-release process and, 105–10 (*see also* Tension); time, place, and position (posture) for, 22, 76–78, 79, 80, 85, 109, 133, 134ff., 175–77; under catastrophic circumstances, 129–31; under physical stress, 131; vacations from, 177–82; when ill, 124–26; why it works, 287–305, 306–16, 320–27

Meditation room, 339–40

Meditative mood, 3–5, 22, 30–31, 33, 36, 92, 93–95, 184, 240, 299, 300, 323, 326, 334; benefits of, 331–42; body rhythms and, 142–56; effect of specific sounds (mantras) and, 161–65, 166–68, 170–71, 172–74; fear of pleasure and, 255–60; flow experiences and play and, 241–44, 256–57; generalization of, 335–42; music and chanting and, 172–74; research on, 57–58, 61, 67–70; spontaneous, 4–5; and tension-release process, 93–95ff.

Meerlo, Joost A., 303, 359

Memories (memory), 134, 263; meditation research on, 58–59; recalled in meditation, 89–90; repressed, 212–17, 219

Menninger Foundation, Biomedical

Electronics Laboratory of (Topeka, Kans.), 37

Mental association. *See* Associations, mental

Mental health (mental illness), 189–204, 309 (*see also* Emotional disturbances); and creativity, 224ff.; meditation as an adjunct to psychotherapy and (*see under* Psychotherapy); meditation and personal growth and, 190–204ff., 210, 211–25; overmeditation and, 262–70

Mental states (*see also* Consciousness; Emotions; Mental health; Thoughts): altered, 37–54 (*see also* Altered states of consciousness); meditation and changes in personality and, 306–16ff., 320–27; meditation as a governing apparatus and, 289–95

Mescaline, 38

Metabolism (metabolic changes), 15, 25, 56–58

Meyers, Ronald, 307

Migraine headaches, 207

Mind, 9. *See also* Consciousness; Mental health; Mental states; Thoughts

Mini-meditations, 111–15, 116, 117; limitations of, 113–15

Minnesota Multiphasic Personality Inventory (MMPI), 192, 224

Mirror Star Tracing Task, 120

Miskiman, Donald E., 209, 349

Moltz, Douglas, ix, 161, 354

Monasteries (monks): Eastern, 41, 42–45; Western, 23, 147

Mood: effect of specific sounds on, 161–65, 166–68; meditative (*see* Meditative mood); music and chanting and, 172–74

Moon, Sun Myung, 268

Moslems, 21, 146

Motor skills, meditation and, 120–24

Mt. Sinai Hospital (N.Y.C.), 140, 141

Moving meditation, 81–83, 85, 245n; two methods of, 81–83

Mudra meditation, 85

Muscular tension, relaxation techniques for, 31–33, 95, 336, 339

Music, 158; brain organization and sensitivity to, 308–9; and chanting, 172–74; overstimulation and, 297–98; soothing effects of, 303, 304

Narcotics, 198. *See also* Drugs

Index

Index

Rama, Swami, 37

Ramah (mantra), 79

Reaction times, meditation research and, 59–60

Relaxation Response, Benson's. *See* Benson, Herbert

Relaxation techniques, 13, 15–19, 111–32 (*see also* specific techniques); autogenic training, 26–28; biofeedback, 33–36; desensitization and, 321–25 (*see also* Desensitization); free association and, 29–31; future of meditation and, 331–42; mantras and, 170–71; physiology of meditation and, 45–51, 55–72; progressive relaxation and (*see* Progressive Relaxation); research, 37–54, 55–72, 191 (*see also* specific kinds, studies); self-hypnosis and, 23–26; side effects, 93, 94–95ff.; and stress, 111–32; and tension-release process, 92–110, 111–32 (*see also* Tension)

Religion, meditation and, xviii, xx, 7–8, 19, 21–23, 146–47, 153, 336–37, 340 (*see also* Spiritual meditation): and prayer, 21–23

REM sleep (Rapid Eye Movement sleep), 138–39, 140, 141–42, 309–10; as a stress state, 150–52

Repetitive movements, meditation and, 81–83, 85, 305. *See also* Moving meditation; Rhythms, natural

Replication failure, meditation research and, 57, 60

Repressed emotions and memories, 212–17, 219–20

Respiration. *See* Breathing

Rest: and activity cycles, 138–44; alternating meditation with, 128–29

Restlessness, 160, 295–96; effect of sound and, 160; in tension-release process, 96, 104–5

Reverie states, 299, 309–11. *See also* Trance states

Rhythms, natural, 133–56, 299, 300–5, 341–42; and tension-release process, 300–5

Rimol, A. G. P. (Andy), ix, 119–24, 352

Rock music, 297–98

Rod and Frame Test, 217–19

Roffwarg, Howard, 159, 353

Roles (role-playing), social, 26, 242, 340

Rorschach inkblot test, 227–28

Roshi, Miura, 238

Ross, Christopher A., ix, 272–75, 357

Rutgers University, 209

Salk, Lee, 302–3

Salvasana, 176

Samadhi, 42–43, 44, 291–92

Sanran, 26n

Sanskrit: mantras, 10, 14, 17, 23, 79n, 88, 157n, 159, 160, 163, 168–69; scriptures, 146

Schizophrenia, 98, 108, 193, 294

Schools. *See* Education (schools)

Schulman, Arnold, 238–40

Schultz, J. H., 26–27

Schwartz, Gary E., 34–35, 50, 123, 236–37, 352

Science, meditation and, xx–xxii: future of meditation and, 331–32, 342; and knowledge and discoveries, 227, 229, 230, 283, 311; and meditation research (*see under* Meditation); scientific method, meaning and use of term, xx–xxii

Science of Creative Intelligence (SCI), 11, 165n

Self-acceptance, meditation and, 211–12, 217–25

Self-assertiveness, 293–94

Self-awareness, meditation and, 217–25 (*see also* Self-identity): and creativity, 226–40; resistance to change and, 245, 248, 250–53

Self-blame (self-criticism): breaks from meditation and, 177, 179, 181–82; guilt feelings and meditation and, 211, 276, 282, 326–27, 368–69; meditation and reduction of, 326–27; and resistance to meditation, 257–58, 368–69

Self-control, resistance to meditation and fear of loss of, 245–46, 250

Self-development. *See* Personal growth

Self-education, meditation and, 327

Self-hypnosis (self-suggestion), 23–26ff., 36, 131–32

Self-identity (self-concept, self-image, self-worth), 217, 271, 325–26, 333, 335; field independence and, 217–19, 274; meditation and psychotherapy and, 189ff., 250–53, 271, 274, 275, 333, 335; and resistance to meditation and

Index

Vision. *See* Eyes (eyesight, vision);
  Hallucinations; Visual meditation;
  Visual-motor co-ordination
Visual meditation, 83–84, 85–86, 87. *See
  also* Guided-imagery meditation
Visual-motor co-ordination, 60
Vogt, Oskar, 27

Wada, Toni, 139–40
Walking meditation, 334
Wallace, R. Keith, 15, 18, 49, 55–56, 57,
  190–91, 197–98, 199
Walton, Bill, 123
Water immersion, isolation experiment
  and, 289, 290–91
Weil, Andrew, 201–2
Weitzman, Elliott D., 151, 353
Wenger, M. A., 41–42, 346
West, Michael, 58–59, 351
White, Robert, 25
Wilson, A. F., 207
Wilson, Bradford, ix–x
Wolpe, Joseph, 32
Woolfolk, Robert L., 19, 80, 108, 209,
  336; and breathing meditation
  technique, 19, 20, 80

World Plan Organization, U. S., 11n, 12,
  18n, 62, 110, 165, 277
Writers (writing ability and
  productivity), meditation and, 231–33,
  238–40

Yoga (yogis), 25, 26, 40, 41–45, 46, 48,
  77, 106, 231, 316–17, 337 (*see also*
  specific individuals, kinds); and
  breathing exercises and postures,
  109–10, 175, 176; and mantras, 14n,
  166–67, 169n; and meditation
  scheduling, 126, 136–37, 147; and
  prana concept, 316–18; research on,
  40, 41–45, 46, 48, 60–61
Yogi, "Maharishi" Mahesh, 12, 110,
  172, 277–78, 317, 344, 358

Zazen meditation, 41, 44, 182, 218, 238,
  263–64, 265, 284; techniques, 20, 85,
  116, 176
Zen beliefs and tradition, 19, 26, 77,
  175, 230, 231, 263–64; and koans,
  228–29; research on monks, 41, 42–45,
  46, 47
Zevin, Wendy A., ix, 274, 357

384